Sowing Seeds for the Future

Andrew Rigby

Sowing Seeds for the Future
Exploring the Power of Constructive Nonviolent Action

Andrew Rigby

Andrew Rigby

Sowing Seeds for the Future

Exploring the Power of Constructive Nonviolent Action

Published by Irene Publishing

Sparsnäs, Sweden

First edition 2022

ISBN 978-91-88061-54-6

Copyright: Author and Irene Publishing

Layout and cover: J. Johansen

Photos used in this book and on the cover are in Public Domain, under Creative Common License or owned by the author.

www.irenepublishing.com

irene.publishing@gmail.com

ISBN 978-91-88061-54-6

9 789188 061546 >

Contents

Preface   i

1   Introduction   1

2   Intentional Living and the Power of Exemplary Action   19

3   Reconstruction and Resistance: Gandhian Satyagraha in
    Theory and Practice   45

4   Constructive Action in Civil Resistance for Political Change   81

5   Constructive Action and Resistance in Wartime   123

6   Constructive Resistance to Organised Crime   159

7   Constructive Action in the Sphere of Production   191

8   Concluding Observations   219

Bibliography   229

Index   241

PREFACE

In writing this book I found that in so many instances it touched upon aspects of my personal and professional life, such that in the end I decided to allow the personal to show through. I don't apologise for this, I just hope that I have not been too self-indulgent in the process. I have spent my professional career researching and writing about other people, so it has been an interesting exercise to allow myself to come openly onto the stage, so to speak, in writing about the many different facets of constructive nonviolent action for change that have touched me in one way or another in the course of my life.[1]

This book has had an incredibly long period of gestation. The first seed, I suppose, was my quite early conviction that killing people was wrong. That basic pacifism led to an interest in anarchism, as part of my search for non-coercive modes of radical change. This, in turn, led me to an interest in exploring the significance of exemplary action – seeking change by the power of example rather than by force. As will become clear in chapter two of this book, this interest led to my doctoral research into intentional communities, forms of constructive action for change whereby people get to live together in order to pursue a particular purpose – seeking to embody in their lives the changes they hope to see adopted on a broader scale over time, letting their lives speak for them.

There have been other, more personal, reasons for my choice of constructive modes of nonviolent action as a theme. One reason for my fascination with the topic is, I believe, my own lack of personal confidence in public arenas, and my general reluctance to draw attention to myself in the public sphere. Despite my radical tendencies, I have never been one of those folk with the gift of oratory and the capacity to touch people's emotions by means of the spoken word. Hence, I have never been to the fore in public protests – I am one of those folk you can rely on to

---

1   Of course my values and my politics have played a part in all the research and writing projects I have undertaken over the years. They have influenced my choice of topics, my research methodology, and my methods of carrying out research. Indeed, over the years I have found my own experiences and emotions a vital research resource and an ongoing source of ideas and insights.

i

turn up, but don't expect more than my presence on your demonstration! Hence my interest in modes of socio-political change activity that can be pursued in the more private everyday spheres of life rather than the realm of public protest.

Another factor that I think might well have fed into my interest in the more quietistic approaches to radical change is my mild claustrophobia, and the consequent horror I have always had of being locked up in some kind of 'paddy wagon' en route to a holding cell as a consequence of my involvement in some kind of nonviolent protest. (I was always the driver or the observer in the affinity groups to which I belonged during the 1980s protests against nuclear weapons.) Moreover, I have always been a little sceptical of what my old friend Howard Clark used to call 'Catholic worker types' – and I am aware I am being unfair here – who always seemed to us to be too enthusiastic about presenting themselves as 'front-line' activists in search of martyrdom.[2]

Another seed that has eventually germinated in this book was sown by my dear friend Bob Overy. I first met Bob in the offices of the pacifist publication *Peace News* back in 1968, when he was part of the editorial team and I was doing a survey of their readership. We stayed in touch, and when I moved to Bradford in West Yorkshire in the late 1970s Bob was involved in researching his thesis on Gandhi as an organiser. It was Bob who brought to my realisation (and that of others) the significance of Gandhi's focus on the constructive programme as an integral dimension of his theory of change. And I have a memory of him saying to me one day that I ought to write a book about constructive action. He probably would deny all knowledge of this, but it has stayed lodged at the back of my consciousness over the years.

After I retired from my post at what was then called the Centre for Peace and Reconciliation Studies at Coventry University I had the time to pursue my own interests, and this is where Jørgen Johansen enters the causal chain. He encouraged me as I started tentatively to broach

---

2   People associated with the Catholic Worker movement are incredibly dedicated and admirable folk who take their values seriously, and have often been to the fore in nonviolent activism for the sake of peace, anti-militarism and social justice. Howard died in 2013, and I continue to find it difficult to forgive him.

the idea of a book on constructive action. Eventually I went over to the small hamlet in the forests of southern Sweden where he lives and works, and his enthusiasm and encouragement gave me the final push to start seriously planning, researching and writing. I remain extremely grateful to him, not least because he promised to publish the finished manuscript!

I would also like to register my deep appreciation of the generosity of Brian Martin, over there in Wollongong, Australia. Brian is a prolific scholar-activist, but he made time to read some of my draft chapters – and his encouragement was one of the factors that enabled me to persevere with this project. Finally, I want to say a great thankyou to Carol Rank – not only did she proof-read my final draft, she remains my love and my companion.

1

INTRODUCTION

This book is about constructive nonviolent direct action for change. Let's start off with a personal account of a nonviolent protest in Norway in the late 1970s, provided by Jørgen Johansen. It illustrates some of the points that will recur throughout the book.

Innerdalen case study

In the late 1970s plans were announced to create a hydro-electric power station on the River Orkla in central Norway. The construction of a dam was proposed, which would result in significant parts of the Innerdalen Valley being flooded. Environmentalists and others were appalled at this and decided to campaign against it. As Jørgen Johansen recalled:

> We wanted to bring the value of soil and land to the centre
> of the discussion. This time not by directly preventing
> the building of the dam, but by occupying the valley and
> start using it for food production. Our idea was that such
> a constructive action would be difficult for politicians and
> industry to ignore. 'Green Action Innerdalen' started by
> repairing old farm houses and starting a wide variety of positive
> activities in the valley. Local farmers let us take their sheep and
> cows up there and start production of cheese, butter and meat.[1]

They invited parliamentarians to visit the site – none of them accepted the offer. Despite coverage and discussion within green-circles there was no interest shown by the national media. In Jorgen's words, 'They were not interested in a bunch of activists living out in the mountains'.

> After three years of constructive resistance in Innerdalen, with
> close to zero attention from authorities and media, we lost

---

1   Personal communication.

1

patience and decided to 'force' the media to recognise what we were doing. One early morning we walked the three kilometres down to the dam area and blocked the construction road. A few hours later national media was on their way to cover a story 'about some activists blocking the road'. The big media houses rented an aeroplane to be first with the spectacular photos of confrontations between police and activists. Result: huge headlines and coverage of us being arrested in all national media. Not a single media representative bothered to walk the three kilometres up to our camp, Green University, sheep and farm.

One of the core lessons to be drawn from this experience is that in liberal parliamentary democracies like Norway and the UK, the greater the friction caused by nonviolent direct action, the greater the likelihood of attracting media attention. And for many activists media attention is the life-blood of their campaign. Without media coverage their means of communicating their cause to wider publics is severely circumscribed.[2] This is one of the reasons nonviolent activists can be critical of constructive modes of nonviolent action, insofar as they can fail to cause any discernible disruption to the normal flow of mainstream life. Others, however, could argue that paradoxically this can be one of the strengths of relatively quiet forms of constructive action, insofar as such forms of activity are far more sustainable over time than the more contentious forms of nonviolent action.

Underlying much of the analysis that follows in the different chapters is the exploration of the different kinds of relationships that can exist between the more contentious forms of protest (that have the capacity to generate friction) and the more constructive modes of action that can persist over time without causing any major concern on the part of defenders of the status quo. For now a few tentative working hypotheses can be presented.

i.   Contentious protest activities can create opportunities for change through the friction the activities cause and which

---

2   For discussion about the importance of media coverage in relation to nonviolent civil resistance, see B. Martin, *Backfire manual: Tactics against injustice,* Sparsnas: Irene Publishing, 2012.

can contribute to the erosion of the supports on which the established order depends. For example, public protests can draw the attention of the media, creating an 'issue' that can become a matter of public concern and debate, thereby creating a situation about which 'something must be done'.

ii. Where a protest movement creates too much friction by threatening the vested interests of elites, particularly in authoritarian and repressive regimes, the activities are likely to provoke counter-measures, involving different levels of sanctions, which can undermine the strength and vitality of the movement, imposing severe costs on those engaged in the protest activities.

iii. When action does not result in friction, when it fails to disturb the defenders of the status quo, as can be the case with many forms of constructive action for change, then the likelihood of actors being subjected to sanctions is reduced, as is the likelihood of significant change taking place in the short-to-medium term as a consequence of the constructive activities.

But hold on a second. I have just thought of a counter-illustration of how constructive action that caused minimal friction with the established order contributed to significant cultural changes. In his famous essay *Civil disobedience* Henry David Thoreau urged us to let our lives be a 'counter-friction' to the smooth operation of government when the state requires us to act as agents of injustice:

> If the injustice is part of the necessary friction of the machine of government, let it go, let it go: perchance it will wear smooth--certainly the machine will wear out... but if it is of such a nature that it requires you to be the agent of injustice to another, then I say, break the law. Let your life be a counter-friction to stop the machine. What I have to do is to see, at any rate, that I do not lend myself to the wrong which I condemn.[3]

Powerful stuff. Thoreau wrote it after he had encountered a tax collector in July 1846 who demanded that he pay his six years of back taxes.

---

3   H. Thoreau, *Civil disobedience* in P. Mayer, ed., *The pacifist conscience,* Harmondsworth: Penguin, 1966, pp. 140-159, p. 148.

Thoreau refused because of his opposition to the Mexican-American War and slavery. 'Friction' ensued and Thoreau spent the night in jail. Much to his chagrin he was released the next day after a relative paid the taxes against Thoreau's wishes.

At the time the writer was living out his vision of the simple self-reliant life in the woods around Walden Pond, near Concord in Massachusetts. This was a form of peaceable constructive living, creating no significant friction whatsoever with the established authorities. But Thoreau was able to use his experience to write *Walden*, which subsequently came to be viewed as a classic American work in its exploration of natural simplicity, harmony, and beauty as models for just social and cultural conditions.[4] This reminds me of a phenomenon that I noticed decades ago. Throughout history there are examples of artists and radical creative people who start to initiate change in some aspect of their lives, and frequently they are dismissed as 'cranks' or eccentrics, out of touch with the 'real world'. But overtime this prophetic function can exercise an influence, and what was once only adhered to by a weird minority enters into the mainstream. An illustration from my own biography: way back in the early 1970s the radical pacifist publication *Peace News*, based in London, published a 'green sheet' full of ideas and recommendations about how to live a more ecologically responsible life. Now, nearly half a century later, the imperative of living more responsibly for the sake of our planet's future is 'common-sense'. We never know where the ripples from our actions might spread.

But I am getting too far ahead of myself here, generating working hypotheses, reflecting on the mysteries of cultural change … all this before I have even defined the terms being used.

---

4   A significant number of contemporary reviews of Walden made reference to Thoreau as quaint or eccentric. See B. Dean & G. Scharnhorst, 'The Contemporary Reception of "Walden"' in Studies in the American Renaissance, 1990, pp. 293-328. Accessible at http://www.jstor.org/stable/30227595 (22 July 2021).

Problems of terminology

i) Constructive resistance or constructive action?

The focus of this book is constructive nonviolent direct action for change. That is a bit of a mouthful, but I have worked with that label primarily because I have had problems deciding whether this should be shortened to constructive action or constructive resistance. Initially I was reluctant to use the term 'resistance' - preferring the label constructive action. The main reason for this was my sense that too many researchers and writers on civil resistance appeared to be over-enamoured with the more contentious and confrontational forms of direct action. I wanted to counter such tendencies by championing forms of action with the potential to bring about change without involving any overtly recognisable form of confrontation. I wanted to be able to lay claim to drinking fair-trade tea as a political act with the potential to bring about change, however unheroic or placid such an activity might seem. In contrast, some of my friends and comrades, with a more significant personal history of involvement in the more contentious forms of nonviolent direct action, like to use the term constructive *resistance* as a way of broadening the parameters of 'resistance' to embrace everyday activities that are not in themselves contentious.

This led me to reflect on the nature of 'resistance'. It seemed to me that where modes of constructive action have a clear oppositional target, such as an occupation regime or a particular institutional practice, then it seemed appropriate to class such activities as 'resistance'. Furthermore, when the mode of constructive action was highly likely to be considered contentious or provocative by the target of the action, and by the activists themselves, then once again it seemed appropriate to use the term constructive resistance.

Let me try and illustrate the points I am trying to make. In 2019 a group of people in Coventry, the city in the UK where I live, obtained a property in order to provide a home for migrant women caught up in the tortuous process of obtaining refugee status in the UK. At the most obvious level this was a humanitarian initiative to care for those in our midst who fall outside most institutional 'safety-nets', and are at serious risk of abuse and destitution. By most definitions it is a form of constructive action – it is creating something new. But is it constructive resistance? From one point of view such an initiative can be categorised as a form of constructive resistance, insofar as it constitutes a nonviolent form of action that is presenting an alternative to, and thereby challenging, the violence embodied in the UK government's treatment of asylum seekers. However, the challenge posed by the project does not manifest itself in any contentious way, and most of those involved might be reluctant to use the term 'resistance' as a descriptor of their activities. The 'resistance dimension' remains relatively obscure.[5] Accordingly I would use the label constructive action to refer to this type of activity.

ii) The significance of context

What is clear from this illustration is that the socio-political context within which action takes place is a crucial determinant of whether an action might be considered a form of resistance or not. For example, providing the means whereby migrant women might live tolerably 'normal' lives in a liberal-democracy such as the UK would not appear to be contentious in the eyes of many citizens, neither does it carry any significant risk of sanctions. By contrast, creating a safe space within Israel, where Palestinian women claiming their 'right to return' might live, would be viewed by the majority of Israeli citizens (and state bodies) as highly contentious and carry significant risk of a range of reprisals.[6]

A related observation is also relevant here. Whether or not an action is viewed as oppositional or not lies in the eyes of the beholder. It is conceivable that some xenophobic citizens within Coventry who became

---

5   Whilst people involved in such initiatives might not define their activity as a form of constructive resistance, even though it might be depicted as such by observers such as myself, the important point is that such actors would be able to understand how their activities might be portrayed as constructive resistance if they were made familiar with the frame of reference being applied by observer. See Alfred Schutz's discussion of first and second order constructs in *Collected papers I: The problem of social reality*, The Hague, Martinus Nijhoff, 1971, p. 6.

6   See J. Cook, 'Crossing the divide', *Al-Ahram Weekly*, 21 August 2003. Accessible at https://tinyurl.com/vgrzose (17 March 2020).

aware of the existence of a house providing shelter to migrant women might consider such an initiative as highly undesirable and provocative.[7] The same observable activity can be defined differently according to the context in which the activity takes place and the particular perspectives of the observers and the actors themselves. Consequently, it would seem appropriate to use the label of resistance in cases where the oppositional dimension of the activity is recognised as such by the actors themselves, and by significant observers, including state authorities. [8]

Here another illustration comes to mind that underlines the importance of the socio-political (and legal) context within which objectively similar activities take place. In the UK 'dumpster diving', the reclamation of food products consigned to waste skips by retailers and other suppliers, can be seen as a political act and a form of constructive action. Whilst for some obtaining sustenance from food deemed to be 'waste' is vital for their food security, for a significant number reclaiming 'waste' food products reflects their desire to live sustainably and their rejection of 'consumerism'.[9] Hence my surprise when I discovered that in Germany the activity is prohibited – it is illegal to reclaim food from dumpsters. Consequently, in the UK reclaiming food in this manner might appropriately be labelled a form of constructive action, whilst in Germany we might feel it is more appropriate to use the label constructive resistance, insofar as the activity has a provocative dimension and could incur the risk of legal sanctions.[10]

---

7   As I learned in my Sociology classes so many years ago: If a situation is defined as real, it is real in its consequences.

8   The concept of constructive action/resistance should be viewed as a sensitising concept, that is one where there is no exhaustive specification of the conditions for the correct use of the concept, but there are core characteristics or attributes that are displayed to some degree by all phenomena to which the concept might appropriately be applied. They are open-textured concepts that are somewhat 'fuzzy' with blurred boundaries but certain common denominators or core characteristics. See H. Blumer, 'What is wrong with social theory?', *American Sociological Review*, v. 18, 1954, pp. 3-10, p. 7.

9   See M. Cyr, 'Sustainability spotlight: An urban harvester', 12 September 2019. Accessible at https://tinyurl.com/jh5ax6xh (22 July 2021).

10 'A crash course in dumpster-diving', *Spiegel International*, 2 September 2019. Accessible at https://tinyurl.com/yzn95nzy (22 July 2021).

Core characteristics of constructive action/resistance

I have been presuming that anyone who got this far in the text would have a common-sense understanding of the phenomena being referred to as constructive action for change – construction involves building something new, like constructing a garden shed or a new concept. But for the sake of clarity I want to try and unpack this a little more.

i. Nonviolent direct action

For me constructive action is a form of nonviolent direct action. That is, it is an activity carried out by people themselves in order to bring about change in relationships and conditions that are perceived to be violent insofar as they cause damage and harm to people. In other words, it involves nonviolent action against violence that is carried out by people directly targeting the violent conditions themselves, rather than delegating or petitioning others to act on their behalf.[11]

ii. Prefigurative dimension

Constructive action for change is driven by the intention to bridge the gap between what-is and what-ought-to-be. That is, the action involves some attempt to create a change in the here-and-now that will contribute to wider processes of change towards a hoped-for future. But the key feature of this activity is that it involves a prefigurative element, with people trying to embody in their activities the kind of values and relationships they hope to see brought into being on a wider scale sometime in the future.

iii. Continuity between means and end

Given the second main dimension of the working definition of constructive action for change, it follows that in this type of action the means and the end are intrinsically linked. In the words of Martin Buber, 'we must create here and now the space now possible for the thing for which we are striving, so that it may come to fulfilment then'.[12]

---

11 See S. Vinthagen, *A theory of nonviolent action: How civil resistance works*, London: Zed Press, 2015, pp. 68-71.

12 M. Buber, *Paths in utopia,* London: Routledge & Kegan Paul, 1949, p. 13.

Typologies of constructive action for change

If by constructive action we are referring to any action that is intended to help bridge the gap between what is and what ought to be, and which also incorporates some element of prefiguration – then such a definition spans a vast range of phenomena. The question then arises – is it worthwhile to try to develop some kind of classificatory scheme whereby a distinction can be made between different types of constructive action for change?

One option would be a typology based on the nature of the agents performing the action – states, civil society groups, individuals. For illustration – when a state agency channels funding into the creation of new wind farms, this could be described as a form of constructive action in response to the climate crisis. When a local group sets up an advisory centre to counsel those who have suffered from some form of sexual abuse, this can be presented as a form of constructive action. When individuals start to use public transport rather than their private vehicles, this could also be deemed to be a form of constructive action. [13]

An alternative classificatory scheme might be based on the different spheres of life within which the activities take place. For example: squatters occupying vacant dwellings to provide shelter for the homeless;[14] groups setting up intentional communities in order to create alternatives to the institution of the nuclear family;[15] workers occupying a factory to continue production as a cooperative;[16] people living in a particular neighbourhood establishing their own social media network to

---

13 Classificatory schemes could be created that distinguished between different types of individual actors. Individuals with significant economic, social, financial and political power have contributed to change through their constructive action. The case of George Cadbury comes to mind. He developed housing in the Bourneville suburb of Birmingham for his employees in the late 19th century, driven by his Quaker conviction and commitment to improve the living standards of others. (G. Darley, *Villages of vision*, London: Granada, 1978, p. 140.)

14 See C. Ward, *Cotters and squatters: Housing's hidden history*, Nottingham: Five Leaves, 2002.

15 See A. Rigby, *Alternative realities: A study of communes and their members*, London: Routledge & Kegan Paul, 1974.

16 See https://www.uk.coop (25 September 2019).

foster mutual aid within the locality;[17] a local municipality making land available for allotments to enable people to grow their own produce;[18] a rural community setting up its own renewable energy scheme.[19] These are all examples of constructive action for change taking place within different spheres of life.

The key criterion by which to judge any classificatory scheme is whether it is useful for the purpose in hand. Truth to tell, throughout this book different ways of typifying constructive action for change will be adopted, as and when it appears useful and appropriate to the context. But one variable upon which a typology of different forms of constructive action for change can be based seems particularly significant - the degree of friction with the established order (and the defenders of the status quo) generated by the activities. So, in the remainder of this introductory chapter, I want to make a number of observations pertaining to this topic, which will crop up again and again in the following chapters.

Backstage – the space for constructive solidarity

One of the reasons constructive modes of resistance can be relatively 'friction-free' is because of the space where they take place, which is frequently backstage, away from the spotlights that public performances of protest can attract. There is a whole stratum of such action that exists largely hidden from public view and frequently overlooked by civil resistance scholars. I am referring to what might be termed everyday acts of constructive solidarity: the range of actions that can be taken by people during the course of their everyday lives as part of their attempts 'to make a difference' in support of some cause or other.

We might buy fair-trade groceries and favour Palestinian produce, maybe we volunteer with charitable organisations and contribute financially to worthy causes. All these activities that are integrated into our everyday life, can be influenced and informed to some degree by a broader commitment to do what we can in the here-and-now to bring about a fairer more caring world. Such activities can be labelled as forms

---

17 See https://nextdoor.co.uk/ (25 September 2019).

18 See D. Crouch & C. Ward, *The allotment: Its landscape and culture,* Nottingham: Five Leaves, 1997.

19 See https://tinyurl.com/yyj53uay (25 September 2019)

of constructive solidarity because they are carried out in support of those 'causes' with which we identify. Such activities are political with a small 'p'. They are not confronting the state or corporate interests in any dramatic fashion, neither do they typically create animosity and bitterness amongst one's fellow-citizens. But such actions can be seen to be addressing and to some extent challenging established relationships and institutional structures. Within the interstices of dominant power structures, such people are exercising their relative autonomy to do what they can, on however miniscule a scale, to create a better future for their fellow human-beings. The prefigurative element in this kind of solidarity activity is embodied in the fact that such people are acting in accordance with values that they hope to see embodied in institutions and relationships on a far wider scale in the future.

Such activities, integrated as they are into the mundane routines of people's lives, can be viewed through the frame of everyday resistance. Much of the research and scholarship on everyday resistance draws on the insights of James Scott, who focused on the 'hidden transcripts' of resistance as enacted by subalterns within authoritarian regimes where open resistance would result in severe repression.[20] Following Scott's lead, others have defined everyday resistance as 'resistance that is done routinely, but which is not politically articulated or formally organised … a form of activity that often avoids being detected as resistance.'[21] But resistance is not the preserve of subalterns. Resistance against particular targets (whether this be identifiable groups, individuals, institutional structures or worldviews) can be integrated into the lives of anybody who feels strongly enough about an issue. For example, many people who are concerned about Israel's ongoing occupation of Palestinian territories, and the accompanying abuse of basic human rights, engage in selective shopping in order to avoid purchasing Israeli-produce in general and Israeli settlement products in particular. For people like me the routine of checking the origins of produce before deciding whether or not to make

---

20 J. C. Scott, *Domination and the arts of resistance: Hidden transcripts*, London: Yale University Press, 1992.

21 S. Vinthagen & A. Johansson, 'Everyday resistance: Exploration of a concept and its theories', *Resistance Studies Magazine,* n. 1, 2013, p. 10. Accessible at https://tinyurl.com/yx8pfllb (7 September 2019).

a purchase is just a natural extension of our commitment to 'the cause'. For such people everyday resistance is what they do as activists, and there is no hard and fast distinction between everyday and 'normal' activism.[22]

The fact that our 'selective shopping' and kindred activities takes place 'backstage' as a mundane feature of everyday life means that relatively little friction is generated. The activities remain relatively 'low cost', and consequently can be sustained over significant periods of time.[23] Once again we are encountering a case where quiet forms of constructive activity can exercise a significant degree of influence on their oppositional targets, without generating any significant kind of friction at the micro-level. Cumulatively, the pressures generated by such grass-roots solidarity activities can exercise significant pressure, as evidenced by the successes of the Palestinian boycott, divestment and sanctions (BDS) movement.[24]

Front-stage - Contentious forms of constructive action

It needs to be emphasised that, in certain contexts, forms of constructive resistance do create friction and are seen as highly contentious by those committed to maintaining the status quo. This is particularly so if the activities are performed frontstage and seen to be a challenge to some aspect of the established order. Here, the most appropriate illustration that comes to mind is the example of Gerrard Winstanley and the Diggers who, in 1649, took over some common land in the south of England and began cultivation, in the hope that poor people elsewhere would follow their example. Within a week outraged local landowners had ousted them and incarcerated them in a local church.[25] Other illustrations come to

---

22 See P. Simi & R. Futrell, 'Negotiating white power activist stigma', *Social Problems*, v.56, n. 1, 2009, pp. 89-110.

23 On occasions, when a high-profile person exercises their ethical judgement in relation to the implications of their sense of solidarity with a particular cause, this can create significant friction with associated 'costs' for the activist. In September 2019 the German city of Dortmund rescinded its decision to award a literary prize to Kamila Shamsie because of her support for the BDS movement. See https://tinyurl.com/yxbncapk (26 September 2019).

24 A few days before writing this the news came that Ben and Jerry's Ice-cream would no longer sell their products in the Occupied Palestinian Territories (including East Jerusalem). See https://tinyurl.com/7mrw6p98 (23 July 2021).

25 The case of Winstanley and the Diggers is reviewed in more detail in the next chapter.

mind, like the blocking of the entrance to a nuclear power construction site by a windmill constructed by activists.[26] I also seem to remember years ago community activists constructing a temporary children's adventure playground on a site due for commercial redevelopment, whilst at the site of the proposed nuclear power station at Torness, in East Lothian, Scotland in May 1979 there was a weekend of activities (the Torness Gathering) that combined a whole panoply of constructive activities alongside highly contentious attempts to occupy the construction site.[27]

Contentious & constructive modes of action levels of participation

Another dimension to the relationship between protest performances and constructive activities relates to the level of participation. In a study of the popular unarmed Palestinian resistance to occupation, carried out by Marwan Darweish and myself, one of the activists interviewed in 2015 observed that what the Palestinians called 'popular resistance' was no longer popular, insofar as the local people were no longer prepared to participate. She went on to present the increasingly widespread view that there was insufficient reason to risk injury, imprisonment or a large fine by participating in protest actions that no longer seemed effective in terms of achieving tangible results.[28] Many of us who are not living under occupation are also averse to seeking nonviolent martyrdom through getting arrested on some protest demonstration or civil disobedience project. But we are prepared to go about our daily lives quietly, if not covertly, making such changes as we can in order to sow small seeds of the future in the here-and-now.

Gandhi was perhaps the best-known historical advocate of constructive action as a basis for change, with his emphasis on the primacy of his constructive programme as the foundation for *Swaraj*

---

26 Personal communication.

27 See R. Edwards, 'When SCRAM began', 25 March 1994. Accessible at https://tinyurl.com/2cxwvxdk (23 July 2021). See also the film *On site Torness 1979* accessible at https://tinyurl.com/z54zfjjc (29 July 2021).

28 M. Darweish & A. Rigby, *Popular protest in Palestine: The uncertain future of unarmed resistance*, London: Pluto Press, 2015, pp. 97-99.

(independence). One of the key strengths of the constructive programme, from his perspective, was the opportunity it created for large swathes of the population to play an active role in the freedom struggle.

Constructive modes of resistance and movement resilience

Other things being equal, one of the strengths of many forms of constructive resistance is that they are more sustainable than the more contentious and confrontational modes of challenging the status quo. Gandhi also recognised the sustainability of constructive work for change as against the more offensive forms of nonviolent protest. Involvement in the constructive programme, he believed, provided cadres with a safe-haven to which they could withdraw from the 'front-line struggle' in order to avoid burn-out and re-charge their batteries. By engaging in the constructive programme they would be able to sustain their sense of activism and involvement in the struggle, particularly during the relatively quiet phases of what was – in Gramscian terms - a drawn-out war of position.[29] In chapter three the centrality of constructive action within Gandhi's theory and practice of change is examined in some detail.

Constructive action as preparation for other forms of direct action

Mahmoud Soliman, a Palestinian active in the popular resistance against the continuing Israeli occupation in the West Bank, has given an example of how his father's steadfastness (*sumud*) in continuing to farm his land, in the face of settlers trying to dislodge him, helped prepare his father to engage in other modes of civil resistance – a contemporary example of

---

29 B. Chandra, *India's struggle for independence*, New Delhi: Penguin, 1989, p. 510. The Italian Marxist, Antonio Gramsci used the terms 'War of Position' and 'War of Manoeuvre' to indicate two different phases in the class struggle. The war of manoeuvre referred to the phase of open conflict between classes, where the outcome is decided by direct clashes between revolutionaries and the State. War of position, on the other hand, referred to the slow, hidden cultural struggle to gain influence and power through swaying people's hearts and minds. See D. Egan, 'Rethinking war of manoeuvre/ war of position: Gramsci and the military metaphor', *Critical Sociology*, v. 40, n. 4, 2014, pp. 521-538.

how constructive resistance can strengthen and reinforce involvement in broader forms of resistance.

> My father believes that farming his land is the most important thing. He is always arguing with me about the symbolic resistance that we carry out every Friday at the entrance to the village. He rejects all of the Israeli policies on the ground and he always refuses to cooperate with the Israeli Civil Administration, but he believes that the real resistance is to be on the land and to plant trees and to cultivate it. One day, he was rehabilitating a piece of land next to the illegal settlement of Efrat to the west of the village, when the security guard of the illegal settlement came to stop him by asking him to prove that this was his land. My father ignored him and refused to talk to him, and, rather than kick the security guard away, he took off his trousers and started releasing himself from them in front of the security guard, who was forced to leave. My father used his body as a form of nonviolent action to defend his land. Through the continuity of the weekly demonstrations at the entrance to the village and his work on his land, my father was convinced to transition from sumud and agricultural work to a more organised form of resistance. He understands that Jerusalem is more at risk than the village, so he volunteers his time to stay in Jerusalem in the Al-Aqsa mosque every Friday and even on other days. He has been involved in organising nonviolent demonstrations and sit-ins, and he has also become involved in organised resistance to prevent settlers from entering the mosque. This is an empirical example of how sumud leads to organised resistance.[30]

Once again the Palestinian unarmed resistance struggle against occupation provides a contemporary illustration of this complementary relationship between the constructive and the more confrontational modes of resistance.

---

30 M. Soliman, *Mobilisation and demobilisation of the Palestinian society towards popular resistance from 2004-2014*, Coventry University, unpublished Ph.D. thesis, 2019, p. 275.

The limits of contentious repertoires of civil resistance: Beyond counting arses!

Front-stage protest performances designed to cause friction can result in severe reprisals, particularly in more repressive authoritarian regimes. In such circumstances activists might well decide that the most significant form of opposition is through less contentious modes of constructive action to make change happen, largely hidden from the opponent's view.

Moreover, even in societies where there is considerable space available for protest politics, there have been persistent threads of criticism of movements that devote the bulk of their energies to publicity-seeking protest actions. In 1963, during the first phase of the nuclear disarmament movement in the UK, some libertarian socialists critical of the campaigning focus of the Campaign for Nuclear Disarmament (CND) issued a pamphlet with the great title *Beyond counting arses*. It was reprinted for circulation during the 'second wave' of the nuclear disarmament movement in the 1980s. It was a coruscating critique of those who believed that nuclear weapons could be removed through the power of public opinion driven by ever larger protest demonstrations and marches. The authors critiqued such 'weekend activism' and urged readers to engage in ongoing subversive action 'to hinder the warfare state in every possible way'.[31]

A similar view was expressed by Kingsley Widmer in the pages of *Anarchy* in 1965. In an article entitled 'The limits of pacifism' he urged a more covert and more sustainable style of resistance:

> Among the choices against a destructive order, many pacifists (like myself, people with violent feelings) often show an inadequate appreciation of, and even a moral antipathy towards, the slyer forms of resistance, institutional and ideological sabotage, and general 'Good Soldier Schweikism'. The desire to 'witness' to the truth by heroic confrontation is essential, and often admirable, but there are many more modest mansions in the house of protest.
>
> Pacifist gestures of peace marches and strikes, of refusing taxes and drafts, of public (and publicity conscious) civil

---

31 'Beyond counting arses', reprinted in *Solidarity*, II, n. 11, 1963, p.12.

disobedience, have their place, but is it not a limited one? Much such direct action is small-time political competition with the big boys at their own games of publicity and pressure. If, to put the issue fancifully, one were Inspector-General of pacifists, the best question might not be 'What public protest have you made?' Rather it could be such questions as 'What have you done today to undermine the efficiency, unity, blandness, and ideology of the authoritarian bureaucracies?'[32]

To that we might add another (more constructive) question: 'What have you done today to sow the seeds necessary for a better future?'

---

32 K. Widmer, 'The limits of pacifism', *Anarchy 52*, June 1965, pp. 161-66, p. 163. In the same article Widmer argued persuasively that negation was a necessary complement to constructive action.

2

INTENTIONAL LIVING
AND THE POWER OF EXEMPLARY ACTION

Personal preface

Many decades ago, as a schoolboy, I came to the realisation that I was a pacifist. The origins of this commitment to nonviolence and abhorrence of killing was the basic Christian ethic that I absorbed at the Sunday School attached to our local church. I adopted that basic injunction to love our neighbour as oneself and all that went with it. I guess that from this grew the notion that if we were enjoined to love our neighbour, our fellow human-beings, then there was no way it was morally acceptable or ethical to kill them. That was the start, manifested to some degree by my involvement with the local nuclear disarmament group, in which a leading role was played by our next-door neighbour at that time, a member of the pacifist *Peace Pledge Union*.

When I made it to university I started to read some of the classic pacifist texts. I was also exposed to a passionate presentation made by Ronald Sampson of the famous Russian novelist Leo Tolstoy's anarcho-pacifism, which has stayed in my mind ever since. Later I came across Sampson's publication, *The anarchist basis of pacifism* – a powerful advocacy of what I would now call a politics of everyday life:

> In order to abolish war, it is certainly necessary to refuse to take part in it, but it is also necessary to live in a way that is conducive to peace and not to war. The way of life that leads to war is one that is based on competition in wealth-getting in order to secure primacy of power and prestige over others ...[1]

---

1 R. Sampson, *The anarchist basis of pacifism*, London: Peace Pledge Union, 1970, pp. 17-18.

By this time, in the mid-1960s, I was reading and selling *Peace News* around the university and it was in the pages of the paper during that period that I was introduced to the writing of people like Thomas Merton and Paul Goodman.[2]

I started to appreciate our own responsibility (and even complicity) in regard to the ongoing social injustices perpetuating the multiple horrors in the world – the linkages between personal change and wider social transformation. One of the core messages that came across was that the creation of a more peaceful and just way of life was an essential dimension too often overlooked in the protest politics of the later 1960s. 1968 found me at the University of Essex and it was there, as a postgraduate student in Sociology, that this mix of Tolstoy, Merton and Goodman was enriched by my growing interest in anarchism as a 'natural extension' of my pacifism and radical idealism. The monthly magazine *Anarchy*, edited by Colin Ward, was a wonderful source of insight throughout this period of my life. What resonated with me was Ward's conviction that the free society, one organised without domination, would never be achieved through some cataclysmic revolutionary overthrow of the old order. The challenge was to work constructively to extend the already existing spheres of free action within society. In his book *Anarchy in Action* he wrote on the first page:

> How would you feel if you discovered that the society in which
> you would really like to live was already here, apart from a
> few local difficulties like exploitation, war, dictatorship and
> starvation? The argument of this book is that an anarchist
> society, a society which organises itself without authority,
> is always in existence, like a seed beneath the snow, buried
> under the weight of the state and its bureaucracy, capitalism
> and its waste, privilege and its injustices, nationalism and its
> suicidal loyalties , religious differences and their superstitious
> separatism. ...

---

2 Thomas Merton (1915-1968) was an American Trappist monk, poet and social activist. Paul Goodman (1911-1972) was an American writer, poet, bi-sexual and draft-resister, best known nowadays perhaps as the author of *Growing up absurd.*

> … once you begin to look at human society from an anarchist point of view you discover that the alternatives are already in the interstices of the dominant power structure. If you want to build a free society, the parts are all at hand. [3]

Great stuff! The historian David Goodway, in one of his appreciations of Colin Ward, quoted some lines written back in 1958 highlighting the relationship between the micro-level of our everyday lives and the macro-level of 'big issues'. His words still resonate:

> … the conflict between authority and liberty is a permanent aspect of the human condition and not something that can be resolved by a vaguely specified social revolution. … the choice between libertarian and authoritarian solutions occurs every day and in every way, and the extent to which we choose, or accept, or are fobbed off with, or lack the imagination and inventiveness to discover alternatives to the authoritarian solutions to small problems, is the extent to which we are their powerless victims in big affairs.[4]

This was the background that fed into my decision in 1969 to devote my doctoral research to a study of the emerging commune movement in the UK. To my mind the communes were significant cells of what people were starting to call the 'alternative society', emerging within the interstices of the status quo. What I did not realise at that time was that the commune-dwellers and kindred spirits of the late 1960s and 1970s were the contemporary carriers of a long tradition of what we might call intentional living – seeking systemic change through the power of constructive action.

The aim of this chapter is to provide the reader with a sense of this historical thread within the UK – people who have sought to live their lives according to an ideal and a set of values that they hoped would be adopted at a societal level, seeing their own attempts to live according to their chosen precepts as a form of exemplary action that others might follow.[5]

---

3   C. Ward, *Anarchy in action*, London: Freedom Press, 1996, p. 18.
4   Quoted in D. Goodway, 'Colin Ward and the New Left', in C. Levy, ed. *Colin Ward: Life, times and thought*, London: Lawrence and Wishart, 2013, p. 60.
5   The thread I trace in the following pages is restricted to the UK, for the simple

Gerard Winstanley and the Diggers
– constructive action as contentious resistance

> In the beginning of Time, the great Creator Reason, made the
> Earth to be a Common Treasury, to preserve Beasts, Birds,
> Fishes, and Man, the lord that was to govern this Creation …
> not one word was spoken in the beginning, that one branch
> of mankind should rule over another. … when once the Earth
> becomes a Common Treasury again ….Then this Enmity in all
> Lands will cease, for none shall dare to seek a Dominion over
> others, neither shall any dare to kill another, nor desire more of
> the Earth then another …

These were the words with which Gerrard Winstanley opened his
manifesto of the True Levellers or Diggers, written in 1649.[6]

Many in England during this period felt they were living in a
momentous and earth-shaking time, with the established order crumbling
and old prophecies and dreams about to be realised. The Civil War had
resulted in the defeat of the Royalists, the king had been beheaded – it
was a revolutionary period and many envisioned a new world about to
be born.[7] But the English Civil War had brought disruption in its wake.
There had been disastrous harvests that led to widespread hunger and
unemployment. Mutinies broke out in the army when men who refused
to volunteer for service in Ireland were demobilised without payment of
arrears. The cost of living rocketed whilst wages lagged, and disbanded
soldiers and other 'master-less men' were trying to find a way to make
a living. There was a genuine fear amongst property-owners that their
world was about to be turned upside down.[8]

---

reason that this is the tradition with which I am most familiar. For those
seeking a broader and more comprehensive coverage of this tradition, there are
a number of sources that can be consulted.

6   Accessible at https://tinyurl.com/ax5hrsw (30 June 2021).

7   The English Civil War (1642-1651) was essentially a battle for control of
English government fought between the Royalists supporting the monarch and
the 'Roundheads' supporting Parliament. The main constitutional outcome
was that henceforth no English monarch could rule without the consent of
parliament.

8   The standard historical work on this period remains C. Hill, *The world turned*

This was the context out of which emerged a small group of visionaries who called themselves the True Levellers, better known as the Diggers. On 1 April 1649 they took over some 'common' land on St George's Hill near Walton-on-Thames in Surrey. They started to cultivate it communally, hoping that poor people everywhere would follow their example and that property owners would voluntarily surrender their estates and join in communal production. They were joined by others, but within a week outraged local landowners had instigated armed raids on them and had them incarcerated in a local church. Taken before Lord Fairfax, Oliver Cromwell's Commander-in-Chief, Winstanley and his companion William Everard explained to him their purpose:

> ... to restore the Creation to its former condition. That as God promised to make the barren land fruitful, so now what they did was to restore the ancient community of enjoying the fruits of the Earth, and to distribute the benefits thereof to the poor and needy, and to feed the hungry and to clothe the naked.[9]

Over the next twelve months perhaps thirty similar initiatives came into being, albeit short-lived. The local inhabitants of Walton continued their assaults on their unwelcome intruders, who moved their community a few miles to land at Cobham Manor owned by a local minister. By April 1650 they had eleven acres under cultivation and had built themselves seven dwellings. But the attacks from local landowners and state authorities continued, and by the end of 1650 the communities had been routed and their members dispersed. So it goes. But their vision of Mother Earth as a common treasury for all has continued to inspire later generations. As Peter Marshall wrote,

> Despite the brief shining of their candle ... the inspiring creed and example of the Diggers lives on. ... The Diggers are the true ancestors of all those who wish to live in harmony with each other and close to the earth and who insist that they can

---

upside down: Radical ideas during the English Revolution, Harmondsworth: Penguin Books, 1975.

9   W. Armytage, *Heavens below: Utopian experiments in England 1560-1960*, London: Routledge & Kegan Paul, 1961, pp. 20-21.

manage their own lives without the burden of external laws and government.[10]

Winstanley and his comrades expressed themselves in the Biblical language of the day, and many of their ideas and activities were inspired by visions and direct experience of 'God's Word'. His vision was of a time when Reason, which he saw as God's immanence, pervaded all social institutions and peace in its deepest sense would prevail. This is reminiscent of the Quaker injunction dating from the same period that we should live our lives so as to take away the occasion of all war. Indeed, amongst those that emerged out of the religious and socio-political ferment of the post-Civil War period in 17th century England there was little to distinguish the early Quakers from other seekers and dissenters who shared the belief that they could access the Divine directly, without the intercession of a priestly caste. As the historian Christopher Hill observed,

> From, say, 1645 to 1653, there was a great overturning, questioning, revaluing, of everything in England. Old institutions, old beliefs, old values came in question. Men moved easily from one critical group to another, and a Quaker of the early 1650s had far more in common with a Leveller, a Digger or a Ranter than with a modern member of the Society of Friends.[11]

Religious dissenters and the cooperative vision

Early Quakers were repeatedly prosecuted and imprisoned on charges of blasphemy and causing disturbances, including the holding of religious

---

10 P. Marshall, 'Digging for freedom', in C. Coates, ed., *Utopia Britannica: British utopian experiments: 1325 to 1945*, London: Diggers & Dreamers, 2001, pp. 21-25, p. 25.

11 C. Hill, 1975, p. 14. Ranters believed that if the spirit of God was within you, then you were free from all external constraints. 'Sin hath its conception only in the imagination ... No matter what scripture, saints or churches say, if that within thee do not condemn thee, thou shalt not be condemned.' Such antinomianism provided a free-pass for licentiousness and George Fox, the founder of The Religious Society of Friends (Quakers), devoted considerable efforts to distance his followers from such tendencies.

assemblies outside the established churches and refusing to affirm oaths of allegiance to the state. As a consequence some of their number were attracted by the promise of a life free from persecution in the New World of North America.[12] Amongst these was a group of 'Shaking Quakers' from the north-west of England, led by Mother Ann Lee. In 1772 she had received a vision that a place had been prepared for them in America and a small group of them arrived in New York in 1774. Two years later they bought some land in upstate New York. Over the ensuing years their numbers grew, based on a philosophy that had been revealed to Mother Ann in a series of visions. God was bi-sexual, male and female. Hence, all people, regardless of gender or race, were fundamentally equal. Celibacy, the regular confession of sins, separation from the outside profane world and communal living (as a living witness of the bonds of love between all believers) were the key tenets by which they lived.[13] They were convinced they were establishing the nuclei of the Kingdom of Heaven on earth in the full expectation that the millennium – the thousand years of heavenly order - was in the process of becoming. Their numbers expanded and by 1850 they had almost 4000 members. The Shakers were the most successful communal sect in American history, with estimates that around 20,000 people spent at least some of their life within their intentional communities over their 200 year history.[14]

By their example religious communities such as the Shakers had an impact that resonated far beyond their co-religionists. Crucially they fed the social imagination of radicals seeking alternative and non-exploitative modes of organising social life. Word of the material prosperity of the Shakers reached Germany and helped convince Frederick Engels of the virtues of communism, whilst some 30 years earlier the utopian socialist Robert Owen observed that the community life of the Shakers showed that 'wealth could be so easily created for all'.[15] According to Edward

---

12 Pennsylvania, founded by William Penn in 1681, guaranteed religious freedom and attracted many Quakers.

13 Ann Lee believed that sexual relations were the origins of the human fall from grace and the root of all sin.

14 C. Coates, 2001, p. 31.

15 E. Spann, *Brotherly tomorrows: Movements for a cooperative society in America, 1820-1920,* New York: Columbia University Press, 1989, p. 7.

Spann the millenarian sects appealed to hopeful radicals searching for a sure and nonviolent way to utopia. He wrote, 'The success of the millenarian sects seemed to demonstrate that brotherly cooperation was a realistic alternative to competitive individualism that had grown into the weakening bonds of traditional community.'[16]

The big question, of course, for those who sought to remake the world along nonviolent communitarian lines, was whether the success of millenarian sects was due to their sectarian faith or their cooperative formula? Robert Owen believed he had the answer.

Robert Owen: The prophet of New Harmony

During the early decades of the 19th century Robert Owen played a significant role, at least in the English-speaking world, as a visionary who believed that humanity could create a paradise for itself here on earth by following his advice and example. It was his fundamental belief that human character was moulded by the environment, that people had become selfish and competitive as a result of irrational social arrangements – particularly the 'trinity of monstrous evils': religion, marriage, and private property. Hence the over-riding need to transform all those circumstances that promoted 'the principle of individual interests over the principle of union and mutual cooperation. He announced, 'We can only change human nature by changing the circumstances in which man lives, and this change we will make so complete, that man will become a totally different being.' In 1816, at the opening of a new institute for learning in New Lanark, Scotland, he proclaimed:

> Individuals may attach to the term millennium I know not;
> but I know that society may be formed so as to exist without
> crime, without poverty, with health greatly improved, with
> little, if any, misery, and with intelligence and happiness
> increased an hundred-fold; and no obstacle whatsoever
> intervenes at this moment, except ignorance, to prevent such a
> state of society from becoming universal.[17]

---

16 Spann, p. 8.
17 Robert Owen: *An address to the inhabitants of New Lanark.* Accessible at https://tinyurl.com/yxpzlzkv (15 October 2019).

Robert Owen

A Welshman who had proven himself a successful businessman, by 1800 he had become a part-owner of the textile mills at New Lanark where he soon developed a reputation as a pioneer of what we might call welfare capitalism – providing pensions, cheap housing and medical care for his workers whilst cutting working hours and increasing profits. Convinced he had discovered the 'science of the influence of circumstances', he developed the idea of a network of what he called 'Agricultural and manufacturing villages of unity and mutual cooperation'.

There are grounds for believing that in developing his plans for cooperative villages Owen was influenced by his familiarity with the cooperative settlement established by members of the Moravian Church at Fairfield near Manchester in 1785. Owen was based in Manchester from 1788 – 1799 prior to moving to New Lanark and could hardly have been unaware of the new community established at Fairfield. Gillian Darley has highlighted the significance of the example set by the settlement which was planned and built by its own people, who lived in community houses and worked in the settlement, which had its own inn, shop, bakery, farm, laundry, fire-engine, night-watchman, inspector of weights and measures, an overseer of roads, and even its own physician.[18]

> The obvious contentment of those who lived there proved that the level at which employees elsewhere were expected to live was inhumane and bestial. In addition it exemplified the success of a system of cooperation and self-sufficiency, provided that the administration was efficient and the principles upon which the settlement was based were adhered to.[19]

Robert Owen envisaged villages that would house between one and two thousand people in areas of intensive agriculture, with factories built

18 See https://tinyurl.com/weneh8a (30 December 2020).
19 G. Darley, *Villages of vision*, London: Paladin, 1978, p. 153.

to employ the labour not required on the land. They would be built as parallelograms of inter-connected buildings in order to maximise the cooperative way of life, with dormitories for the children and provision for communal eating and socialising.[20] In 1824 he heard that a religious community (the Rappites) in Indiana wished to sell their settlement. He went out there and in 1825 bought the property. It spread over 20,000 acres, consisting of a complete village with houses, churches, dormitories, textile factory, distillery and brewery etc. New Harmony was ready for immediate occupation, and as the Rappites moved out some 900 newcomers moved in, answering Owen's public invitation to 'the industrious and well-disposed of all nations' to join in recreating the world.

Owen's refusal to make any sort of selection amongst the applicants was a key reason for the subsequent instability of the community. During its two years of existence there were seven different constitutions and several divisions into smaller offshoot communities. Eventually New Harmony lapsed into individualism, with much of the property being leased or sold as individual holdings.[21] Owen returned to Britain where he continued his involvement in the promotion of communities based on cooperation and economic equality. Unfortunately most of these had short, crisis-ridden lives and by the mid-19th century there was little material evidence of their existence.[22]

---

20 Owen was convinced that his Villages of Cooperation could be brought into being with the assistance of capital from landowners and industrialists. They would be induced to support the ventures by appealing to a range of motives: anticipated profit, benevolence, belief in cooperation, avoidance of violent class conflict etc.

21 About ten Owenite communities were founded in North America in the 1820s but none lasted more than two or three years. J.F.C. Harrison, 'The Owenite socialist movement in Britain and the United States a comparative study', *Labor History*, v. 9, n. 3, pp. 323-337, July 2008, p. 325.

22 See R. G. Garnett, *Cooperation and the Owenite socialist communities in Britain, 1825–45*, Manchester: University of Manchester Press, 1972.

From Villages of Cooperation to model industrial villages

Be that as it may, the Owenite plans and experiments of 1825– 845 had a significant impact on British movements for change during the latter half of the 19th century. There were numerous threads of influence. One was town planning and housing. By the turn of the century new model villages were being established by paternalistic factory owners with a concern for the social and moral welfare of their employees. Sir Titus Salt was to the fore in creating the village of Saltaire to house the workers at his woollen mill on the outskirts of Bradford.[23] His example was followed by the Quakers George Cadbury and Joseph Rowntree, who were responsible for the construction of Bourneville in the Birmingham suburbs and the 'garden village' of New Earswick outside York. Port Sunlight was constructed in the same period by William Lever (Viscount Leverhulme). Each of these owed something to the principles that had informed the Owenite communities.[24] Furthermore, the campaigning and the personal example set by people like Cadbury and others was of tremendous importance in applying pressure on the British political establishment to take up the challenge of housing reform.[25]

Owenism and the cooperative movement

Another sphere within which the influence of Owen's schemes to transform society can be traced is the cooperative movement in Britain and beyond. In the early decades of the 19th century in Britain the growth of 'Owenism' reflected the yearning of so many to escape and forge an alternative to the poverty and hardship that accompanied the burgeoning industrial revolution and the accompanying loss of more traditional

---

23 See Armytage, 1961, pp. 251-4.

24 Garnett, p. 33. It should be noted in passing that these industrial villages were visited by overseas specialists concerned with addressing the challenges of providing adequate and healthy housing for working people in their own societies that were undergoing periods of rapid industrial and urban expansion.

25 Darley, p. 140. The Housing of the Working Class Acts of 1890 and 1900 empowered local municipalities to purchase land by compulsory order and to construct housing for working people.

sources of solace and support. This interest in practical steps to alleviate suffering manifested itself in various ways, including the development of the cooperative movement. As the historian John Harrison noted, out of Owen's (unsuccessful) efforts to establish sustainable experimental communities as a means of transforming society, 'emerged a new type of Owenite institution - the cooperative trading association. From 1828 cooperative stores increased rapidly and by 1830 The Co-operator claimed that 300 existed in the United Kingdom.'[26]

In 1844 a group of working men in Rochdale met together to form a cooperative society. Amongst their number were several who had been local leaders of the Owenite movement in the town, which one visitor noted stood out in its Owenite zeal, with self-improvement activities taking place almost every night of the week at the local New Social Institution – one of the many mutual self-help initiatives that had been launched in the town in the spirit of Owenite socialism.[27] They shared the vision of their forerunners in the cooperative movement, resolving:

> As soon as practicable, this society shall proceed to arrange
> the powers of production, distribution, education and
> government, in other words to establish a self-supporting home
> colony of united interest, or assist other societies in establishing
> such colonies.[28]

This initiative was a classic form of constructive action – a relatively small-scale project aimed at addressing practical needs in the here-and-now that would also constitute steps towards a much grander vision. By the late 1870s the number of cooperative societies in the UK had grown to over a thousand, and the success of the movement inspired others in Europe and North America to launch their own cooperatives, based to a greater or lesser degree on the Rochdale model.[29]

---

26 Harrison (2008), p. 325.
27 B. Fairbairn, *The meaning of Rochdale: The Rochdale Pioneers and the cooperative principles*, 1994. Accessible at https://tinyurl.com/uzg9427 (5 December 2019).
28 Quoted in Armytage, p. 239.
29 Fairbairn, p. 12.

Edward Carpenter and search for new ways of relating and desiring

Some 45 miles from Rochdale across the Pennines is the city of Sheffield. In Sheffield, as in Rochdale, Robert Owen and Owenism exerted a significant influence on the development of working class organisation in the city during the first half of the 19th century. One institutional outcome of this influence was the establishment of a Hall of Science, which was opened by Owen himself on 17 March 1839 as a centre for workers' education and mobilisation. It was recorded in one of the local papers that many of the early lectures were devoted to 'developing the principles on which to establish home colonies, which are the only remedies for the numerous evils that are now affecting all classes of the community.'[30] According to Sheila Rowbotham,

> The Owenite Hall of Science in Rockingham Street provided a centre for a plebeian underground of rebels and utopians, embracing men and women affected by the radicalism of the first half of the century, along with Secularists, Unitarians and Quakers.[31]

Amongst the many activities taking place were discussion groups on the nature of communism, and in the early 1870s a number of the participants decided that in order to live as communists they should establish a communal farm. They began saving a penny a week, then the art critic and philanthropist John Ruskin offered to lend them the money needed to buy some land to the south-west of Sheffield.[32] One of their neighbours and kindred-spirits was Edward Carpenter who came to live a few miles away at Millthorpe in the early 1880s.[33]

Carpenter, perhaps best known nowadays as a pioneer advocate for sexual freedom and gay rights, was one of the most significant figures in the nascent socialist movement that was emerging in Britain during the

---

30 Quoted in J. Salt, 'The Sheffield Hall of Science', *The vocational aspect of secondary and further education,* v. 12, n. 25, 1960, pp. 133-138, p. 133.

31 S. Rowbotham, *Edward Carpenter: A life of liberty and love,* London: Verso, 2008, p. 60.

32 A penny would buy you a daily newspaper in the 1870s.

33 Rowbotham, p. 66.

late 19th century.[34] There was a buzzing utopianism about the decade between the mid-1880s and 1890s. Becoming a socialist had some of the characteristics of a 'conversion experience'. Katherine St John Conway read Carpenter's *England's Ideal* (1887) and recalled that 'the vision of a new world had been shown me; of the earth reborn to beauty and joy.'[35] For many new socialists their 'conversion' meant joining a new crusade requiring a change in their way of life. As Stephen Yeo has pointed out, it was Carpenter's *Towards democracy* (1883) that was the fullest expression of what it felt like to experience this unity between revolutionary change on a societal level and the transformation in the taken-for-granted routines of everyday life, the fusion between politics and morality, in which moral imperatives themselves were part of the social agency to herald in a new social order.[36] Speaking at the opening of the Commonwealth Café in Sheffield early in 1887 Carpenter emphasised that socialism was more than the transfer of capital from private to public ownership, it 'meant the entire regeneration of society in art, in science, in religion and in literature and the building up of a new life

Edward Carpenter

---

34 An indicative timeline: 1881 - Social Democratic Federation; 1884 – Fabian Society; 1885 - Socialist League; 1893 - Independent Labour Party; 1900 - Labour Representation Committee (morphed into British Labour Party).

35 Quoted in S. Yeo, 'A new life: The religion of socialism in Britain, 1883-1896', *History Workshop Journal*, n. 4, 1977, pp. 5-56, p. 12.

36 Yeo, p. 14.

in which industrial socialism was the foundation.'[37] Carpenter practised what he preached, buying a cottage at Millthorpe, some eight miles to the south of Sheffield, where he lived the simple life – one of the early members of the 'brown rice and sandals brigade' – eventually to be joined there in the late 1890's by his partner George Merrill. [38]

Carpenter came early to the conclusion that if attitudes towards same-sex relationships were to change, then society itself would need to change. Accordingly, alongside pursuing his own alternative lifestyle, he campaigned on a whole range of issues, all driven by his quest for a new and more caring way of living and relating to other human beings and to nature. Sheila Rowbotham attempted to capture some of the scope of his concerns in the introduction to her biography:

> During the early 1880s, when the first socialist and anarchist groupings emerged in Britain, Carpenter was among the first to challenge capitalism as a social and economic system, linking external transformation with new forms of relating and desiring. … Carpenter devised a flexible version of socialism with anarchist stripes which put the emphasis on changing everyday living and behaviour. Stretching socialism towards environmental and humanitarian causes, he campaigned for clean air, prison reform and animal rights. He came to symbolise the possibility of a new lifestyle without the trappings of Victorian bourgeois respectability …[39]

One of the dilemmas that a free spirit like Carpenter faced as his fame spread was that his life at the cottage in Millthorpe came to be viewed as a model to be emulated by those who were also seeking social transformation through personal liberation. This was an anathema to Carpenter, who had a strong thread of anarchism running through his being. He hated the idea of replacing one set of constricting rules by a new frame of inhibiting normative prescriptions, a stance which was also reflected in his refusal to adumbrate a specific vision of the new social

---

37 Quoted in Rowbotham, p. 112.
38 From a wealthy family, Carpenter embraced a simple life-style but used his inheritance to keep his escape routes open – taking off from time to time in pursuit of sun, sex and spiritual enlightenment! (Rowbotham, p.7)
39 Rowbotham, pp. 1-2.

order except in the most general of terms. Scientific socialists tended to dismiss as faddish Carpenter's back-to-nature enthusiasms and the practice of simple living, but he did strike a resonant chord with many of his contemporaries who shared his ethical concern about how to live the good life. Moreover, his writings and his lived example continued to inspire kindred spirits long after his death in 1929, as Sheila Rowbotham concluded:

> The utopian energy which carried Carpenter and his friends along in the early 1880s overflowed into subsequent decades, inspiring ventures in communal living and working, progressive educational experiments, alternative diets, fashion and décor. It also fostered ideas about ethical consumption and a conviction that theorising social change involved living some part of the future in the here and now.[40]

Tolstoyan 'communities of saints'

In 1894 Tolstoy's *The kingdom of God is within you* was published in English. In her preface the translator expressed the view that 'his destructive criticism of the present social and political regime will become a powerful force in the work of disintegration and social reconstruction which is going on around us.'[41] Tolstoy urged absolute nonviolence, believing that all forms of coercion were contrary to the Christian 'Law of love' – hence his condemnation of the institutions of the state which were based on coercion and violence, manifested most clearly in the practice of war. Aligned with his uncompromising nonviolence and fundamental rejection of the core institutions of the state was the conviction that the greatest force at hand for socio-political transformation was the capacity of individuals to refuse to cooperate with the state and obey its immoral diktats. Individuals had a duty to observe a higher moral code than that of the state – the purpose of life was to exemplify goodness and abstain from participating in any form of violence.[42]

---

40 Rowbotham, p. 103.
41 Constance Garnett, translator's preface to L. Tolstoy, *The kingdom of God is within you*, New York: Cassell, 1894.
42 Tolstoy wrote, 'You need only free yourself from falsehood and your situation will inevitably change of itself. There is one and only one thing in life in which

In developing his ideas Tolstoy had been influenced to some degree by the example of world-rejecting anabaptist groups such as the Doukhobors who sought to follow their divinely-ordained way of life by living and working together as communities of believers. In fact Tolstoy had little confidence in the capacity of 'communities of saints amongst sinners' to bring about change.[43] Despite this, idealists in Britain and elsewhere created something of a Tolstoyan movement, setting up cooperative communities where they sought to live simple lives untainted by the evils of capitalism and the state and, by so doing, demonstrate to others that a more moral and fulfilling life was possible. In 1894 a Brotherhood Church was established in Croydon to the south of London and two years later a group of men and women from the church established a Tolstoyan community at Purleigh in Essex.[44] In 1898 some of their number created a new community, Whiteway, on 42 acres of land just a few miles from the town of Stroud in Gloucestershire. One of the founders, Nellie Shaw, later wrote a history of Whiteway in which some of the early members explained something of their motivation and mission:

> To live a happy, idyllic life, free from carking care and the responsibility of property? Yes, that and something more.
> We do not set ourselves up as reformers of society, but try to reform ourselves. If we cannot be actively useful and good we can at least cease doing evil by competing with others …. To live as far as possible up to our ideals is what we are striving for.[45]

---

it is granted man to be free and over which he has full control – all else being beyond his power. The one thing is to perceive truth and profess it.' Quoted in J. Hunt, 'Gandhi, Tolstoy, and the Tolstoyans', in H. Dyck, ed., *The pacifist impulse in historical perspective*, Toronto: University of Toronto Press, 1996, pp. 260-277, p. 261.

43   Quoted in A. G. Higgins, *A history of the Brotherhood Church*: Stapleton: Brotherhood Church, 1982, p. 7.

44   See M Holman, 'The Purleigh Colony: Tolstoyan togetherness in the late 1890s', in M. Jones, ed., *New essays on Tolstoy*, Cambridge: Cambridge University Press, 1978, pp. 194–222.

45   Quoted in N. Shaw, *Whiteway: A colony on the Cotswolds*, London: Daniels, 1935, pp. 59-60.

There was also a small group in the Beeston neighbourhood of Leeds who formed a producers' cooperative making stockings. Dennis Hardy has recorded how this anarchist community, however small it was in terms of numbers, became a thorn in the side of the authorities – refusing to register the birth of their children and refusing to complete census forms. They also engaged in a long-running battle with the local education authority about their right to educate their children at home and not send them to a state school. Then, in 1914, they refused to support the British war effort.[46] After the First World War, in 1921, they bought some land in the countryside at Stapleton, near Pontefract in Yorkshire, and proceeded to build their community. The clashes with the local state authorities continued – homes demolished because they did not correspond to building regulations, refusal to send children to state schools and the refusal to complete census returns were just some

Entrance to Brotherhood Church, Yorkshire (2007)

of the confrontations. During the Second World War the remaining colonists refused to accept ration books or to sign up to any other special arrangements, and were active in the Peace Pledge Union. The community at Stapleton remained in existence into the post-Second World War period – a complete anachronism in the 'modern world', remaining stubbornly beyond the pale of mainstream society.

My own experience of the Brotherhood Church at Stapleton goes back to me growing up in the 1950s. Our next-door neighbour had been a 'conchie' (conscientious objector) during the Second World War and remained an active member of the Peace Pledge Union. Occasionally a van would be parked outside our house – it belonged to Len Gibson,

46 See D. Hardy, *Utopian England: Community experiments 1900-1945,* London: E & F.N. Spon, 2000, p. 177.

one of the members of the Brotherhood Church, who showed anti-war films around the countryside. Later, when I was living in West Yorkshire, we used to go over to Stapleton once a year for their annual Strawberry Tea. That was a weird gathering with its liberal sprinkling of eccentrics and odd-balls – but I could not help but admire the determination of the Gibsons to maintain their way of life, a feeling that I suspect Denis Hardy shared when he wrote, 'Stapleton was an act of faith, achieving no significant material feats but flying the anarchist flag proudly in the face of overwhelming odds.'[47]

Second World War and the politics of creative living

The Brotherhood Church at Stapleton was one of the few of the original experiments in communal living established in the early years of the 20th century to still be in existence at the outbreak of the Second World War. However, this tradition of constructive living refused to die and within two years of the start of the war agriculturally-based communities were being established all over Britain. By the Spring of 1940 pacifist appeals for a negotiated peace seemed increasingly irrelevant – the world was sinking ever-deeper into a totalitarian pit of violence – and pacifists had no immediately practical alternative to offer. What they could do, however, was to bear witness to an alternative way of life. As Margaret Corke phrased it in her contribution to a conference organised by the Community Service Committee in 1939,

> We believe that the international and social problems, which threaten to overwhelm us, cannot be solved by political action alone, but that we can begin at once to live out in small groups and in all sorts of ways the vision of human community which we have seen.[48]

A group of people around the pacifist publication *Peace News* began to reframe their views regarding the role of pacifists in war-time in a similar

---

47 Hardy, 2000, p. 182. See also K. Osgood, 'Life at one of England's last Tolstoyan communes', *The New Yorker,* January 6, 2016. Available at https://tinyurl.com/stghvdg (30 December 2020).

48 M. Corke, in L. Stubbings, ed., *Community in Britain*, West Byfleet: Community Service Committee, 1940, p. 88.

direction. If the dominant trend was the expansion of totalitarianism, perhaps the time had come for pacifists to revert to their traditional role as prophetic witnesses to an alternative set of values and way of life that might one day save the world from destruction. One of the editors of *Peace News* during this period, Wilfred Wellock, began to argue that in such circumstances the key role of the pacifist was 'to envisage the future and to seek ways and means of saving and introducing those values without which human existence ceases to have any meaning'.[49] He advocated a 'politics of creative living' – the way to render war obsolete was to transform society from the grass-roots upwards, starting with our own lives. Wars would cease when people had learned how to live cooperatively.[50]

Eventually over 50 community projects were established – some of them land-based agricultural colonies but others urban income-sharing ventures. In March 1941 *Peace News* began publishing a monthly supplement devoted to the coverage of community projects. Unfortunately the lived experience of those seeking to sow the seeds of a new civilisation proved to be more problematic and troublesome than many had anticipated. As with the Owenite communities of the 19th century many of the members were ill-prepared for the routine chores and hard grind of agricultural work. Dennis Hayes identified three types of people who were attracted to these agricultural colonies: those with a definite calling, those who were seeking an escape, and those who needed a job to fulfil the conditions of their exemption from military service. The majority of the predominantly young and single males who gravitated towards the communities would appear to have belonged to the latter two categories.[51]

Cyril Wright, however, was one with a genuine vocation. He helped to establish a community at Charney Bassett in Oxfordshire. In his words,

---

49 W. Wellock, *Peace News*, 14. June 1940.

50 Much of this section draws on A. Rigby, 'Be practical, do the impossible: The politics of everyday living', in G. Chester & A. Rigby, eds., *Articles of peace: Celebrating fifty years of Peace News*, Bridport: Prism Press, 1986, pp. 90-105.

51 D. Hayes, *Challenge of conscience: The story of the conscientious objectors of 1939-45*, London: George Allen and Unwin, 1949, p. 217. For a fuller examination of the pacifist communities of the Second World War in Britain, see A. Rigby, 'Pacifist communities in Britain in the Second World War', *Peace and Change*, v. 15, no. 2, April 1990, pp. 107-22.

The idea was we should put all our available capital in a pool and purchase a farm. ... This would not only be a source of livelihood and subsistence for a number of people, but would also illustrate to the world, we hoped, ways in which people could live together without fighting one another - a very small example of a peaceful world. And we would put into practice our ideas on tolerance, nonviolence and love towards one another at a time when other people were engaged in smashing themselves to bits.[52]

The communal life at Charney Bassett lasted just over two years. Cyril Wright attributed its eventual collapse to interpersonal difficulties between people who were such strong individualists.

For Wilfred Wellock the collapse of so many of the pacifist communities by the end of the war was a major disappointment. However, he continued to advocate and practise a simple life-style, emphasising the themes of self-reliance, non-acquisitiveness, organic horticulture and continually urging people to develop the art of 'localising, nationalising and internationalising neighbourliness.'[53] Writing in 1947 Aldous Huxley maintained that Wellock, along with Ralph Borsodi in the USA, was one of the few isolated voices advocating the old doctrine of self-reliance and mutual aid within a localised cooperative community.[54]

The counter-culture and the creation of an alternative society

Wellock died in 1972 but maybe he was able to derive some satisfaction from the fact that in the years before his death the emphasis on pacifism as an integral way of life had begun to encroach in again from the margins of the wider peace movement in the guise of what became known as the counter-culture. In the 1960s there was a confluence of factors in Britain, the USA and beyond that helped nurture a widespread questioning of

---

52 Quoted in A. Rigby, 'The Peace Pledge Union: From peace to war, 1936-45', in P. Brock & T. Socknat, eds., *Challenge to Mars: Essays on pacifism from 1918 to 1945*, pp. 169-185, p. 180.
53 *Peace News*, May 18, 1945.
54 A. Huxley, *Science, liberty and peace,* London: Chatto & Windus, 1947, p.43.

the taken-for-granted patterns of everyday life by a younger generation brought up during the years after the Second World War. Amongst the more significant radicalising factors, certainly within Britain, was the emergence of a popular protest movement against nuclear weapons in the late 1950s, the struggle for civil rights in the south of the USA and American involvement in the Vietnam War. [55] Within the broad counter-cultural movement there was a renewed emphasis on creating alternative institutions within which non-exploitative relationships were possible, thereby creating cells of a new society in the here-and-now. Self-change for social change became a recurring theme informing the creation of an imaginative range of alternative projects such as free schools, free universities, communes, food cooperatives and a new wave of workers cooperatives. It was a period of amazing creativity and alongside the mushrooming of new institutions there were radical reappraisals and critiques of established approaches to health and psychiatry, family life and sexual morality, economics and environmental sustainability. It was a wonderful time to be young – at times I recall feeling that the possibilities were endless. The times really were 'a-changing'.

Looking back now it was such a vastly different world we occupied and in these harsher times when so many dreams remain unfulfilled, it is too easy to dismiss the counter-culture or alternative society movement as an aberration, a cultural blip created by disaffected youth that was closer to a fashion movement than a substantive challenge to the established order. There may be some truth in such a judgement, but the movement also had its strengths. There was the amazing creativity that came from the utopian confidence that anything was possible. Moreover, there was a widening and deepening of the understanding of the foundations of the social order that needed to be challenged beyond that of class. Furthermore, the emphasis on embodying the future in the present means of struggle, especially the concern with developing non-hierarchical modes of organising, became quite central to a number of

---

55 The cultural shift in Britain took place against a background of relatively full employment, which resulted in young people experiencing a greater degree of freedom to pursue their ideals as against being trapped in the '9 to 5 routine' that so many of that generation feared.

social movements that emerged out of the counter-culture – especially the women's movement.

The women's movement and 'the personal is political'

In some ways one could say that the 'second wave' of the women's movement emerged out of, and in reaction to, the perceived gap between the rhetoric and the practice of the counter-culture and related movements of the late-1960s and early 1970s. Certainly the women's liberation movement shared the call made by some opinion-leaders within the alternative society movement for the re-evaluation of social roles in which the established sexual division of labour had cast men and women. But, in reaction to the perceived gap between the rhetoric and the practice of the counter-culture and its related movements, the feminists demanded that this restructuring should extend beyond the confines of the outposts of the new society into the realm of mainstream everyday life. Under the promptings of the women's liberation movement the mantra 'the personal is political' took on a much wider and deeper significance. Moreover, in its emphasis on patriarchy as the defining feature underpinning domination in all its different forms, the feminist movement developed an analysis that resonated with wide swathes of people – women and men. One of the key contributions of the feminist movement was to cast the whole of our daily life as an arena of struggle and contestation, thereby helping us to see the relationship between our everyday patterns of life and the societal institutions and structures that we reproduce in our daily lives.

Climate change and intentional living

In this chapter the focus has been on those who could be said to have dedicated their lives to acting as agents of change, believing that they might bring about systemic change through the exemplary power of their own lives. As such they have invariably been cast in the role of 'utopians', 'outsiders', eccentrics, cranks or plain 'nutters' by those firmly entrenched within mainstream opinion. A typical critique coming from political activists might be 'Yes – beautiful vision and admirable ideals, but sadly not relevant to the practical and pressing needs of everyday people

41

struggling to live decent lives in the here and now.' I recall many years ago the disparaging response from a colleague (and friend) of mine when I remarked that I would not be voting in the upcoming general election – 'God Rigby', she exclaimed, 'Have you no politics?' For her, the fact that I would not vote for any party that supported the UK holding on to its nuclear weapons arsenal meant that I was threatening the welfare of my fellow-citizens by refusing to vote for the Labour Party, of which she was an active member, even though she herself was opposed to the nuclear deterrent and an active campaigner for disarmament.

It has always been a difficult ethical and political dilemma – how to act to change the world? Max Weber, the distinguished German social scientist, contrasted two ideal-types of ethical systems pertaining to this problematic. First there was the ethic of ultimate ends or conviction, characterised by uncompromising commitment to a set of values and ideals; against this he set the ethic of responsibility which acknowledges the need to be guided in one's political conduct by the sense of what is realistically possible in the prevailing circumstances. Unlike the actor who follows the ethic of conviction, who refuses to compromise their values for the sake of short-term gain, he or she who is guided by an ethic of responsibility is prepared for pragmatism and the necessary choosing between lesser evils in order to operate effectively within the profane world of politics.[56]

It was Weber's pessimistic conclusion that neither ethic was infallible as a guide to political action. For the advocates of the ethic of conviction, who scorn any half-measures or compromise of their values and commitment, it can lead to the belief that the good end justifies any means – a path that can lead to genocide and the Gulag. Alternatively it can lead to the rejection of all but the purest of means, with a consequent failure to resist immediate evils in any effective manner. But the ethic of responsibility also has its pitfalls. You compromise your values once, and then a second time, and you are on the slippery slope that results in the loss of vision. Is there a way of reconciling the two modes of political conduct – a way of combining conviction with responsibility?

---

56 See M. Weber, 'Politics as a vocation', in H. Gerth & C. Wright Mills, eds., *From Max Weber: Essays in sociology,* London: Routledge & Kegan Paul, 1967, pp. 120-126.

At the present juncture of our civilisation, it does seem as if the ethic of responsibility and that of conviction have come into some kind of alignment in response to the immediate and escalating threat posed by the climate crisis. If we are not to forfeit the right of future generations to enjoy some kind of fulfilling and sustainable life, then it seems imperative that not only states, commercial institutions and manufacturing behemoths should implement far-reaching measures to reduce their carbon-footprint, but citizens – particularly those in the industrialised and relatively affluent 'north' – must also start to change aspects of their own everyday lives and begin to live as responsible citizens of our shared planet, our common home. And the indicators are that this change is taking place. In the UK, with which I am most familiar, people have been implementing quite significant changes in their lifestyles in response to the climate threat – switching from animal to plant-based diets has been the most obvious change.[57] In Sweden one reads that internal air travel has declined in response to 'flight-shaming'.[58] Intentional living - seeking to bring about wider transformation by means of changes in one's own lifestyle is moving into the mainstream – the ethics of conviction and responsibility have come into some kind of conjunction.

57 Ethical Corporation, 'Growing fears for climate help fuel rise in plant-based diets', May 28, 2019. Accessible at https://tinyurl.com/wbevupv (21 January 2020).

58 See BBC report, 'Sweden sees rare fall in air passengers, as flight-shaming takes off', January 10, 2020. Accessible at https://tinyurl.com/yt7jyj64 (21 Jananuary 2020).

3

THE CONSTRUCTIVE DIMENSION OF GANDHIAN SATYAGRAHA

Introduction

In the late 1970s I moved to Bradford in West Yorkshire to teach Peace Studies at the university. It was there that my friendship with the eminent Gandhian scholar Bob Overy deepened. We had met a few times at gatherings of people associated with the pacifist publication *Peace News* and we recognised each other as kindred spirits. Bob was and remains one of the deepest thinkers about pacifism and nonviolence – stemming primarily from his research on Gandhi as a movement organiser. During my early years at Bradford Bob was trying to finish his Ph.D., which he eventually completed after spending some time away from his family occupying a spare room in the house I owned in the city. A revised and updated version of this thesis was eventually published in 2019.[1]

There was a group of us at Bradford who were interested in non-violent action for change in general and nonviolent (social) defence in particular. The group met regularly, facilitated by Michael Randle.[2] One of the themes that Bob would return to time and again was the fundamental importance of grounding nonviolence as a means of change upon a 'philosophy of nonviolence' that embraced such core values as respect for the sanctity of life, acknowledgement of the humanity of 'the other' and recognition of the multifaceted dimensions of violence. We also explored the manner in which taken-for-granted mundane activities

---

1   B. Overy, *Gandhi as an organiser: How he shaped a nationwide rebellion: India 1915-1922,* Sparsnäs, Sweden: Irene, 2019.

2   For a fascinating insight into Michael's commitment to nonviolent direct action, see M. Levy, *Ban the bomb! Michael Randle and direct action against nuclear war,* Stuttgart: Ibidem, 2021.

in our everyday lives might sow the seeds of such violence. It was one of Bob's recurring critiques of Gene Sharp, for whom we all had huge respect, that his attempt to divorce nonviolence as a technique for wielding power in conflict situations from the value base out of which it grew was misplaced.[3]

Another member of our group was Howard Clark, who also lived in my house in the early 1980s. During this period, when the anti-nuclear weapons movement had become resurgent once again, Howard spent quite a bit of time conducting training workshops for people prior to embarking on demonstrations of one sort or another. We would talk together about how the focus of the workshops was almost entirely upon techniques for action – how to form an affinity group, how to act when being restrained or arrested by the police, the necessary division of roles within an affinity group and the like. There was very little time spent discussing the positive values and principles underpinning such nonviolent actions. This phenomenon, the prioritisation of techniques and method above values and principles of right living by theorists and practitioners of nonviolent direct action, has become even more pronounced over the last few decades with the different civilian-based challenges to authoritarian regimes.

One feature such movements have shared has been the use of unarmed means of pressure to undermine the pillars of support upon which the targeted regimes relied, thereby bringing about a nonviolent transfer of state power.[4] Unfortunately, whilst the exercise of nonviolent power has proven successful as a means of dislodging authoritarian regimes, the wielders of this technique have been less successful in bringing about

---

3   One outcome of this group was a conference on social defence held at Bradford University in April 1990. See S. Anderson & J. Larmore, eds, *Nonviolent struggle and social defence*, London: War Resisters International, 1991. Accessible at http://www.wri-irg.org/books/nvsd.htm (13 February 2020).

4   The standard sources on the role of unarmed civil resistance in the overthrow of authoritarian regimes include E. Chenoweth & M. J. Stephan, *Why civil resistance works: The strategic logic of nonviolent conflict*, NY: Columbia University Press, 2011; S. E. Nepstad, *Nonviolent revolutions: Civil resistance in the late 20th century*, Oxford: Oxford University Press, 2011; K. Schock, *Unarmed insurrections: People power movements in nondemocracies,* Minneapolis: University of Minnesota Press, 2005.

significant socio-economic change in the wider post-revolutionary society. Chabot and Sharifi have pointed out that the consequences of the nonviolent overthrow of authoritarian regimes (which I would liken to nonviolent coup d'états) has been the establishment of neo-liberal states characterised by i) a narrow form of democracy, where the political participation of the citizenry is limited to voting in elections; ii) the opening up of the economy to global corporations; iii) the spread of free-market rationality in which the prime role of the state is deemed to be the promotion of economic growth and consumerism, instead of social equality and human well-being.[5]

They go on to suggest that one of the prime reasons for such outcomes, that end up reinforcing rather than reducing multiple forms of exploitation, domination and dispossession, is that the participants failed to incorporate into their movement methodology Gandhian political ethics. They maintain that 'these people power struggles mostly focused on mass mobilization and civil disobedience against the authoritarian regime, while mundane constructive work in everyday life and local communities toward individual, relational, and social transformation was sporadic and short-lived.'[6] Their thesis is that the statist focus of too many civil resistance movements has been misguided, and that those who envision a more human world would be better advised to prioritise constructive work to change ways of life in their neighbourhoods: 'experimenting with Gandhian self-rule, truth-seeking, and nonviolence in their everyday lives and local communities.'[7]

It is certainly true that activists and analysts of civil resistance who have sought lessons to be learned from Gandhi's leadership of the Indian freedom struggle have tended to have a rather narrow focus on the large-scale satyagraha campaigns such as the Salt March of 1930 that inaugurated a mass civil disobedience campaign and the 1942 'Quit India' campaign. Less attention has been paid to exploring the significance

---

5   S. Chabot & M. Sharifi, 'The violence of nonviolence: Problematizing nonviolent resistance in Iran and Egypt', *Societies without borders*, v.8, n. 2, 2013, pp. 205-232. Accessible at https://tinyurl.com/uf4fc6s (12 February 2020).

6   Chabot & Sharifi, p. 22.

7   Chabot & Sharifi, p. 23.

and contemporary relevance of the other major dimension of Gandhi's approach to transformation – constructive action to lay the foundations of new ways of living, which has been termed pre-figurative politics by more recent generations of activists and scholars. For Gandhi the constructive work was far more important than the active 'political satyagraha'. As he advised his co-workers in 1944, through the constructive programme 'you can make the villages feel self-reliant, self-sufficient and free so that they can stand up for their own rights. If you make a real success of the constructive programme, you will win Swaraj for India without civil disobedience.'[8]

The aim of the first section of this chapter is to explore why Gandhi placed such emphasis on constructive action. In the second section the focus is upon how the Gandhian constructive workers in India developed their movement in the years following Gandhi's assassination. In presenting this historical overview I could have followed a myriad threads but I chose to follow the movement in the south-eastern Indian state of Tamil Nadu. The reason is that this is the thread with which I am most familiar – let me explain.

In 1981 I was granted a sabbatical term from my academic post to enable me to travel round India visiting Gandhian centres and interviewing Gandhian sarvodaya workers and activists. I considered myself a 'peace-nik' as well as a peace researcher, and I was keen to learn as much as I could about the Gandhian *sarvodaya* (welfare of all) movement. The most significant encounter during my travels took place in October 1981 at Gandhigram in Tamil Nadu where I first met a married couple - Jagannathanji and his wife Krishnammal. I had been told by my host at Gandhigram Rural University that Jagannathan was an important Gandhian leader, so I was a little nervous prior to our first encounter. I did not anticipate that he and Krishnammal would welcome me into their wider 'family' and exercise such a profound influence on me. In the years following that first encounter I made regular trips to Tamil Nadu just to spend time in their company and recharge my batteries, and be challenged by their example to try and live a life a little more aligned with

---

8   Quoted in G. Ostergaard & M. Currell, *The gentle anarchists: A study of the leaders of the sarvodaya movement for non-violent revolution in India*, Oxford: Clarendon Press, 1971, p. 3.

Andrew Rigby & Jagannathan, 1988

the pacifist values that I have always professed, and which took me to India in the first place. Jagannathan was in his sixties when we first met. He died in February 2013 at the age of 100. However, for the last decade of his life he had been relatively inactive due to poor health. During the 1990s I carried out a series of interviews with him and Krishnammal. It is on these conversations and the field notes taken on my many visits that I have drawn in the second part of this chapter.

In the third section of the chapter the focus will be upon the more contemporary people's movements in India that continue to draw upon the insights and practical examples of the Gandhian emphasis on the importance of constructive nonviolent action for social transformation.

Constructive action as foundation of the new society

Gandhi's understanding of *Swaraj* (independence) was far deeper and broader than political independence from Britain. Self-rule for Gandhi was premised on a fundamental moral-psychological transformation that each person had to experience for themselves – it could not be granted by some external agency. As he wrote in *Hind Swaraj*, 'It is *Swaraj* when we learn to rule ourselves ... But such Swaraj has to be experienced by each one himself.'[9] From his perspective, to the extent that people individually and collectively practised self-rule and self-reliance, then they would make British rule irrelevant. As such there was no distinction between means and ends insofar as he contended that the attempt to win *Swaraj* was Swaraj itself. In this we can see how Gandhi in effect held his

---

9   M.K. Gandhi, *Hind swaraj or Indian home rule*, Ahmedabad: Navajivan Publishing, 1938, p. 65.

fellow-citizens responsible for their own subjugation. The way to achieve the necessary individual and collective transformation that would make Swaraj a reality was for people to transcend the practices that prevented them from achieving their potential as free human beings. And it was in his constructive programme that he began to explore the types of changes necessary.

His vision of the constructive programme embraced many overlapping dimensions. They included the development of village-based industries as one of the foundations for economic self-reliance, the use of local resources and the spinning of locally grown cotton for the production of hand-woven cloth (*khadi*), the promotion of community cohesion through the eradication of untouchability and the promotion of economic equality, the improvement in the status of women and the pursuit of communal unity between Hindus and Muslims. [10]

The constructive programme functioned as a series of experiments in self-rule, and as such constituted the necessary preparation for Swaraj/ independence. As with so many other aspects of his life Gandhi was continually developing his ideas on the changes necessary to throw off the hegemonic domination of the British Raj, and it was in his ashrams that they were most fully put into practice. As Judith Brown has noted, the ashrams or intentional communities which housed his most devoted co-workers, 'were places akin to laboratories where he could attempt to solve in microcosm problems that affected India on a much larger scale.'[11] The ashrams also provided a training ground from which cadres of workers went out to develop a wider network of constructive initiatives, acting in the capacity of community development workers and animateurs

---

10 Khadi was a central element in Gandhian economics. Not only did it provide employment and meet a basic need for clothing, it also symbolised i) the values of economic freedom and equality, ii) the swadeshi mentality of self-reliance, iii) the weakening of the city's traditional exploitation of the countryside, iv) the transcendence of the traditional division between mental and manual labour, and v) the decentralisation of production and distribution.

11 Judith Brown, in J. Brown & A. Parel, eds., *The Cambridge companion to Gandhi*, Cambridge: Cambridge University Press, 2011, p. 55.

throughout the countryside. As Krishnalal Shridharani, who participated in the Salt March, observed, the ashram graduates became 'the nuclei of the economic and spiritual regeneration of India's countryside.'[12]

Satyagraha and constructive action

It should be clear from the above that a central theme of Gandhi's approach to social transformation was a kind of life-style politics – the creation of spaces within which individuals and communities might attempt to bring about the changes necessary for them to 'live the future now'. The practice, in and of itself, was integral to the whole liberatory project, embodying the end in the means. However, Gandhi was aware that there were inevitable institutionalised 'blockages' that would be encountered in the struggle for change. In such circumstances it was necessary to consider political action to try to overcome the barriers. He urged people to use all the constitutional space available in the pursuit of the necessary changes, but once these had been exhausted then it became necessary to consider other forms of pressure, including civil disobedience and forms of nonviolent resistance - obstructive rather than constructive direct action.

For Gandhi civil resistance was a nonviolent alternative to armed struggle, and just as engagement in armed revolt required training, so it was with civil resistance – and the training ground for developing the discipline and commitment necessary for sustained civil resistance was the sphere of constructive work. Indeed, he was convinced of the imperative of training potential participants in civil disobedience campaigns in the disciplines of nonviolent resistance. Otherwise he feared that any attempt to launch a large-scale civil disobedience campaign would be likely to deteriorate into violent confrontations once people's passions were aroused. The key medium for this training was involvement in different forms of constructive action. As he wrote in *Constructive*

---

12 K. Shridharani, *War without violence: A study of Gandhi's method and its accomplishments*, London: Victor Gollancz, 1939, p.150. Accessible at http://tinyurl.com/kgwraxm (21 May 2020).

Programme, 'Training for military revolt means learning the use of arms ending perhaps in the atomic bomb. For civil disobedience it means the constructive programme.'[13]

He did not believe that small-scale local level satyagraha required trained participants, so long as there was a cadre of disciplined activists to lead and coordinate the action. But, as he wrote in 1941,

> ... when Civil Disobedience is itself devised for the attainment of Independence, previous preparation is necessary, and it has to be backed by the visible and conscious effort of those who are engaged in the battle. ... Civil Disobedience in terms of Independence without the cooperation of the millions by way of constructive effort is mere bravado and worse than useless.[14]

So how was involvement in the constructive programme necessary for a sustained and large scale civil resistance movement?

i. Popular movements require participation

In a study of the popular unarmed Palestinian resistance to occupation by Marwan Darweish and myself, one of the activists we interviewed, in 2015, observed that what the Palestinians called 'popular resistance' was no longer popular, insofar as the local people were no longer prepared to participate. Why should they risk injury, imprisonment or a large fine by participating in protest actions that no longer seemed effective in terms of achieving tangible results?[15]

A key feature of the Gandhian constructive programme was that it created the opportunity for everyday people, particularly the peasantry, to play an active and significant role in the liberation movement. As Gandhi noted in a letter to Nehru following the Civil Disobedience movement of 1934-5.

> With civil resistance as the background we cannot possibly do without the constructive activities such as communal unity, removal of untouchability and universalization of the spinning-

---

13 M. Gandhi, *Constructive programme: Its meaning and place*, Ahmedabad: Navajivan Publishing, 1941 , p. 4.
14 *Constructive programme*, p. 35.
15 See Darweish & Rigby, 2015, pp. 97-99.

wheel and khaddar. I am as strong as ever about these. We must recognize that whilst the Congressmen can be counted by hundreds of thousands, civil resisters imprisoned have never amounted to more than one lakh (100,000) at the outside. I feel that there is something radically wrong if paralysis has overtaken the remaining lakhs. There is nothing to be ashamed of in an open confession by those who for any reason whatsoever are unable to join the civil resisters' ranks. *They are also serving the cause of the country and bringing it nearer to the goal who are engaged in any of the constructive activities* I have named and several other kindred activities I can add to the list.[16]

ii. Maintaining involvement during 'quiet times'

In his analysis of the Indian liberation movement Bhipan Chandra, using Gramsci's terminology, likened it to a protracted war of position, a struggle to undermine the hegemonic influence of the Raj in all walks of life.[17] This was the battle of ideas, the sustained struggle to get increasing numbers of people aware of the ways their acquiescence sustained British rule, and hence the extent of their power to challenge and undermine the colonial power by thinking and acting differently. According to Chandra,

> … it was the law-breaking mass movements of the post-1918 period which basically performed the task among the mass of the Indian people. The basic objective of these movements was to destroy the notion that British rule could not be challenged,

---

16 *Collected works of Mahatma Gandhi,* v. 55, p. 429. (Emphasis added) Accessible at https://tinyurl.com/srutfwd (29 January 2020).

17 The Italian Marxist, Antonio Gramsci used the terms 'War of Position' and 'War of Manoeuvre' to indicate two different phases in the class struggle. The war of manoeuvre referred to the phase of open conflict between classes, where the outcome is decided by direct clashes between revolutionaries and the state. War of position, on the other hand, referred to the slow, hidden cultural struggle to gain influence and power through swaying people's hearts and minds. See D. Egan, 'Rethinking war of manouver/ war of position: Gramsci and the military metaphor', *Critical Sociology,* v. 40, n. 4, 2014, pp. 521-538.

to create among the people fearlessness and courage and the capacity to fight and make sacrifices, and to inculcate the notion that no people could be ruled without their consent.[18]

But no movement can sustain extended periods of mass mobilisation without exhausting its followers and 'burning out' its cadres. So, given the prolonged nature of the struggle, periods of intense mobilisation and contestation were interspersed with longer 'passive' periods when ideological work was carried out. A key medium for this was the constructive programme, which helped fill the political space left vacant by the withdrawal from civil disobedience, thereby enabling people to sustain a sense of activism and provide a medium for continued involvement in the movement during the relatively quiet phases, whilst at the same time providing something of a 'safe haven' for the cadres where they could withdraw from the front-line struggle in order to recuperate and recharge their batteries.[19]

iii. Developing the self-discipline of satyagrahis

As noted above one of Gandhi's ongoing concerns was the propensity to violence of those engaged in confrontational struggle that was intended to be nonviolent.[20] To maintain the commitment to nonviolence in the face of an opponent prepared to use violence required a significant degree of self-discipline on the part of the satyagrahis. Gandhi believed that the experience of working in the constructive programme enabled participants to take on as their own the world-view and values on which it was based, particularly the importance of self-reliance. This, he felt, was a necessary preparation whereby people could develop the self-discipline and emotional control necessary for them to engage in nonviolent confrontational resistance without resorting to violence.

---

18 Chandra, p. 508.
19 Chandra, p. 510.
20 See K. Mantena, 'Another realism: The politics of Gandhian nonviolence', *American Political Science Review*, v. 106, n. 2, May 2012, pp. 455-470, p. 458.

iv. Steel-frame of the movement

Given Gandhi's preoccupation with maintaining a nonviolent discipline during civil disobedience and other forms of confrontational resistance, he placed considerable emphasis not only on the self-discipline of the activists, but also the importance of trained cadres with the capacity to direct and control the rank-and-file activists during their contentious encounters with opponents. Once again, the bulk of his lieutenants were graduates of many years of community organising as part of the constructive programme. As Bhipan Chandra noted:

> As a whole, constructive work was a major channel for the recruitment of the soldiers of freedom and their political training - as also the choosing and testing of their 'officers' and leaders. Constructive workers were to act as the steelframe of the nationalist movement in its active satyagraha phase. It was therefore not accidental that *khadi bhandar* workers, students, teachers of national schools and colleges, and Gandhian ashrams' inmates served as the backbone of the civil disobedience movements both as organizers and as active *Satyagrahis.*[21]

Gandhian constructive work post-Independence

For Gandhi the achievement of national independence was only the first stage in the Indian revolution. The second, and more important stage, was to be a non-violent social revolution. Shortly before he was assassinated he wrote: 'The Congress has won political freedom, but it has yet to win economic freedom, social and moral freedom. These freedoms are harder than the political only because they are constructive, less exciting and not spectacular.'[22]

---

21 Chandra, p. 246. Another related function of the constructive programme was that it made the urban-based and upper caste cadres familiar with the conditions of the villages and went some way towards bridging the gulf between the leadership and the peasantry.

22 Quoted in D. Dalton, *Indian idea of freedom*, Gurgaon, Haryana: Academic Press, 1982, pp. 187-8.

He urged Congress to transform itself into a voluntary organisation of *Lok Sevaks* (Servants of the People), with workers going amongst the villagers to help them achieve true swaraj, full self-reliant independence – economic as well as political. Gandhi's ideal of sarvodaya (the welfare of all) envisaged a reconstructed Indian village society with people using simple hand-tools in agriculture and industry, engaged in production for local use rather than profit. It was to be a society of equals, a kind of pure communism wherein each individual would place the common welfare above their own selfish interests, and the principle of 'from each according to their ability, to each according to their need' would be paramount. This vision of a society of small, largely self-sufficient village communities, a just and nonviolent political, social and economic order, was far removed from the modern industrial society that Nehru and many of the other congress leaders eagerly anticipated,

Following Gandhi's death in January 1948, those of his co-workers who remained committed to his vision of a sarvodaya society and his emphasis on the necessity for constructive work amongst the villages gathered together to form a loosely structured organisation of *Lok Sevaks*, which eventually became known as *Sarva Seva Sang* (Association for the Welfare of All). Their third conference was held at Hyderabad in 1951. After the conference Gandhi's spiritual heir, Vinoba Bhave, travelled to the Telangana district of Andhra Pradesh where a violent struggle was taking place between the landless peasants and their feudal landlords, At one of the villages he visited on 18 April 1951 he was approached by a number of landless *dalits* who asked him for help in obtaining land. According to Arthur Koestler, Vinoba 'turned to the people of the village and asked whether there was somebody among them willing to give land to his brethren so that they may not die of starvation; and a man came forward and offered a hundred acres of land.'[23] This was the birth of what became known as the *Bhoodan* (land gift) movement.

Bhoodan-Gramdan: Towards a nonviolent revolution

Vinoba was quite consciously searching for an answer to the problems of India's landless which would serve as an alternative to a violent revolution.

23 Quoted in A. Koestler, *The lotus and the robot,* London: Hutchinson, 1966, p. 301.

He decided to embark on a series of *padyatras* (walking tours/ pilgrimages) throughout India, appealing to the consciences of the landlords, begging for land on behalf of the landless, achieving social reform through individual acts of charity. His goal was a three-fold revolution: 'Firstly I want to change people's hearts. Secondly I want to create a change in their lives. Thirdly I want to change the social structure ... We do not aim at doing mere acts of kindness, but at creating a Kingdom of Kindness.'[24] It was through his initiative and example that Vinoba revitalised the Gandhian constructive movement.

So great was the enthusiasm for bhoodan that a target of 50 million acres was set to be reached by the end of 1957, designated as the Year of the Land Revolution. In fact a total of 4.2 million acres had been donated by the end of the year. By that time, however, the movement was calling not for the individual's surrender of a proportion of their land but for the complete surrender of property rights in favour of the village community. This was the call for *gramdan*, gift of the village - the pooling of all the village land and vesting its ownership in the community. According to Geoffrey Ostergaard, who carried out a number of detailed studies of the post-Independence Gandhian movement in India, 'The substitution of gramdan for bhoodan represented a move from a basically individualist to a basically socialist programme.'[25] Whereas in a bhoodan village the basic structure was similar to a normal Indian village except for there being a fairer distribution of land, in a gramdan village (in theory at least) the landless ceased to be recipients of individual acts of charity and became equal members of the village community which owned the land in common.

This revolutionary character of gramdan made it difficult to promote. Nevertheless, in the wake of Vinoba's padyatras throughout the country, village after village declared itself for gramdan. By 1964, 6807 villages had declared themselves gramdan villages. By this time, however, the movement was slackening, whilst the gramdan villages themselves were generally small, very poor, and concentrated in low caste and tribal areas. Therefore a new approach was developed called *sulabh* (simplified) gramdan which represented a concession to the principles of

24 *Bhoodan*, 18 April 1956.
25 Ostergaard & Curry, 1971, p.10.

private ownership. Under the revised scheme the private use of land was to continue, whilst the formal ownership of the land was vested in the village community as organized in the *gram sabha* or village assembly. In other words, the landowner would continue to retain possession of the land for cultivation purposes and could also pass it on in inheritance, although the actual legal title to the land was held by the gram sabha. In addition landowners were required to donate at least 5 percent of their holding to the gram sabha for distribution to the landless, Also a village fund was to be established into which every family would contribute a portion of their income equivalent to one fortieth of their agricultural produce. The common affairs of the village were to be managed by the gram sabha, membership of which would be open to all adult members of the village. Disputes between villagers would not be taken to the courts but would be settled in the village itself by a special committee set up for the purpose. A village was to be declared a gramdan village when at least 75 percent of its residents had expressed their approval and sufficient numbers of landowners were involved so that at least 51 percent of the total land in the village would be covered by the gramdan scheme.

By 1971 it was claimed that 168,108 villages had declared for gramdan, over one quarter of the total number of villages in India. However, the majority of these were mainly 'declarations of intent'. Only in about 5,000 cases had the land titles actually been transferred to the village assembly and the village officially registered as a gramdan village whilst, according to Ostergaard and Curry, little more than 500 of these villages would have revealed to an observer signs of development and social reconstruction.[26] Basically what seems to have happened is that villages would declare themselves for gramdan in a wave of enthusiasm following a visit from the saintly Vinoba or one of his lieutenants like Jayaprakash Narayan (JP). The leaders would then move on to the next village or location, leaving the local sarvodaya workers on their own to try to implement the declaration of intent. The movement clearly lacked the financial resources and the necessary number of suitably trained personnel to carry out such a task. As a consequence a vast gap remained between the ideal picture as it might appear on paper, and the reality.

---

26 Ostergaard & Curry, 1971, p.14.

Furthermore, of the 4.2 million acres donated by over half a million landowners under the bhoodan scheme, 1.85 million acres proved to be either uncultivable or subject to legal dispute. By the late 1970s, only 30 percent of the total land received as bhoodan had been distributed to the landless through the various state bhoodan boards which had been formed to allocate the land to the landless. Furthermore, even when land was distributed, it was found that in many cases the allottees were not in a position to benefit from the land gift. They lacked the finances and the resources to reclaim land that was often un-irrigated and in need of levelling. They lacked the means to acquire the necessary implements, seeds, fertilizers and draught power to start cultivation. In addition, they lacked the experience and self-confidence to manage their own land - theirs had always been a life of complete and utter dependency on the local landowners. Indeed, in many cases they were too poor even to contribute their own labour to the development of their land, as they were so dependent for their day-to-day survival on the wages received as day labourers for local landowners.[27]

During the late 1950s and 1960s, various attempts were made to deal with this situation. Bhoodan co-operatives were formed, government loans were obtained for irrigation and land reclamation purposes, development agencies intervened to offer funds for specific projects. On the whole these efforts had only a marginal impact. Many of the schemes omitted crucial inputs - finance might be made available for irrigation but not for the purchase of draught animals or seeds. Other schemes concentrated on the economic development of the land at the cost of the necessary social and educational work amongst the villagers, with the result that the project crumbled once the sponsoring agency had withdrawn. The lessons drawn from these experiences by certain key figures involved in the Gandhian constructive work movement was that the full development of the bhoodan and gramdan lands required

---

27 These observations are drawn primarily from my own discussions with Gandhian sarvodaya workers in the 1980s and Geoffrey Ostergaard's definitive study, *Nonviolent revolution in India,* New Delhi: Gandhi Peace Foundation, 1985. Geoffrey was one of the people I sought for advice prior to my first field research into the post-Independence Gandhian movement in India. His advice has stayed with me: 'Keep the faeces away from the food!'.

their concentration upon the promotion of the necessary qualities of self-confidence and self-reliance, and the capacities for self-management and co-operative endeavour amongst the allottees, in addition to the provision of the physical and technical inputs required for the full utilisation of the newly acquired land. Amongst those who decided to act on these insights was a veteran of the freedom struggle and a senior figure in the sarvodaya movement in Tamil Nadu, Sankaralingam Jagannathan.

Land for the landless – the struggles of Jagannathanji

Vinoba Bhave with Jagannathanji (R) & Keithanji (L)

As a college student in Madurai in 1930 Jagannathan was swept up by Gandhi's non-cooperation campaign. He gave up his studies and on the advice of Gandhi joined an ashram in the north of Tamil Nadu to work with the poor. It was there that he met an American missionary, Ralph Richard ('Dick') Keithahn.[28] They became lifelong companions and comrades, devoting their lives to the pursuit of the Gandhian vision of a sarvodaya society.[29] During the freedom struggle Jagannathan was imprisoned by the British twice, and Keithahn deported back to the USA.

Reunited after independence they commenced organising trainings for constructive programme workers from the base they established

---

28 See K. Arunachalam & C. Sadler, *On the frontiers: Essays in honour of Rev. Dr R.R. Keithahn,* Madurai, TN: Koodal, 1977; K. Arunachalam & K.M. Natarjan, eds., *Integrated rural development*, Madurai, TN: Koodal, 1977, pp. 3-28.

29 Much of this section is based on my field-notes and interviews with Jagannathanji, carried out over many years from our first encounter in 1981 into the 1990s during which period I recorded a number of lengthy interviews with him. See A. Rigby, 'The nonviolent activism of the radical Gandhian, Jagannathanji, 1912-2013', in D. Hardiman, ed., *Nonviolence in modern Indian history,* Hyderabad: Orient Blackswan, 2017, pp. 179-206. Accessible at https://tinyurl.com/vxssejm (30 January 2020).

for themselves at Gandhigram, mid-way between Madurai and Trichy in Tamil Nadu. In 1952 Jagannathan was tasked with organising the bhoodan campaign in Tamil Nadu, and by the time Vinoba Bhave reached the state in 1956 some 3,500 acres of land had been pledged. By this time the focus of Vinoba's campaign had shifted to gramdan – the target he set for the Tamil sarvodaya workers was 500 gramdan villages. Jagannathan, Keithahn and the Gandhian economist J.C. Kumarappa accompanied Vinoba as he toured the state.[30] But after a few months Kumarappa challenged Vinoba. According to Jagannathan's recollections:

> For the whole of the Tamil Nadu padyatra, Kumarappa was with us. Kumarappa used to say, 'This is a mightier movement than Gandhiji's freedom movement. Freedom movement was easier, to fight the Britisher. To fight landlordism and feudalism by nonviolence - it is a great thing.' ....
>
> After following him for two or three months, Kumarappa wanted to tackle Vinoba. He said, 'There should be three departments. One is getting bhoodan-gramdan. Secondly, immediately you should have an implementation programme. Third, your ideology of gram swaraj. Like that the Gandhian economy should be applied in the villages, on the land. What kind of agriculture now the land has come under your control? So please have these sections. First you propagate and convince the people about gramdan. Then, what sort of cultivation are we going to have? Individual or group cultivation? Then scientific application for self-sufficiency. Immediately you should have three departments.' He warned Vinobaji.
>
> Vinobaji ... 'Ah, I don't care for that. I only set fire, but then let anything happen, I don't care. I am only the fire-lighter. ... I only set fire, I don't care for what will follow.'

---

30 I have always found Kumarappa's *Economy of permanence* to be the most valuable source of insight into the principles of Gandhian economics. Accessible at https://tinyurl.com/ww9e28d (13 February 2020). Other sources include M. Lindley, *J.C. Kumarappa: Mahatma Gandhi's economist*, Mumbai: Popular Prakashan, 2007; R. Guha, *An anthropologist among the Marxists*, Delhi: Permanent Black, 2001, pp. 81-86.

So Vinobaji did not heed Kumarappa's advice. I was close by, watching this discussion between Kumarappa and Vinobaji. If Gandhi was a practical man, this man Vinoba was not a practical man. A spiritual man, a mighty spiritual man, mightier even than Gandhi we can say, but not a practical man. Gandhi would have said immediately, 'Come on Kumarappa, take charge'. He would have taken charge of the economic use of the land, a section of the movement would have been created and Kumarappa would have been in charge, guiding the movement in a constructive way. But Vinoba discouraged that. [31]

J.C. Kumarappa

Kumarappa abandoned the padyatra and urged Jagannathan to do likewise, but as the key organiser in the state Jagannathan felt committed to continue accompanying Vinoba as he walked across the state – but he could see the strength of Kumarappa's critique.

After Vinoba's padyatra through the state had been completed Keithahn proposed that he and Jagannathan should relocate to an area around a place called Batlagundu, where 300 villages had declared themselves for gramdan. Their intention was to follow Kumarappa's promptings and work with the villagers to bring about the social, cultural and economic revolution that was at the heart of the gramdan vision. Whilst engaged in constructive work in the Batlagundu area Jagannathan continued to launch satyagraha to do with land. As he informed an Italian interviewer,

> Some had the objective of making people respect their donation papers, because many people had promised land but never got around to actually giving it. Other satyagrahas were directed against social and economic injustice, such as when we

---

31 Interview, 25 December 1995.

discovered that the land of a temple was cultivated by a single large landholder instead of it being distributed to the landless as it should be by law, or the time we came to know that a certain landlord had much more land that the government allowed under recent land ceiling acts.

Vinoba was opposed to these satyagrahas. … But I thought it was critical that the promises made were kept so the people wouldn't lose faith in nonviolence as a means to obtain land to cultivate. Many times I went against Vinoba's will and organised satyagrahas, so in Tamil Nadu the Bhoodan-Gramdan Movement became a true people's movement, not Vinoba's movement only.[32]

The 'NGO-isation' of constructive work

It was during this period of constructive work at Batlagundu that Jagannathan was approached by an Italian nonviolent activist, Giovanni Ermiglia, who offered to raise funds in Italy to support the constructive rural development work. As a consequence of this encounter it was decided to establish a non-governmental agency to continue the work developing the bhoodan lands and the Association of Sarva Seva Farms (ASSEFA) was established in 1969 with Jagannathan as its chairperson. Since then under the direction of one of the experienced constructive workers from Batlagundu, Logannathanji, ASSEFA has grown into one of the largest and most respected rural development agencies in India.[33] One more example of the way in which constructive work by movement

32 L. Coppo, *The Color of Freedom*, Monroe, ME.: Common Courage Press, 2005, p. 112. In 1957 both Jagannathan and Keithahn were imprisoned in Madurai for their part in protesting against the failure of the Meenakshi Temple authorities to distribute their land to the landless. By 1969, when he was elected president of Sarva Seva Sang, Jagannathan's reputation for militancy was well-established. (Ostergaard, 1985, p. 30).

33 See Y. Poirier & K. Loganathan, *ASSEFA India: 50 years of sustainable development*, 2019, accessible at https://tinyurl.com/uqxahcf (6 February 2020). See also A. Rigby, 'Practical utopianism: a Gandhian approach to rural community development in India', *Community Development Journal*, v. 20, n. 1, 1985, pp. 2-7. Accessible at https://tinyurl.com/rggqx2n (7 February 2020).

activists can sow the seeds of more sustainable and institutionalised programmes of constructive work for social transformation.[34]

Movement for total revolution

Jagannathan was not 'at home' working within institutionalised structures

Jayaprakash Narayan (JP) 2001
Indian stamp

such as ASSEFA – he was a movement person, a '*Bhoodan wallah*'. One of his abiding concerns was that in situations of gross injustice people would resort to violent means of redress if nonviolent resistance proved ineffec-tual. This was what had happened in the rich paddy-growing area of East Thanjavur in eastern Tamil Nadu where violent clashes between landowners and landless resulted in the killing of 44 people on Christmas Day 1968 in the village of Kilvenmani. On receiving the news Jagannathan and Krishnammal left their base in Batlagundu and headed for Thanjavur District. Once again their practice displayed a joint focus on peacekeeping, constructive work to strengthen the village communities and satyagraha campaigns in pursuance of legitimate claims for land. After one note-worthy struggle in 1972 which resulted in the redistribution of over 1000 acres of land, Jayaprakash Narayan (JP) came to visit them. [35] According to Geoffrey Ostergaard the main object of his visit was to express his solidarity with Jagannathan, Krishnammal and their co-workers who, in the previous few years, had been pursuing what

---

34 It is relevant to note that international aid and development agencies such as Oxfam and Save the Children amongst others had their origins in initiatives launched by peace activists mobilising against the horrors of war. See M. Black, *A Cause for Our Times: Oxfam the First 50 Years*, Oxford: Oxford University Press, 1992.

35 For an account of this satyagraha, see Coppo, pp. 137-44.

JP saw as a 'judicious mixture of nonviolent persuasion, direct action and constructive work.'[36] JP invited Jagannathan and Krishnammal to come to Bihar where there were similar problems of landowners retaining control of vast tracts of land, despite the land-ceiling acts.

JP had been a leader of the Congress Socialist Party during the freedom struggle and had embraced Marxism, before throwing himself into the Bhoodan-Gramdan movement as Vinoba's lieutenant. However, after spending some time in Bihar where a significant number of villages had declared for gramdan on paper, he realised that in reality little had changed on the ground.[37] Much of the land acquired as gift remained undistributed, much of it was poor quality, subject to legal dispute, and the impact of the movement on the life-situation of the bulk of the oppressed and down-trodden of rural India was revealed as minimal. This was the context within which JP began to revise his approach to nonviolent socio-economic and political transformation. He began to consider the need for large scale 'negative satyagraha' and the challenging of state power over a number of issues, as it became increasingly apparent to him and his followers that Congress, led by Indira Gandhi, was leading the country towards dictatorship rather than democratic decentralisation.

This shift was directly counter to the direction Vinoba was taking. A deeply spiritual man, Vinoba was opposed to all forms of nonviolent coercion which he felt had no place in a democracy like India. As he noted, 'In Gandhi's days, there was no freedom of thought and expression .... But in India today we enjoy the highest measure of freedom in the world .... Satyagraha as practised by Gandhi has therefore become quite irrelevant in India.'[38] Rather than offering 'negative satyagraha', as an increasing number of the movement's activists were demanding, Vinoba urged an approach of 'gentle, gentler, gentlest' in order to assist people in 'right thinking' – conversion rather than coercion.[39]

---

36 Ostergaard, 1985, p. 70.

37 In October 1969 he had declared that 'in the Gramdan states, such as Bihar, the entire social, economic, and political picture might be transformed in the next five years.' Quoted in Ostergaard, 1985, p. 25.

38 Quoted in Ostergaard, 1985, p. 63.

39 T. Weber, *Gandhi's peace army: The Shanti Sena and unarmed peacekeeping*, Syracuse, NY: Syracuse University Press, 1996, p. xx.

In January 1974 student protests began in Ahmedabad which soon escalated into a popular movement against what was perceived to be a corrupt state government in Gujarat. At the same time the outbreak of student-initiated agitation against the corrupt state government of Bihar provided JP with the opportunity to apply the revised strategy. Under his influence the agitation began to be framed as a movement for a total transformation of the political and social order. Many sarvodaya workers from throughout India went to Bihar to join in the struggle for 'Total Revolution', including Jagannathan and Krishnammal.

After spending a few days in Patna with JP and meeting state officials they relocated to Bodhgaya where they encountered conditions far worse than in Tamil Nadu. The head of a monastery there controlled some 30,000 acres, mainly by means of registering ownership in false names and maintaining a reign of terror over the local people. Whilst Jagannathan devoted most of his time to working as an advisor to JP in his role as leader of the opposition movement in the state, Krishnammal focused her considerable energies on travelling round the villages, meeting with the womenfolk, finding out about their living conditions and slowly gaining their trust and building up their confidence in their capacity to bring about change. Eventually she succeeded in organising women-only protests and fasts in front of the Bodhgaya Monastery. It was a difficult and dangerous time, as the local police and state officials were under the sway of the head of the monastery.

The example of the 'Bihar Movement' inspired similar protests beyond the boundaries of Bihar and when, in 1975, Indira Gandhi was found guilty of electoral malpractice by a court in Allahabad, JP was to the fore in demanding her resignation. She responded to this threat by declaring a state of emergency in June 1975 and thereby inaugurating two years of state repression. JP was arrested and many of the leaders and activists of the opposition, including Jagannathan, were imprisoned.[40] Jagannathan served 18 months, and by the time he was released in 1977 the sight in one of his eyes had been severely impaired. He returned

---

40 Krishnammal was arrested in April 1976, but she escaped from the police van while her guards were taking tea. She fled south to Tamil Nadu.

to Thanjavur District to re-join Krishnammal in their work with the landless.[41]

The failure of the movement appeared to vindicate the criticisms of that minority of sarvodaya workers who claimed the support of Vinoba in their opposition to JP's programme and methods. However, in the 1977 general election the Janata party, a coalition of opposition parties brought together under the influence of JP, resoundingly defeated Indira Gandhi - once again it seemed as if 'state power' might be used alongside 'people's power' to transform Indian society. The disintegration of the Janata government almost as soon as it achieved power rapidly frustrated such hopes. JP died in October 1979, shortly before Mrs Gandhi regained power in 1980. Vinoba died in November 1982. In the following years the Gandhian sarvodaya movement in India was focused on trying to mend the divisions and define for themselves a common and comprehensive programme for the future.

LAFTI – expanding the constructive repertoire

Back in Tamil Nadu Jagannathan and Krishnammal resumed their pursuit of their overwhelming vocation – land for the landless. In 1980 82 acres of land were put on the market in the neighbourhood of a village called Kulamanickam, a few kilometres north of Thanjavur. The villagers were desperate to obtain the land but faced seemingly insurmountable problems in raising the necessary purchase price. Krishnammal approached the banks and eventually they agreed to loan the necessary funds as long as the amount could be guaranteed by a legal entity. So Krishnammal established LAFTI – Land for the Tillers Independence/Freedom. The 82 acres were duly purchased and distributed to 162 families.[42]

Since that time LAFTI has obtained in excess of 13,000 acres on behalf of some 13,000 families. In addition to negotiating with landowners, banks and government ministries, much of LAFTI's work has been along the classical lines of Gandhian constructive work - with

---

41 The struggle to claim the land controlled by the head of the monastery in Bodhgaya continued and some years later 25,000 acres were released.

42 See A. Rigby, 'LAFTI—Making offers the landowners cannot refuse', *Community Development Journal,* v. 22, n. 4, 1987, pp. 310-321.

LAFTI workers spending time with the villagers, helping to establish gram sabhas and facilitating social and economic development.

Prawn satyagraha[43]

Whilst the scale of LAFTI's development activities continued to grow, Jagannathan retained his commitment to organising and mobilising movements, 'lighting fires' as opposed to establishing and tending institutions. In 1992 he embarked upon a one year padyatra in the main areas of LAFTI's operations. The aim was to spread the gospel of *gram swaraj* or village independence. It was in the twelfth month of the padyatra

that they reached a coastal area where the women came forward to express their concerns about the damage to their well-being caused by the establishment of prawn farms along their coastline.[44]

From that time until the end of his active life Jagannathan devoted himself to organising a nonviolent movement

Krishnammal & Jagannathan at protest rally against prawn fisheries

against the prawn farms. He drew on his long experience to organise collective fasts, processions, training camps, public meetings, and active satyagraha to prevent the construction of prawn tanks, to bring pressure

---

43 This section draws heavily on my own fieldwork and research papers. See A. Rigby, 'Gram Swaraj versus globalisation: Popular resistance against the spread of prawn farms in India', *Peace and Change*, v. 22, n. 4, October 1997, pp. 381-413.

44 They claimed that fertile land was being taken over for the tanks, this in turn resulted in a loss of employment whilst the prawn-tanks caused the salination of the soil and the water supplies, polluting the earth and the atmosphere with their effluent and waste - destroying not only the eco-system, but also the very life of the local agricultural and fishing communities.

on the prawn farm owners and workers, and spread public awareness of this new threat to 'Mother Earth' and the lives and livelihoods of local villagers. In the process he made full use of the constitutional space available in India to make representations at local, state and central levels. It was largely due to these efforts that in May 1995 the Tamil Nadu Aquaculture Regulation Act came into force. In 1996 the Supreme Court, responding to a petition lodged by Jagannathan, issued an interim order prohibiting and restricting the establishment and operation of prawn farms.

Of course it is one thing to obtain a court ruling, it is an altogether more difficult task to ensure its implementation, which became the focus of Jagannathan's ongoing campaign. It has to be said that the movement achieved only limited success in this regard but towards the end of 2004 'nature' intervened with the Boxing Day tsunami that destroyed the majority of the prawn farms along the Tamil Nadu coastline, followed in turn by an outbreak of the Norwalk virus that destroyed the viability of the remainder of the prawn farms.

Analysis of prawn satyagraha campaign

In many ways the Tamil Nadu Gram Swaraj Movement ((TNGSM), the campaign Jagannathan led against the spread of prawn farms along the Tamil Nadu coastline, was an ideal-type Gandhian campaign, one which manifested features that had informed some of Gandhi's own struggles and which revealed the extent to which Jagannathan continued to embrace not only the constructive work to change the living conditions of the landless but also the 'protest work' of challenging the privileged and powerful.

i. Bringing the grassroots into the struggle

During the period of Gandhi's leadership of the independence struggle, he transformed the national movement into a mass movement, involving the poorest sections of the community, declaring that the Indian people 'can have swaraj for the asking' when they 'have attained the power to take it.'[45] In challenging the ideological dominance of British rule, Gandhi orchestrated movements of large-scale civil disobedience, primarily to

---

45 Quoted in Chandra, p. 507.

convince the Indian masses that the British could be challenged and the foundations of their colonial power shaken once people withdrew their consent to be ruled.

In similar vein the TNGSM focused primarily on mobilising the villagers directly affected by the expansion of the prawn farms. Hundreds of women and men proved themselves willing to offer satyagraha – fasting outside the farms and offices, disrupting the construction work of the prawn tanks, and marching in procession at demonstrations. In so doing, the people were challenging, in effect, not only the operations of the companies but also the accepted wisdom of the new economic policies advocated by politicians, state functionaries and the business community in India. Their preparedness to risk arrest and assault by *goondas* hired by the prawn companies reflected the impact of the constructive work of the village workers attached to LAFTI who, over the years, had gained the trust and respect of the villagers, and from whom the villagers had derived their own sense of confidence in their capacity to challenge the perceived threats to their well-being.

ii. Alternating phases in the pace of the movement

During the independence struggle, phases of mass mobilisation and confrontation were interspersed by periods of relative quiescence.[46] As has been observed, Gandhi pursued swaraj through a combination of active satyagraha and constructive work which was intended to lay the seeds of the nonviolent society. There were times during the liberation struggle that he called a halt to confrontations and redirected collective energies towards the constructive programme, with its aim of removing all forms of inequality and oppression within the village society. This reflected his awareness that in a movement based on mass participation, there were limits to the commitment and endurance that could be expected from 'ordinary people' who were not 'professional', full-time freedom-fighters. To sustain a movement it was necessary to allow people to rest, restore their energy, and take care of their family responsibilities. At the same time it was from the ranks of the constructive workers, those

---

46 Chandra characterised this aspect of the nationalist strategy as 'Struggle-Truce-Struggle'. Chandra, p.509.

schooled and disciplined in the work for the uplift of the poorest sections of society, that Gandhi recruited the cadres of the movement.

A similar pattern can be discerned in the prawn campaign. It was from the ranks of LAFTI's constructive workers that the experienced satyagrahis of the TNGSM were drawn. Furthermore, the years of campaigning were characterised by alternating phases of active protest and periods when direct confrontations were avoided - to allow the heat to go out of the situation and avoid the risk of bloodshed, and to allow time for people to recoup their energies and revive their commitment.

iii. Utilising all channels of influence

In 1945 the Indian National Congress adopted a resolution which identified its guiding method as 'negotiation and settlement when possible and non-cooperation and direct action when necessary.'[47] Although British rule in India was authoritarian, there was a degree of constitutional space within which the independence struggle could be pursued, and Gandhi was prepared to use this space. In fact, satyagraha was frequently offered in order to create a situation in which the British had little option but to agree to sit down at the negotiating table. A similar combination of nonviolent direct action with more conventional methods of exercising influence characterised the campaign against intensive prawn farms. The aim was to catch the prawn companies in a pincer movement, between the grass-roots pressure from below and the judicial pressure from above.

The development of a multi-pronged approach ranging from direct action through to lobbying and resort to the courts helped broaden the constituencies of support for the struggle, and thereby increased the number and salience of the pressure points on the prawn companies and state authorities. In all this the active satyagraha at the grassroots was central. Thus, on a number of occasions protesters at construction sites were met with violence by employees of the prawn companies and the police. The result was increased media attention and an escalation in public concern. State authorities and politicians began to view the issue through the lens of 'law and order'. As the profile of the movement rose, so did the feeling grow that 'something must be done'. This growth in public awareness and

---

47 Chandra, p.512.

concern sensitised politicians to the political capital to be gained from the issue. As a consequence different political parties and groupings began to take an interest in the campaign. The Tamil Nadu Aquaculture Regulation Act of 1995 was one consequence of this set of pressures.

iv. Creating networks of support in the process of struggle

A key feature of Gandhi's direction of Congress strategy during the freedom campaign was the attempt to impress upon all sectors of India's population that they had a role to play in the overall movement. In particular, non-Congress leaders and constituencies were invited to participate in the struggle to undermine British hegemony. As part of this overall project, British public opinion was also targeted. In this process an important part was played by anti-colonialists who did their utmost to represent the views of Congress to British political leaders and publics, acting as links in what Johan Galtung characterised as 'the great chain of nonviolence'.[48] Organisations like the India League and individuals such as Fenner Brockway, Reginald Reynolds and Wilfred Wellock were integral to the whole network of relationships through which the nonviolent pressure and persuasion embodied in the freedom movement was conveyed from the grassroots in India right through to the metropolitan centre of British colonial power.[49]

In similar fashion, during the campaign against the spread of prawn fisheries the TNGSM forged important links with other groupings, networks and constituencies of support at the local, national and international level. In September 1994 a regional networking body, Campaign Against Shrimp Industries (CASI), was formed, followed by the establishment of the all-India People's Alliance Against Shrimp Industries (PAASI) at a meeting in Madras/Chennai in May 1995. The director of PAASI, the well-known author and environmentalist Dr Vandana Shiva, was the Indian representative for the Third World Network which, from its base in Malaysia, initiated an international campaign against unsustainable aquaculture. Closely associated with this campaign was the Mangrove Action Project (MAP), based in the United States and established in

---

48 J. Galtung, *Non-violence and Israel/Palestine*, Honolulu: University of Hawaii, 1989, p 19.

49 See F. Brockway, *Inside the Left*, Leicester: Blackfriars Press, 1947.

order to raise public awareness of issues related to mangrove forest areas around the world. Through these organisational developments links were established that connected the local, grassroots-based groups through to a global network of environmental activists and agencies. This meant that news of satyagraha actions at remote hamlets along the coast of Tamil Nadu spread around the world through different communication networks.[50]

v. Practical steps towards a utopian goal

In pursuing the goal of swaraj prior to the 1942 'Quit India' campaign, Gandhi tended to mobilise people around issues that directly affected their life chances. He interpreted the significance of such struggles in terms of the continuity between the immediate issues and the longer term goal. Thus, with reference to the Bardoli 'No Tax' satyagraha that took place in Gujarat in 1928, he observed: 'Whatever the Bardoli struggle may be, it clearly is not a struggle for the direct attainment of swaraj. That every such awakening, every such effort as that of Bardoli will bring swaraj nearer and may bring it nearer than any direct effort is undoubtedly true.'[51] In the same spirit, Jagannathan emphasised that whilst the impact of the prawn farms was the issue around which people mobilised, his vision remained that of gram swaraj.

vi. Constructive action and resistance

As was noted much earlier in this chapter, when Gandhi initiated struggles against particular instances of injustice and oppression, he emphasised not merely the aim of overcoming evil, but also the importance of creating positive alternatives to the violent structures and practices which were targeted. In demanding a boycott of foreign cloth, he also urged people to produce their own clothing. In confronting the British by refusing to pay the Salt Tax, he also emphasised the importance of people making and distributing their own salt. In similar vein, a considerable amount

---

50 A related network of influence was created through non-governmental development agencies. In May 1996 Christian Aid, the official relief and development arm of British and Irish churches, which had supported the work of LAFTI in Tamil Nadu and PREPARE in Andhra Pradesh, launched a campaign to highlight the social and environmental costs of intensive prawn farming. See K Blundell & E Maybin, *After the prawn rush: The human and environmental costs of commercial prawn farming,* London: Christian Aid, 1996.

51 Quoted in Chandra, 1989, p.209.

of effort was expended by the TNGSM in establishing gram swaraj committees through which villagers might start to exercise an increased degree of control over their collective lives.[52] It was through these village committees that the mobilisation of local people for collective action during the campaign was organised.

The continuing relevance of the Gandhian constructive vision in contemporary India

By the late 1990s Jagannathanji's energies were much diminished with advancing age, and I confess that I had the growing sense that his Gandhian vision of an India characterised by a radical devolution of power to self-reliant villages and neighbourhoods was increasingly out-of-step with the dominant trends in Indian society at that time. During the 1980s India had been borrowing significant amounts and its external debt was rocketing. By the early 1990s India's economic situation had come under severe stress and faced serious balance of payments challenges. Turning to the World Bank and the International Monetary Fund for assistance, the Finance Minister at that time, Manmohan Singh, was required to open up the previously relatively protected Indian economy to international corporations as part of the structural adjustment policies required by the international financial institutions. In 1991 India announced its New Economic Policy (NEP), which included such standard structural adjustment measures as the devaluation of the currency, increase in interest rates, reduction in public investment and expenditure, reduction in public sector food and fertilizer subsidies, and the opening up of the domestic markets to imports and foreign investment. This was how globalisation came to India, and the upsurge in the numbers of prawn farms being established along the Tamil coast was just one of the many consequences of this 'liberalisation' of the Indian economy.

But the resistance to the spread of the prawn farms was just one of the many popular movements that emerged during the 1990s and later in response to the deleterious impact of the NEP on the environment,

---

52 Although the gram swaraj committees were seen by Jagannathan as the seed-beds of a new society, their main function during the prawn campaign was as agents of mobilisation for the struggle.

community well-being and people's livelihoods. One of the people with whom Jagannathan made contact during the prawn campaign was Thomas Kocherry, who was president of the National Fishworkers Forum and the convenor of the National Fisheries Action Campaign Against Joint Ventures. In the mid-1990s he led a nationwide campaign to stop the Indian government from opening up the country's fishing industry to a growing fleet of large foreign trawlers. With 10 million Indians dependent on a sustainable fishery for their survival, the stakes were high. The movement against the introduction of joint-venture deep sea fishing eventually led to the Indian government withdrawing the legislation – one of the first and most significant victories against corporate globalization.[53]

Another of Jagannathan and Krishnammal's contemporaries was 'Baba' Amte (1914-2008) who, like them, had been active in the freedom struggle. Following independence he devoted his energies to the establishment of a number of ashrams for the care and treatment of people with leprosy in the state of Maharashtra. The life within the ashrams followed the guidelines laid down within the Gandhian constructive programme. As with other Gandhian sarvodaya workers, the time and the devotion spent working with villagers to meet their basic needs established the legitimacy they enjoyed when engaging in nonviolent satyagraha against perceived injustices and threats to human well-being. In the case of Baba Amte the cause he pursued in the later years of his life was the Narmada Bachao Andolan (NBA) – the Save the Narmada Movement.

The Narmada River is one of the major waterways of India, flowing west through three states and entering the Arabian Sea at the Gulf of

---

53 See 'Tom Kocherry: Fisher for justice', *New Internationalist*, 1st May 2012. Accessible at https://tinyurl.com/3h9fuftu (20 February 2020). The Gujarati social activist Anand Mazgaonkar has pointed out that in his experience effective movements take off only when a traditional community identity is involved, where people live and work together and experience the same challenges to their well-being. Fisherfolk are one such group, as are the indigenous people (adivasis) of India. (M. Mazgaonkar, 'India – macro-violence, micro-resistance: Development violence and unarmed grassroots resistance', in H. Clark ed., *People power: Unarmed resistance and global solidarity,* London: Pluto, 2009, pp. 76-85, p. 83.)

Khambhat. In 1979, after many years of deliberations, proposals and counter-proposals about how best to utilise the water resource, approval was granted for the construction of around 30 dams along the length of the river. It was claimed that around 40 million people would benefit from the irrigation networks and hydro-electric power supply which would result. The centre-piece of the whole scheme was to be the Sardar Sarova Dam, where construction started in 1987. The NBA launched its resistance campaign in the mid-1980s when it became apparent that the flooding of the gorge upriver from the dam would result in the displacement of up to 250,000 of people, mainly adivasis (tribal peoples) and poor peasants living in 245 villages.[54] Under the leadership of Medha Paktar the NBA succeeded in generating a debate throughout India and beyond, pitching the dam construction project as a potent symbol of the violence of a development paradigm hugely destructive of the natural environment and the social fabric of those who happen to be in the way of 'progress'.

One dramatic indicator of the 'price of progress' borne by the poor and vulnerable in India has been the rising rate of suicides amongst farmers and peasants. Between 1995 and 2014, more than 300,000 farmers – cultivators and agricultural labourers – committed suicide in India. That is roughly equivalent to one farmer suicide every 30 minutes.[55] A number of studies have suggested that a prime reason for this rise has been the growing indebtedness of marginal cash-crop farmers, consequent upon the opening up of Indian markets to international producers and suppliers combined with the reduction of state support – all part of the liberalisation of the agricultural sector that has been a central plank of the NEP since the early 1990s.[56]

---

54 Figure taken from *Bretton Woods Observer*, October 2017. Accessed at https://tinyurl.com/tpk2rsb (24 February 2019).

55 D. Basu et al, *Farmer Suicides in India: Levels and Trends across Major States, 1995-2014*, University of Massachusetts – Amherst: Economics Department Working Paper Series, 2016. Accessible at https://tinyurl.com/ut6cjdy (24 February 2020). The authors note that the majority of the Indian workforce is still dependent on agriculture for its livelihood. According to data from the 2011 census about 55% of Indian workers were employed in agriculture, either as cultivators or as agricultural labourers.

56 J. Kennedy & L. King, 'The political economy of farmers' suicides in India:

One of the most significant responses to the plight of the rural poor in India has been the emergence of the people's movement *Ekta Parishad* - Unity Forum (EP). Ekta Parishad quite specifically seeks to mobilise people against a development model that creates and reproduces violence (structural, cultural and interpersonal) through escalating levels of inequality. Established in 1991 out of a grouping of non-governmental training organisations for village development workers, it has grown into a phenomenal network of organisations and groups with volunteer activists working in thousands of villages in many of India's 28 states. It is firmly grounded in the Gandhian tradition. Their mission statement affirms:

> Ekta Parishad is a people's movement dedicated to non-violent principles of action. Our activists work towards building community-based governance (gram swaraj), local self-reliance (gram swawlamban) and responsible government (jawabdeh sarkar). Our aim is to see India's poorest people gain control over livelihood resources, especially land, water and forest.
>
> We believe that the grassroots, the village, is the perfect space in which to plant and nurture the seeds of unity and non-violence that can create positive changes at the social, political and economic levels. We believe that through non-violent struggle … the rural communities of India can secure Gandhi's vision of self-rule *gram swaraj*. *Srijan*, or the creation of a self-reliant society, is possible when community ties are strengthened through mutual respect and social equity. It is our responsibility as activists, as citizens of this country and as human beings to make sure that the needs of the deprived communities are no longer brushed aside. Our willingness to trust the principles of truth and non-violent civil disobedience is the way to see that happen.[57]

---

indebted cash-crop farmers with marginal landholdings explain state-level variation in suicide rates', *Globalization and health,* v.10, no.16, 2014. Accessible at https://doi.org/10.1186/1744-8603-10-16 (17 January 2020).

57 Ekta Parishad's statement of mission, https://tinyurl.com/tf8pja4 (25 February 2020).

Just as Jagannathanji pursued both dimensions of Gandhi's approach to transformation – constructive work and the protest politics of satyagraha, so EP characterises its core activities as falling into the same two categories of action: constructive work involving economic and development activities at the village level, alongside the mobilisation of people in pursuit of land and associated rights through various forms of nonviolent action. However, there are at least two features of EP that sets it apart from other Gandhian social movements for change in India. One is the size and scale of the movement. The second is their adoption of large-scale padyatras as a means of mobilisation and method of leverage on policy-makers and political leaders. In 1999-2000, the first state-level foot-march was organised, which traversed the central state of Madhya Pradesh from west to east.[58] According to EP it was on this padyatra they discovered:

> … walking was an enabling tool, one that allowed the marginalized people to participate readily and with dignity, since it only demanded their physical prowess and not funds or political patronage. The foot-march, like Gandhi's Salt Satyagraha of 1931, was also a way for people to highlight their rights and become visible by attracting the attention of the media, policy-makers and the general public.[59]

In 2007 the decision was taken to complement the state-level padyatras with pressure on the central government. On 2 October 2007 (Gandhi's birthday) some 25,000 people set off to walk over 340 kilometres from Gwalior in Madhya Pradesh to the capital, arriving there on 29 October. The Prime Minister met them and gave assurances that the unfinished land reform agenda that they presented would be completed. Of course, like movements for change the world over, EP has learned over time that a statement of intent from a representative of the political elite does not necessarily translate into substantive action for change on the ground, and that continuing pressure at the grass-roots and other levels is necessary for land reform to be implemented. Before

---

58 For details of the organisational infrastructure underpinning such marches, see K. Schock, 'Gandhian struggles for land in India', in Hardiman, ed., 2017, pp. 207-229.

59 See https://tinyurl.com/r3j7yyk (25 February 2020).

the onset of the coronavirus pandemic scuppered their plans, EP had launched a new campaign – a foot-march from Delhi to Geneva due to take place in 2020. As one of their core members explained:

> We continue to organize marginalized communities for their control over land and natural resources, as a way to fight poverty. At the same time we realize that this problem is not limited to India alone and that people from almost every country across the world are experiencing similar challenges. Market driven globalization is depriving millions of people from their land and accessing resources. People are being dispossessed and forced into cities and slums. This means that we need to work at a global as well as at the grassroots level to bring about real change.[60]

The campaign had been called *Jai Jagat 2020*. In English *Jai Jagat* translates as 'Victory to the world'. The phrase was first coined by Vinoba Bhave back in 1957. It expresses the awareness of oneness and inter-relatedness that was – and remains – at the heart of the Gandhian approach to constructive work and 'obstructive' satyagraha. As Vinoba expressed it all those years ago, at the height of the gramdan movement:

> Fifteen years earlier we had begun to use the slogan *Jai Hind*, 'Victory to India'; now the time has come to move on to *Jai Jagat*. The mental outlook is changing all over the world, and very rapidly. Little by little the dividing walls between country and country will be broken down, and it will become more and more possible to create a united world family. The human spirit is being enlarged. So, from now on, our slogan should be *Jai Jagat*.[61]

That call resonates even stronger at a time when the global pandemic, coming on top of the climate crisis, reminds us that the world is one.

---

60 *Call to action for Jai Jagat 2020*, Accessible at https://tinyurl.com/rw6bdmv (26 February 2020).
61 V. Bhave, *Moved by love: The memoirs of Vinoba Bhave*, Wardha: Paramdam Prakachan, 1994, p. 133. Accessible at https://tinyurl.com/57makjha (30 June 2021).

4

CONSTRUCTIVE ACTION IN CIVIL RESISTANCE FOR POLITICAL CHANGE

Personal preface

In the early 1970s I had just started teaching in the Sociology Department at the University of Aberdeen up in the north-east of Scotland. Given my tentative anarchist leanings (I used to label myself a libertarian socialist, being too timid to call myself an anarchist!) I took an interest in a local arts and community workshop where kindred spirits were trying to mobilise local people around various community action projects related to housing conditions, local services and various forms of exclusion and deprivation.

Some of the people involved began to feel that the focus on a single neighbourhood within the city was failing to challenge the residents' view of their problems as 'private troubles' rather than 'public issues' - manifestations of the inequalities and injustices embedded in the wider socio-economic and political structures. There was a need for a medium through which critical perspectives, new ideas for action and visions of alternative futures could be communicated across different communities. From this grew the idea of establishing a city-wide alternative newspaper, alongside a printing service for local groups. I was one of the founding group of seven. I even gave up my academic post so I could devote more of my energies to what had become Aberdeen Peoples Press (APP).[1]

I started thinking about my time with APP because, just as I had started planning this chapter, I received news that there were moves to create an exhibition to commemorate Aberdeen's radical printing and publishing past, exemplified by APP. Thinking back to those days,

---

1   The first issue of the newspaper appeared May 1973.

through the prism of civil resistance movements, it struck me that what we were trying to do, so long ago, was a form of constructive resistance through community action. We had a vision of how we wanted to contribute to the creation of an 'alternative society', which we articulated quite clearly in one of our submissions for funding at the time.

> … We are seeking to create a society where we think of our fellow man's/woman's needs rather than exploit him/her, a society where an individual can grow and develop as a creative being and not live in fear of others, a society where love and cooperation with others are the prime qualities and not the selfishness and power-seeking that characterises the present order of things.

> … such a society will never be achieved unless people actively and collectively seek to create such a world through transforming their own personal lives and relationships with

others in the 'here-and-now' rather than waiting for the 'revolution from above' sometime in the distant future.[2]

This was the deeper, long-term purpose that some of us held – we envisioned a fundamental transformation of society by means of a bottom-up nonviolent revolutionary process. Remember - this was the early 1970s, when the future seemed far more open than it does now, some 50 years later. It was this sense of possibility that informed my friend Howard Clark's vision as he described it in his *Making nonviolent revolution*, which was first published in 1977:

> My vision of nonviolent revolution isn't of a united mass movement sweeping away the institutions of the status quo, but of people acting in their own situations to take control of their own lives and asserting different values, values which have been systematically suppressed.[3]

However utopian such a vision might seem, up in Aberdeen we pursued it by means of providing practical support services for local community groups and activists. So, whilst our visible, surface function was the provision of printing and related communication services for our contemporaries, this was our means towards a deeper goal – the transformation of society by nonviolent means.

Reflecting on my past political involvement as I planned this chapter, it occurred to me that our project with Aberdeen Peoples Press could be seen as a model, in microcosm, of two of the main roles constructive action can perform in the context of civil resistance movements seeking change by targeting state institutions. There is the support function - servicing the needs of those engaged in the more contentious or offensive modes of civil resistance. In addition there is the deeper function of

---

2   *A book of visions: A directory of alternative society projects*, London: BIT Information Service, 1973, p. 107.

3   H. Clark, *Making nonviolent revolution*, London: Peace News, 2012. (An updated version of a booklet first published in 1977.) In the second issue of *APP* (July 1973) we wrote, 'One thing is certain, unless ordinary folk start trying to control their own lives, and this includes creating their own means of communication, then there are plenty of people only too willing to control our lives for us.'.

attempting to create the foundations of new ways of life, exemplifying ways in which different spheres of life might be carried out in the hoped-for future.[4] In the remainder of this chapter an attempt will be made to examine a range of different types of civil resistance movements that have pursued some kind of state-related change, guided in part by the question of how significant these two modes of constructive resistance have been in the overall portfolio of activities pursued by such movements.

Civil resistance 101

Definition

A simple and basic definition of civil resistance is that used by April Carter, Howard Clark and Michael Randle in 2013 in their book *A guide to civil resistance*: 'Civil resistance refers to collective action for political or social ends without any systematic recourse to violence.'[5] Expanding on this, other analysts have affirmed that the adjective 'civil' implies that the collective action is carried out by civilian sectors of the population, actors and institutions from civil society, and without recourse to lethal violence. Others have underlined that the collective action typically takes place outside conventional political channels.[6]

Types of civil resistance movements seeking political change

Reviewing the literature on civil resistance struggles, whose main target is changing the state in some way or another, it is possible to distinguish three main types, according to the goals of the movement.[7]

---

4   These twin dimensions remind me of the distinction between diggers and dreamers: the dreamers spend a lot of time imagining different ways of doing things, and the diggers do the day-to-day work of making it actually happen. The ideal of course is a synthesis – diggers who dream and dreamers who dig! See https://www.diggersanddreamers.org.uk/ (30 January 2021).

5   A. Carter, H. Clark, & M. Randle, *A guide to civil resistance: A bibliography of people power and nonviolent protest*, London: Merlin Press, 2013, p. 15.

6   See A. Roberts & T. Garton Ash, *Civil resistance and power politics: The experience of non-violent action from Gandhi to the present*, Oxford: Oxford University Press, 2009, pp. 2-3; H. Clark, *Civil resistance in Kosovo,* London: Pluto Press, 2000, pp. 2-3; M. Randle, *Civil resistance*, London: Fontana Press, 1994, pp. 10-11.

7   There are a number of publications containing studies of a range of nonviolent

i.   Movements to remove an authoritarian regime.

ii. Movements for liberation from what is perceived to be an occupation regime.

iii. Movements to achieve or extend citizenship rights within constitutional democracies.

Types of civil resistance activity

Gene Sharp identified 198 types of nonviolent action for change, which he grouped into three main categories: protest and persuasion, non-cooperation, and interventions.[8] In my own research into civil resistance movements of one kind or another I have found a five-fold categorisation more heuristically valuable as a framework than that proposed by Sharp. My classification is based on the typology developed by Werner Rings in his study of resistance to occupation in Europe during the Second World War.[9] Drawing on Rings' work I have found it useful to distinguish the following types of unarmed resistance.[10]

- *Symbolic resistance*: 'We display our allegiance to the resistance and its values by means of gestures, actions or dress.'

- *Polemical resistance:* 'We voice our protest and try to influence others by using whatever media available, seeking to communicate our message to our opponents, supporters, bye-standers and third-parties.'

- *Offensive resistance:* 'We are prepared to do all that we can to frustrate and overcome the oppressor by nonviolent means, including strikes, demonstrations and other forms of direct action.'

---

movements for change. In addition to the sources already cited I should also include M. Bartowski, ed., *Recovering nonviolent history: Civil resistance in liberation struggles*, Boulder, CO.: Lynne Rienner, 2013.

8   See G. Sharp, *Waging nonviolent struggle: 20th century practice and 21st century potential*, Boston: Porter Sargent, 2005, especially pp. 49-65.

9   W. Rings, *Life with the enemy: Collaboration and resistance in Hitler's Europe 1939-1945*, NY: Doubleday, 1982.

10 See A. Rigby, *Palestinian resistance and nonviolence*, East Jerusalem: PASSIA, 2010, pp. 3-4.

- *Defensive resistance*: 'We aid and protect those in danger or at risk of sanctions from the regime.'

- *Constructive resistance*

    * *Service provision*: 'We support the struggle by providing essential services to meet the needs of the resisters.'

    * *Prefiguring the future*: 'We challenge the existing order by attempting to practice the values we hope to see flourish more widely in the future.' [11]

Working hypotheses

The analysis that follows is informed by a number of working hypotheses, based on the awareness that the extent and significance of constructive modes of action within a civil resistance movement will vary according to the type of movement, the phase of the resistance struggle, and the context within which the struggle takes place.

1. A basic premise is that where offensive modes of resistance are likely to be met by severe repression and associated sanctions, there is a strong likelihood that many resisters will choose 'quieter' and less contentious modes of action, such as constructive modes of resistance, that do not cause significant friction with the regime, and hence carry a lower risk of incurring costly sanctions.

2. A related working hypothesis is that when people are aware that their identification with a civil resistance struggle for political change will involve a long-term commitment, then – other things being equal – they are likely to develop constructive modes of resistance that can be incorporated into their everyday lives. By so doing they can embody, express and sustain their commitment over time, whilst reducing the risk of 'burn-out' or inviting reprisals from the regime.[12]

---

11 Rings did not have a category of 'constructive resistance'.

12 Here I am reminded of James Scott's distinction between public and hidden transcripts, the contrast between what is said and done in the face of power and what is said behind its back. See Scott, 1990, pp. 1-5.

3. Conversely, when activists feel that their civil resistance struggle is entering a pivotal phase that demands public displays of resistance, then primacy will be given to more offensive and confrontational modes of resistance. Such 'front-stage' activities, aimed at exercising leverage on the regime, will take primacy over the more constructive modes of resistance that typically take place 'backstage', away from public view.[13]

4. In civil resistance struggles against an occupying power, constructive modes of action can be prioritised as a means of affirming and reproducing a culture and way of life integral to the maintenance of an oppositional identity.

5. In civil resistance movements to overcome discriminatory practices and institutions, and achieve full rights within a state, constructive resistance activities are likely to be prioritised as ways of embodying the rights being sought, providing certain services in support of the wider movement, and as a means of preparing people for more offensive forms of action.

Civil resistance against authoritarian regimes

As I started to plan this chapter a military take-over of political power took place in Myanmar, leading to large-scale protests and civil resistance by hordes of people determined to frustrate the anti-democratic impulses of the generals and their cohorts.

Resisting the military coup in Myanmar

The military coup against the democratically elected government took place on 1 February 2021, with Aung San Suu Kyi and other senior political figures detained in a morning raid. As news spread the initial reaction seemed to be of shock and fear. People stocked up on food, withdrew cash, and stayed indoors. On Saturday 6 February activists began marching. Over the weekend more than a hundred cities and towns

---

13 See A. Rigby and M Sørensen, 'Frontstage and backstage emotion management in civil resistance', *Journal of Political Power*, v. 17, n. 2, June 2017, pp.219-235. Accessible at https://tinyurl.com/dmcckaor (18 February 2021).

witnessed a growing campaign of civil resistance, with tens of thousands facing down armed police, water cannons, tear gas, and rubber bullets. As the demonstrations grew the crowds took on something of a celebratory atmosphere. Families started banging on pots and pans in the evening, a traditional way to drive out the devil, creating a huge din in opposition to the coup. This became a daily ritual carried out nightly at 8 p.m. across the country.

One of the first demonstrations against the coup was organized by doctors at a Yangon hospital who staged a protest wearing their blue scrubs, surgical masks and red ribbons. The colour signified support for Aung San Suu Kyi and her political party, the National League for Democracy. Protestors also adopted a three-finger salute, a symbol from the *Hunger Games* series of films that was first used after the 2014 coup in neighbouring Thailand.[14] The international media coverage of the civil resistance movement focused on the different types of protest, with special attention paid to the symbolic protests and the civil disobedience campaign, with a widespread general strike at its heart. By 10 February economic activity was paralysed as bank employees, workers at power plants, civil servants, health workers, teachers and others joined the strike. Significantly, ship-yard workers and river-transport officials also joined the strike, paralysing river transport on the Irrawaddy, the country's main commercial waterway. It was there, on 20 February 2021, that two young people were killed when armed police and military used live ammunition whilst confronting protesters who were trying to defend the shipyard from attempts to force striking workers back to work.[15]

The Myanmar civil resistance movement during the early weeks was characterised by intense offensive resistance, characteristic of similar phases in other cases of civil resistance launched to challenge authoritarian regimes elsewhere in the world. During such periods, when emotions are high, the sense of urgency ever-present, and the level of public protest

---

14 The crosscurrents of protest flew both ways, with a Thai youth group adopting the pots and pans campaign from Myanmar for a protest in Bangkok in mid-February. H. Beech, 'Paint, poems and protest anthems: Myanmar's coup inspires the art of defiance', *New York Times*, 17 February 2021.

15 *Radio Free Asia*, 21 February 2021. Accessible at https://tinyurl.com/5xbhstqp (22 February 2021).

intense, the main civil resistance activities tend to be offensive, defensive, polemical and symbolic. During such high-intensity phases the main forms of constructive resistance are those focused on providing the basic services and support for the activists in the front-line – medical aid, legal support, human rights monitoring, media coverage and the like. Where normal public services are disrupted there is also space for neighbourhoods to organise their own alternatives, such as garbage collection, transport, communication and other community services.

Most people can only sustain the high intensity of offensive public protest for a limited period of time – alongside the incidence of exhaustion, emotional and physical 'burn-out', there are the more mundane de-mands of putting food on the table, avoiding impoverishment through unemployment, fear of sanctions. If the pillars of the regime remain firm and their capacity to wield retaliatory violence persists, then there comes a time when the cost of persistent offensive resistance becomes too high to sustain for civilians. There can then follow two possible paths. On the one hand people can revert to less offensive modes of resistance, seeking to keep certain values and political identities and networks alive until such time as factors coalesce in such a way as to bring about a renewal of the more offensive modes of civil resistance. The other path that can emerge is the resort to armed resistance. We have seen this in the case of Myanmar where, by the end of July 2021 more than 900 had been killed by the junta's forces after their seizure of power. However, casualties amongst the military and police began to rise as armed resistance grew in numerous areas, with ethnic armed groups also offering their support to anti-coup forces.[16]

I have neither the knowledge, the capacity nor the will to illustrate this process in anything like a full review of case studies. Instead, and purely for illustrative purposes, I intend to draw on material relating to the civil resistance movements against authoritarian regimes in Central and Eastern Europe during the latter half of the twentieth century.

Civil resistance in Poland and Czechoslovakia - 1989

In Poland the movement around the trade union *Solidarnosc* emerged in 1980 following strike action at the Gdansk shipyard. It morphed into

---

16 *The Guardian*, 2 August 2021.

a broad anti-Soviet movement with support from the Roman Catholic church and also from various support networks in the West. In 1981 the state responded by imposing martial law, followed by several years of repression. But the movement for change did not evaporate. Likewise, in what was then Czechoslovakia, there had been a period of intense hope and liberalisation during the 'Prague Spring' of 1968, only for the Soviet military to intervene on 20 August in order to crush the reform movement. For the next twenty years the Czech regime was arguably the most hard-line and repressive of all the states throughout the Soviet bloc, only for the regime to crumble in the face of large-scale protests in 1989.

Wall of Gdansk shipyard, 1980

In both countries dissidents pursued variants of a two-pronged response during the lengthy periods when a full-scale nonviolent offensive against the state was deemed to be unfeasible. The first was to focus on developing 'civil society' as a 'parallel polis' from below, as a counter to the corrupted state.[17] The aim was to consolidate social networks and ties in order to combat the atomisation created by the repressive state.[18] As Adam Michnik, the Polish dissident and writer, urged, 'The resistance movement must be at the same time the school of liberty ... .'[19] He talked of a 'new evolutionism' that did not seek to overthrow the state so much as expand the sphere of civil liberties and human rights within the existing regime's carapace. As in Czechoslovakia, the aim was not so much to defeat the ruling power but to progressively liberate spheres of civil society from its control, to create oases of freedom as part of the struggle for human rights and independent institutions.[20]

---

17 A. Carter, 'People power and protest: The literature on civil resistance in historical context', in Roberts & Ash, eds., 2009, pp. 25-42, p. 33.

18 A. Smolar, 'Towards "self-limiting revolution": Poland, 1970-89', in Roberts & Ash, eds., 2009, pp. 127-143, p. 133.

19 Quoted by Smolar, p. 131.

20 These ideas resonated strongly with the activists in Serbia who mobilised in

This focus on self-organising in the interstices of the society-state nexus was also at the heart of the second strategic theme – what Vaclav Havel termed 'living in the truth' as against 'living within the lie'. By the latter he was referring to the manner in which everyday people living within totalitarian systems might give vent to their frustration and resentment in the privacy of their own home, whilst keeping their heads down and never questioning the system in public. Such people might not accept 'the lie', but they do accept living *within* the lie – the mythological version of reality propagated by the regime. As a consequence, by living as if they accept the lie, such people become complicit in the perpetuation of the totalitarian system. In the words of Havel:

> Individuals need not believe all these mystifications, but they must behave as though they did, or they must at least tolerate them in silence, or get along well with those who work with them. For this reason, however, they must *live within a lie*. They need not accept the lie. It is enough for them to have accepted their life with it and in it. For by this very fact, individuals confirm the system, fulfil the system, make the system, *are* the system.[21]

In the pages of his essay *The Power of the Powerless* Havel drew on all his strengths as a writer and observer of human life to portray the manner in which regimes, such as existed in Czechoslovakia, drew people into their sphere of power, so that they became agents of its reproduction. To illustrate his thesis Havel presented the case of a greengrocer placing a poster in their shop-window, proclaiming 'Workers of the world unite!' By displaying the sign the shop-keeper was declaring loyalty to the system, by participating in the ritual they were manifesting their acceptance of the rules of the game. This is the 'dictatorship of ritual', whereby compliance is obtained and reproduced through the anonymous power of routine. In such a world people forfeit their dignity as autonomous human beings and become more akin to anonymous cogs in the wheels of repression.

2000 to claim electoral victory over the Milosovic regime. (See I. Vejvoda, 'Civil society versus Slobodan Milosevic: Serbia 1991-2000', in Roberts & Ash, eds., 2009, pp. 295-316, p. 296).

21 V. Havel, 'The power of the powerless' in V. Havel, *Living in truth*, London: Faber & Faber, 1990, pp. 36-122, p. 45.

But Havel then imagines a day when the greengrocer stops putting up the slogans of the regime, stops voting in farcical elections that mean nothing, and actually starts to say what he or she really thinks in political meetings.

> And he even finds the strength in himself to express solidarity with those whom his conscience commands him to support. In this revolt the greengrocer steps out of living within the lie. He rejects the ritual and breaks the rules of the game. He discovers once more his suppressed identity and dignity. He gives his freedom a concrete significance. His revolt is an attempt to *live within the truth.*[22]

From this perspective, when people seek to live within the truth, they threaten one of the main pillars of the system – the routinisation of living within the lie.[23] As a consequence, such dissidents must expect to face sanctions from the state, unless they can find relatively safe spaces within which living the truth can be practised without undue risk. This is where the two threads of the civil resistance strategy adumbrated by people like Havel and Michnik intertwine. The constructive action by individuals seeking to regain their dignity as moral human beings feeds into, and strengthens, the parallel institutions and structures created by dissidents within the broader civil resistance movement. As Havel expressed it:

> For what else are parallel structures than an area where a different life can be lived …? What else are those initial attempts at self-organisation than the efforts of a certain part of society to live – as a society – within the truth ….? What else is it but a nonviolent attempt by people to negate the system within themselves and to establish their lives on a new basis, that of their own proper identity?[24]

---

22 Havel, 1990, p.55. Emphasis in original, as is the gendered language.

23 Havel's 'living in the truth' is reminiscent of Colin Ward's emphasis on the significance of people seeking to embody such ideals as autonomy and mutuality in their everyday lives, thereby sustaining the seeds of an anarchist society that are otherwise buried beneath the weight of the state, capitalism, privilege and nationalism. See C. Ward, 1996, p. 18.

24 Havel, 1990, p. 102.

A number of illustrations come to mind of the manner in which institutional spaces were created within which resisters might nourish and practice their resolve and their resilience. In Poland, after martial law was imposed in 1981, Solidarnosc and other networks and initiatives retained a strong underground existence, and were able to resurface to negotiate with the regime once the Soviet bloc started to crumble.[25] In Czechoslovakia, human rights groups that had been operating underground were instrumental in organising public rallies and demonstrations that pressured the regime to relinquish power in 1989.[26] In the German Democratic Republic (GDR – East Germany), the church networks were crucial in creating the spaces where people could meet and prepare for the demonstrations that were such crucial levers in weakening the regime.

In Serbia, during the 1990s, a significant development was the mobilisation of youth who began to organise human rights groups and social support networks in towns and cities throughout the country, the most prominent nationally being the Centre for Anti-war Action, Women in Black and the trade union Independence.[27] In 1996-7 protests against the Milosevic regime grew once again, resulting in a number of academics losing their posts for supporting the dissidents. They proceeded to establish the Alternative Academic Educational Network (AAEN), a parallel university which acted as a hub for dissident students and academics. It was from these ranks that the Serbian nonviolent movement OTPOR (Resistance) was founded in October 1998, and which was largely credited with bringing about the downfall of Slobodan Milosovic's regime in 2000.

---

25 During this period dissidents could draw on the long tradition of underground organising that has been such a strong feature of Polish history.

26 Michael Randle and other peace movement activists from the UK operated a clandestine courier service delivering books, pamphlets and other materials to dissident groups in Czechoslovakia throughout the 1970s. See https://tinyurl.com/yjb4kjfb (4 March 2021).

27 Vejvoda, in Roberts & Ash, eds., 2009, p. 299.

Observations

What comes across in all these cases is that the political mobilisation and offensive modes of resistance that were vital levers in pressuring the regimes to relinquish power in Poland, Czechoslovakia, the GDR, Serbia, and elsewhere, grew out of the constructive work of individuals seeking to live in the truth. Under the radar, so to speak, such people committed themselves to creating support networks, human rights monitoring groups, educational and information services, underground media outlets. In so doing they not only kept the democratic impulse alive, but they developed the levels of trust and camaraderie, the communication networks and the skill-sets necessary to support and sustain the mobilisation of large swathes of the population when the political opportunity arose for offensive resistance.

Civil resistance against occupation

In this section the focus of attention is the role of constructive resistance in civilian based resistance movements against occupying regimes. The working hypothesis informing this analysis is that in such struggles constructive modes of resistance can perform a number of significant functions – offering a role in the struggle to wide sections of the population, enabling people to maintain their commitment to the cause without experiencing too high a cost, and generally acting as a means of affirming and reproducing a culture and way of life integral to the maintenance of an oppositional identity. However, constructive modes of resistance on their own lack the leverage power to dislodge or bring about substantive changes in the nature of the occupying regime. Illustrative material to examine this hypothesis will be drawn from two case studies: the Kosovan civil resistance against what was perceived as the occupation regime imposed by the Serbian state during the 1990s and the Palestinian struggle against the ever-deepening Israeli occupation.

Civil resistance against occupation – the case of Kosovo

In the early 1990s, whilst the republics of Slovenia, Croatia and Bosnia-Herzegovina fought wars to leave Yugoslavia, Albanians in the autonomous province of Kosovo engaged in an unarmed civil resistance struggle to defend their rights and demand independence from the Federal Republic of Yugoslavia (FRY). This phase of the Kosovo struggle had been sparked by the Serbian leader Slobodan Milosevic's determination to abolish the autonomy status that Kosovo had been granted in the 1974 constitution. In his book *Civil resistance in Kosovo*, Howard Clark examined how Kosovo Albanians frustrated Milosevic's plans by means of a civil resistance struggle in which constructive modes of action played a paramount part.[28] However, according to Clark's analysis, the prudent approach of the leadership in seeking to avoid a direct confrontation with the regime proved too passive a form of 'semi-resistance', and was eventually superseded by armed resistance. This began in 1998 and concluded with the NATO military intervention against FRY in 1999, which ended Serbian rule in Kosovo and paved the way for the February 2008 Kosovo declaration of independence.[29]

In 1974 some acknowledgement had been made by President Tito that Kosovo was home to the largest non-Slav ethnic group in Yugoslavia. As a result Albanian-language secondary and university education was introduced along with formal recognition of Kosovo's special status as an autonomous province. This, in turn, deepened Serbian resentment of 'Albanisation' and fed claims of cultural genocide being inflicted on Serbs living in Kosovo. Milosevic aligned himself with this trend, and after coming to power introduced a host of regulations, including the re-imposition of the Serbian language and curriculum, and efforts to redress the demographic imbalance by encouraging Serbs to settle as part of the effort to 're-Serbianize' Kosovo. This, in turn, sparked resistance on the part of Kosovo Albanians, some of it involving violence. However, the experience of intensified Serb repression in response to the violence contributed to a growing interest in the potentialities of less provocative modes of resistance – constructive resistance.

The Kosovans were also influenced by the relative success of the civil resistance movements in Central and Eastern Europe during 1989, and by the end of the year a network for coordinating unarmed resistance emerged with the establishment of the Democratic League for Kosovo

---

28   H. Clark, 2000.

29   H. Clark, 'The limits of prudence: Civil resistance in Kosovo, 1990-98', in Roberts & Ash, eds., 2009, pp. 277-294, p. 277.

(LDK), led by Ibrahim Rugova. By February 1990 membership of the LDK was estimated to be in excess of 200,000.[30]

Constructive resistance – the 'politics of as if'

A significant dimension of the civil resistance strategy was what Noel Malcolm termed 'political as if': acting as if the independent Kosovo state existed, in order to bring it into being.[31] The prime example of this was the parallel education system that was established, from primary level up to the tertiary level of the University of Prishtina. At one point there were over 18,000 teachers and in excess of 330,000 students.[32] Salaries were funded from voluntary payments levied from businesses and individuals within Kosovo and from the diaspora.[33]

Equally significant was the development of parallel medical services, following the dismissal of more than half the medical staff. Any sign of disloyalty to the regime was a reason for dismissal – treating demonstrators, providing medical treatment to strikers, writing professional scripts in Albanian rather than Serbo-Croat. Dismissed physicians set up their own private practices, offering free treatment to the families of those who had lost their income. The Mother Theresa Association was also established to deliver welfare and social services to those in need. Clark estimated that by Spring 1992 there were 71 clinics and some 7000 volunteers distributing humanitarian aid to as many as 350,000 people.[34]

A third strand was focused on ending the social institution of the blood feud, which had blighted Kosovo society for generations.[35] In the late 1980s it was estimated that the lives of 17,000 men were under threat due to the historic practice.[36] 1990 was declared to be the Year

---

30 Clark, 2000, p. 56.
31 N. Malcolm, *Kosovo: A short history*, London: MacMillan, 1998, p. 348.
32 Clark, 2000, p. 99.
33 Clark, 2000, p. 103.
34 Clark, 2000, pp. 106-7.
35 Blood feuds in Kosovo involve cycles of retaliatory violence based on the principle of collective guilt. When someone has been killed or dishonoured, the relatives of the victim seek retribution by killing the culprit or their male relatives.
36 M. Thompson, *A paper house: The ending of Yugoslavia*, London: Vintage. 1992, p. 141.

of Reconciliation, and every weekend campaigners would go out into the countryside seeking out families trapped in a blood feud. Obtaining a 'magnanimous pardon', to absolve the blood debt, would require a number of visits before people were prepared to consider the path of reconciliation. The campaign also involved enlisting local support to establish structures such as Councils of Elders to arbitrate disputes. The leader of the overall campaign, Anton Cetta, claimed that the blood feud campaign was integral to the Kosovan civil resistance struggle, 'The enthusiasm and sense of fraternity that spread gave courage to our politicians and also encouraged the self-organisation of our population.'[37]

However impressive the parallel institutions and constructive work to bring an end to blood feuds were as symbols of a new and independent Kosovo, criticism began to grow about Rugova's 'passivity'. For all the popular mobilisation and solidarity, young people were missing out on their education and there was no evidence of any progress towards formal recognition of Kosovo's right to independence. People began to feel that more active or offensive forms of nonviolence were necessary. On 1 October 1997 15,000 students challenged the LDK's five year moratorium on protest demonstrations by marching towards Pristina University, with the declared aim of reclaiming the buildings so they might resume their formal education. The march was broken up by police violence, but the clash caught the attention of the international media.

However, the exploration of the potentialities of more offensive forms of civil resistance in Kosovo was too little and too late. During 1996 the Kosovo Liberation Army (UCK) began to declare its existence, and by 1997 it was engaging in skirmishes with Serbian police, declaring parts of central Kosovo to be under its control. This provoked retaliatory measures from the Serbian authorities, and the violence escalated. Thousands fled their homes, whilst a series of atrocities were perpetrated on those who remained, with extended families slaughtered in their own compounds. These victims became more potent symbols of the Kosovo cause than the 'passive' Rugova.

---

37 Quoted in Clark, 2000, p. 63.

International pressure brought a temporary ceasefire in October 1998, only for the violence to be resumed in Spring 1999. After the Serbian authorities refused to countenance the presence of an international peacekeeping force, NATO embarked on a 78-day bombing campaign against targets in Kosovo and throughout the FRY. In June 1999 Serbia agreed to withdraw its forces, and Kosovo was placed under the United Nations Interim Mission in Kosovo (UNMIK). In 2008 the Kosovo legislative assembly declared Kosovo to be independent from Serbia. Serbia refused to recognise the secession, and there then followed an EU-facilitated dialogue which resulted in an agreement in 2013 for Serbia and Kosovo to normalise their relations, although Serbia still refused to recognise Kosovo as a sovereign state.

Observations

According to Tim Judah the 'semi-resistance' in Kosovo was 'an extraordinary experiment' that failed.[38] Certainly, a critical analysis of the Kosovo struggle to secede from Serbian domination reveals some of the weaknesses of constructive modes of civil resistance against an occupying regime determined to hold on to its patrimony. Constructive modes of resistance, such as the establishment of parallel institutions are processes, not events. They lack the drama of a clash between unarmed protesters and violent oppressors. Whilst the constructive actions might embody a morality tale of a just struggle being pursued by just means, when the activities are implemented as a means of avoiding violent suppression and related sanctions, they lack the 'punch' that grabs the attention of significant others, such as the global media. In and of themselves constructive modes of resistance lack the coercive power to impose the level of costs on the opposition necessary to force them to concede.

Moreover, the constructive 'semi-resistance' pursued by Albanians in Kosovo had limited potential for persuasion or conversion of their adversaries. Their target was an occupation regime, whose officials and constituencies of support had been exposed to a widely accepted world-view that portrayed the Kosovo Albanians as 'other', alien, less than fully human. In such circumstances efforts to influence the Serbian police,

---

38 T. Judah, *Kosovo: War and revenge*, New York: Yale University Press, 2000, p. 146.

administrative officials and policy-makers by means of 'shame power' - appeals to morality and conscience, based on claims of a common humanity - were always doomed to be of limited effectiveness.[39]

Despite such weaknesses, Howard Clark pointed out that the constructive work that was at the heart of the 'semi-resistance' was not without its achievements. Firstly, it maintained and reinforced social solidarity within the Kosovo Albanian communities, with Denisa Kostovicova observing: , 'The cause of schooling turned Albanians into a community of solidarity.'[40] Secondly, at a time when anti-Albanian feeling was at its strongest amongst the Serbian population in FRY during 1989-90, the 'non-threatening' form adopted by the Kosovo resistance reduced the likelihood of a full-scale Serbian assault. Thirdly, the constructive approach to civil resistance in Kosovo provided evidence of the legitimacy of the liberation struggle, which in turn strengthened the impact of lobbying efforts for international pressure on Serbia.[41]

Overall, then, we might conclude that whilst the constructive resistance of the Kosovans failed to liberate them from Serbian rule, it played an important role in grounding the struggle amongst a broad swathe of the Kosovo population who, as a result, became active participants in the making of their own history – at least for a short time. Once the overall movement became stagnated, with the failure to develop more offensive modes of unarmed civil resistance, then the space opened up for the weapons of war to be deployed. To quote Howard Clark:

> The case of Kosovo shows civil resistance functioning when other forms of resistance would have been disastrous. However, it then shows the need for civil resistance strategy to renew itself, to build on the basis established, to innovate in its own community and to pose new challenges to the adversary. In hindsight, civil resistance appears … to have been a phase through which Kosovo Albanians survived repression and

---

39 For a brief discussion of the significance of social distance in nonviolent (civil) resistance, see A. Rigby, *Living the Intifada*, London: Zed Books, 1991, p. 174.

40 D. Kostovicova, *Kosovo: The politics of identity and space*, Abingdon: Routledge, 2005, p. 112.

41 See Clark in Roberts & Ash, eds., 2009, p. 287.

succeeded in convincing the world of the injustice and inhumanity of Belgrade's politics. Finally, and belatedly, once armed struggle was underway, the Kosovo Albanian patience was 'rewarded' with an unprecedented military intervention by NATO and later by the unprecedented recognition of an independence that for years they had been told was inconceivable.[42]

Civil resistance against occupation – the case of Palestine[43]

In early December 1987 riots broke out in the Israeli-occupied Gaza Strip and there were violent clashes between Palestinians and Israeli forces. The confrontations spread and developed into a sustained attempt to throw off the burden of Israeli occupation by means of mass protest and non-cooperation. This was the start of the Palestinian Intifada.

The outbreak of the uprising came as a surprise to the leadership of the Palestine Liberation Organisation (PLO) in their headquarters in Tunis. They were even more surprised by its scale and its coordinated nature. This was achieved through the creation of a Unified National Command (UNC) representing the different political factions. This clandestine body attempted to coordinate the resistance through regular communiqués and leaflets. The UNC was supported by an organisational infrastructure of popular committees formed in villages, towns and refugee camps, and together they took on the character of an embryonic state – coordinating activities and administering the provision of basic services. With such an organisational framework, organically linked to the different sections of Palestinian society, the months following the outbreak of the Intifada saw a mass social mobilisation – a horizontal escalation of the struggle which embraced all sectors of society. It was a classic example of civil resistance against occupation: a struggle for a cause that was widely supported by all

---

42 Clark in Roberts & Ash, 2009, eds., p. 294.

43 In this section the focus is on civil resistance since 1987. However, it is important to note that there is a significant historical thread of civil resistance carried out by Palestinians in their quest for their political and human rights since the late 19th century. See A. Rigby, *Palestinian resistance and nonviolence*, East Jerusalem: PASSIA, 2010.

sectors of society, a resistance movement comprised of civilians and civil society networks, and using means that were predominantly unarmed.[44]

Different modes of civil resistance during the First Intifada

Symbolic resistance: Whilst stone-throwing and other direct confrontations with the occupiers was primarily the preserve of young males, the majority of Palestinians bore witness to their resistance by less drastic yet symbolically powerful means. They boycotted Israeli products as much as possible. They wore clothes in their national colours, women wore pendants and jewellery incorporating the outline of historic Palestine. People followed 'Palestinian time' by switching between summer and winter time a week earlier than the Israelis.

Polemical resistance: The authority of the UNC and the popular committees was revealed during the first phase of the intifada by the solidarity of the response to strike calls and the instructions to merchants to restrict their opening hours to the mornings on non-strike days. Moreover, as part of its attempt to undermine the authority of the Israeli occupiers the UNC called on all those Palestinians who worked for the Israeli administration to resign. Those who ignored such instructions faced sanctions - Palestinians referred to this process as 'cleansing our national home'.

Offensive resistance: Whilst the closure of shops and work-places at mid-day represented a powerful display of the authority of the UNC and the solidarity of the population, it also meant that by mid-afternoon the streets and public spaces were clear of 'civilians', creating the space for the strike forces to engage in direct confrontations with the Israeli occupiers. This was the dimension of the Intifada that lent itself most readily to the world's media - stone-throwing youths with *keffiyeh*s wrapped round their faces clashing with Israeli soldiers armed with tear-gas grenades, rubber-bullets and other weaponry. This was the visual representation of the 'David versus Goliath' conflict that the Palestinians sought to communicate to the rest of the world.

---

44 Palestinian resistance could not be characterised as nonviolent - those who threw stones did so in order to inflict physical harm on the targets. However it could be characterised as 'unarmed' insofar as the weapons used (primarily stones) were not designed to maim and kill.

Defensive resistance: Each neighbourhood and community had its own 'strike force' of young men engaged in direct confrontations with the occupier. Rarely would they spend more than one night a week with their families. They moved from house to house (and cave to cave) in order to avoid arrest and imprisonment, depending on a network that also included medical relief and other support services.

Constructive work and resistance during the First Intifada

Less visual than the confrontations was the constructive work that was integral to the first phase of the Intifada. As people began to suffer economic hardship, as a consequence of the calls to disengage from the Israeli economy, the loss of income through strikes, and the boycott of Israeli produce, so families began to develop their household economy. In their efforts to become more self-reliant there was a renewed emphasis on cultivating vegetable plots and rearing poultry. Women's committees were particularly active in promoting new forms of home-based economic activity. Homes were also the base for the clandestine education classes that were held as a means of countering the Israeli closure of schools and colleges.

In 1989 a Palestinian political activist I interviewed in a refugee camp in the West Bank gave voice to the sense of solidarity and hope for the future he was feeling during what was the height of the popular unarmed resistance: 'Everyone helps each other … all the people have the same way now, the same struggle against the occupation – from the children to the old men, all the same, they want to get rid of the occupation. One soul through many bodies, through many voices.'[45]

1990 and the weakening of civil resistance

By the summer of 1990 it was clear that much of the vigour and drive of the uprising had dissipated. There were a number of reasons for this:

i.   *The relative failure of disengagement and non-cooperation*

Palestinians hoped that by their civil resistance they would raise the costs of the occupation to such a level that the Israelis would consider withdrawing. The weakness was that historically Israel has always sought the territory of the Palestinians, not the people. In a nutshell, Israel did

---

45   Quoted in A. Rigby, 1991, p. 41.

not require Palestinian cooperation to maintain the occupation, and this seriously weakened the impact of the unarmed resistance.

ii. *The escalating costs of resistance*

Furthermore, it turned out that in many ways the Palestinians were more dependent on Israel than the other way round. Israel could find replacements for the Palestinians who withdrew their labour, the Palestinians could not find alternative sources of employment and income. Moreover, Israel remained the only source of many of the basic necessities of life within the occupied Palestinian territories.

iii. *Resistance and weakening of political control*

By 1990 the tensions between the different Palestinian political factions increased in the light of the perceived weaknesses of the unarmed struggle, whilst the majority of the experienced cadres who had been able to maintain cohesion in the struggle had been arrested, imprisoned or deported by the Israelis.

iv. *Third parties and the impact of external events*

Palestinians lacked the resources to affect the self-interest of the United States and other international actors and thereby push them to intervene constructively in the conflict. This was highlighted by the USA's response to Iraq's invasion of Kuwait in August 1990, which led directly to the first Gulf War to expel the Iraqis from occupied Kuwait. During this conflagration the hardship and the suffering of the Palestinians intensified, as did their bitterness. By mid-1991, more Palestinians were being killed by their fellow Palestinians than by the Israelis, as anger and resentment turned against those suspected of collaboration and 'betrayal' of the uprising.[46]

Palestinian civil resistance after the 'Oslo Accords'

The contemporary generation of Palestinian popular resistance activists look back towards the First Intifada of 1987-91 as some kind of mythical past, a period when there was mass involvement in the resistance struggle against the Israeli occupation. Those days are long gone, and there are a

---

46 A. Rigby, *The legacy of the past: The problem of collaborators and the Palestinian case*, East Jerusalem: PASSIA, 1997, p. 54.

number of structural factors that make it highly unlikely that they will return.

In September 1993 the Israelis and the Palestinians signed what became known as the 'Oslo Accords', a Declaration of Principles that referred to the commitment of both parties to work towards 'a just lasting and comprehensive peace settlement'. I was not alone in feeling a sense of elation, there was the belief that this was an historic breakthrough that fed our hopes for the future. How naïve we were! This Declaration of Principles was the prelude to an asymmetric negotiation process that culminated in another agreement, 'Oslo II', signed two years later in September 1995. Under the terms of this agreement the West Bank was divided into three administrative divisions categorised as Areas A, B and C. Each zone was to enjoy a different degree of Palestinian self-government until a final peace agreement was established. [47] Area A covered three percent of the West Bank encompassing the main Palestinian population centres, but excluding East Jerusalem, and it was to be under the full civil and security control of the Palestinian Authority (PA). Area B covered 23 – 25 percent of the West Bank, and within this area the PA would exercise civil control, but security would be the joint responsibility of the Israeli and Palestinian authorities. Area C covered the remainder of the West Bank, approximately 73 percent of the territory, and here Israel was to continue to exercise complete civil and security control. It was presumed by naïve folk like myself that over a period of time there would be a transition towards Palestinian self-government over expanding stretches of contiguous territory. As events unfolded it became increasingly clear that Israel had no intention of transferring territory of any significant scale over to the PA.

No grounds for a national civil resistance movement

The combined impact of these developments was to bring about a set of conditions that undermined the possibility of relaunching any mass-based unarmed civilian resistance movement against the occupation.

---

47 A similar pattern had already been imposed in the Gaza Strip, with Jewish settlements divided into three blocs covering about one third of the territory, with the remaining two thirds cut into cantons for the 1.1 million Palestinians.

i. The PA had been tasked by Israel and its international backers with controlling dissent within the Palestinian community. From the start the PA tried to control any civil society organisation that evidenced signs of independence of thought, action and funding.[48]

ii. The leverage power over the Israelis that could be exerted by Palestinian non-cooperation was virtually nil. Drawing the lessons from the First Intifada, Israel had attracted guest-workers from around the globe to take the place of the Palestinian labour upon which significant sectors of the Israeli economy had once depended.

iii. There was a lack of potential leaders of any coordinated unarmed popular resistance movement. The cadres from the First Intifada followed different trajectories, but two career paths were common. Some joined the new PA, whilst others founded or joined non-governmental organisations concerned with themes like democratisation and peace-building, a trend encouraged by foreign donors who directed funds towards the promotion of warmer relationships between Palestinians and Israelis through 'people-to-people' dialogue projects. Such programmes often included conflict resolution training and capacity-building components, but they did not include training for unarmed civil resistance.[49]

iv. A consequence of these developments was an increase in social, economic, geographical and political divisions within Palestinian society which drastically weakened the level of social solidarity and trust necessary for large-scale civilian mobilisation. Moreover, in place of the dense network of civil

---

48 The organisational infrastructure of popular committees that had directed and guided the First Intifada had been superseded by the agencies of the PA.

49 It has been estimated that between September 1993 and October 2000 there were about 500 people-to-people projects involving over 100 organisations and a total budget of $20-30 million. S. Herzon & A Hai, 'What do people mean when they say people-to-people?', *Palestine-Israel Journal*, v.12, n. 4, 2005. Accessible at https://www.pij.org/journal/40 (30 July 2021).

society organisations that had been one of the seed-beds of the First Intifada, Palestinian society was now dominated by foreign-funded NGOs with relatively tenuous links with the grass-roots.

Second Intifada and civil resistance since 2002

By the summer of 2000 the occupation seemed more firmly entrenched than ever. The confiscation of land and the expansion of settlements had continued at an accelerated pace since the signing of the Declaration of Principles. The West Bank had been divided into cantons separated from each other by Israeli controlled territory. Innumerable check-points and barriers had been set up throughout the territories controlling the movement of Palestinians and enabling the Israelis to confine them within their particular enclaves, with disastrous consequences for economic activity and general living standards. Moreover, as Sarah Roy observed, 'In these policies Israel relied on the Palestinian Authority and its vast security apparatus to maintain control of the population, suppress any visible forms of opposition, and provide protection for Israeli actions.' [50]

The consequent build-up of resentment and anger resulting from seven years of a peace process that had served to deepen Palestinian dispossession and deprivation, whilst strengthening the Israeli occupation, fed into the outbreak of the Second Intifada in September 2000. The rapid militarisation of the uprising effectively side-lined any significant role for civil society groups in the struggle. A younger generation of cadres came to the fore who were influenced to a significant degree by the example of Hezbollah in Southern Lebanon, whose guerrilla tactics had succeeded in forcing Israel to withdraw in May 2000. Amidst the violence and the associated destruction of the socio-economic fabric of Palestinian society, there was little space for any large-scale unarmed resistance.

In the Spring of 2002 Israel began constructing its infamous 'Separation barrier', also known as the 'Apartheid Wall', which resulted in the expropriation of even more Palestinian land. What followed was the emergence of a series of localised centres of active popular resistance against the construction of the Wall and the associated expropriation of

---

50 S. Roy, *Failing peace: Gaza and the Palestinian-Israeli conflict*, London: Pluto Press , 2007, p. 245.

Palestinian land. The instances of civil resistance spread to other locations where the expansion of settlements presented a significant threat to local Palestinians. But at no stage was there anything comparable to a mass movement of protest – at the height of the popular resistance during 2010-11 there was a maximum of 40 - 50 villages and neighbourhoods where there was some form of organised unarmed resistance against the on-gong occupation.[51]

Sumud – to exist is to resist

One result of this desperate trajectory has been a significant loss of hope amongst Palestinians (and those who support their cause). As I type these words an image comes to me of a very close Palestinian friend of mine. We have known each other since the early 1980s. He is something of an intellectual and opinion-leader, a significant figure in certain quarters of Palestinian political society. He was ever the optimist. I remember us sitting down one evening in a restaurant in East Jerusalem during the First Intifada having a serious discussion about whether there would be prisons in the new Palestine that we both believed was in the process of emergence. About 20 years after that discussion I was interviewing a senior figure in a Palestinian network of non-governmental organisations. After the formal interview process was over we relaxed and started talking about people we knew in common. I mentioned the name of my close friend, and marvelled at how he always seemed so optimistic and hopeful about the Palestinian future. 'Ah yes', he responded, 'but nowadays his expressions of hope and optimism stem from a sense of political duty and responsibility, not from belief.' It is only now, as I reflect back on this, that I realise that my friend's ongoing display of hope for the future was his own version of what Palestinians refer to as *sumud* – a form of steadfast resilience in holding on to valued ways of life and associated identities in the face of an ever-deepening and pervasive occupation, a Palestinian version of 'living within the truth'.[52]

---

51 Darweish & Rigby, 2015, p. 73.

52 The following analysis draws heavily on the work of Toine van Teeffelen, *The story of sumud*, (2008), accessible at https://www.academia.edu/5596248/ (26 May 2020). See also A. Rijke and T. van Teeffelen, 'To exist is to resist: Sumud, heroism and the everyday', *Jerusalem Quarterly*, n. 59, 2014, pp. 86-99.

Some insight into the challenges faced by people like my friend, living under occupation for more than fifty years, with hopes and dreams having evaporated, can be gathered from the writings of one of his contemporaries, Raja Shehadeh. The first book of his that I read was *The third way: A journal of life on the West Bank*, published in 1982.[53] On the title page there was a succinct explanation of the title: 'Between mute submission and blind hate I choose the third way – I am *sumud* (the steadfast)'. Reading his latest book, published in 2019, one gets a clear sense of the struggle so many Palestinians have had in order to hold on to their humanity and identity whilst living under occupation. As he writes,

> There was a time when we hoped that we were getting rid of the occupation and I worked and lived for that moment. But it dissipated twenty-four years ago with the first Oslo Accord, and since then I've lived without hope, constantly trying to adjust to life and accept that it will only go from bad to worse as the occupation becomes more entrenched, grabbing more of our land and tightening the noose around our necks.[54]

In essence his books have been about how he and others have tried to adapt and cope with the ever-tightening strangle-hold of the occupation, without losing their humanity and giving way to blind hatred or abject submission. Writing has been one of the ways he has continued to assert his commitment to his Palestinian identity, culture and way of life. In his latest book he reconstructs walks around his home town of Ramallah, each of them prompting memories and stories of how the Israeli occupation has impacted on his life and experience. After half a century of life under the sway of the Israeli occupation he recalls:

> For many years I raged in anger at my fate. Now when I look back over my life, I can see that the occupation has provided me with an immense amount of work and great challenges, not only in how to resist but in how to live under its ruthless

---

53 R. Shehadeh, *The third way: A journal of life in the West Bank*, London: Quartet Books, 1982.

54 R. Shehadeh, *Going home: A walk through fifty years of occupation*, London: Profile Books, 2019, p. 169.

matrix of control as a free man refusing to be denied the joys of life.[55]

He is forced to acknowledge that after fifty years of trying, the Palestinians have not succeeded in forcing Israel to end its occupation. But 'the struggle is neither over nor won, and what keeps it going is nothing other than our sumud'.[56]

Shehadeh recognises one of the key motifs of his life under an ever-more tenacious occupation has been 'coping and resisting': summoning up the steadfastness necessary to maintain his humanity and his identity, refusing to be consumed by hatred and resisting the waves of hopelessness, maintaining his resilience under the suffocation of occupation. This is *sumud* - farmers replanting olive trees uprooted by settlers, families rebuilding homes demolished by the Israeli military, people determined to resist by continuing to claim their right to live their everyday life on as much of their own terms as possible.

At the core of the conception of constructive action that has informed this chapter is the recognition that it involves nonviolent activity to change situations deemed damaging to well-being, and which involves a pre-figurative dimension – action that is intended to embody changes in the here-and-now that might contribute to a process whereby such changes take place on a far wider scale in the hoped-for future.[57] These elements are captured vividly in the words of a Palestinian from Aida refugee camp (Bethlehem):

> Sumud is continuing living in Palestine, laughing, enjoying life, falling in love, getting married, having children. Sumud is also continuing your studies outside, to get a diploma, to come back here. Defending values is sumud. Building a house, a beautiful one and thinking that we are here to stay, even when the Israelis are demolishing this house, and then build a new and even more beautiful one than before – that is also sumud.

---

55 Shehadeh, 2019, p. 40.

56 Shehadeh, 2019, p. 182.

57 Sometimes, of course, the dreamed-of future reflects features of a longed-for past, a (mythological?) time when it was possible to be fully human.

> That I am here is sumud. To reclaim that you are a human
> being and defending your humanity is sumud.[58]

Observation

There is something about the poetry of these words that touches me deeply. It reminds me of an observation made by a friend, a German national who has lived in East Jerusalem for most of her adult life. She likened Palestinians to the moles in the fairground 'whack-a-mole' game. No matter how hard you whack them with a mallet, they keep popping up. This degree of persistence and resilience is grounded in the constructive action of those who find the spaces within which to retain their sense of identity and oppositional culture.

But it also needs to be recognised that this form of 'living in the truth' reflects the political impotence of the Palestinians living under occupation. They are entrapped in an asymmetric conflict, without a unified legitimate leadership and without a clear path to achieve their basic human rights. On their own they lack the leverage to weaken the colonial project of Israel. To achieve the most basic of their human rights they require the intervention of significant third parties. But most modes of constructive resistance lack that degree of drama necessary to grab the attention of third-party publics and their political leaders, and convince them that 'something must be done'.[59] What this means is that for the foreseeable future the persistence of those Palestinians who actively seek to maintain their culture, their humanity and their identity, can be little more than a 'holding-operation' until such time as the political climate and context changes in their favour.

Civil resistance and the struggle for civil rights

In this section the focus is on the place of constructive modes of action within the portfolio of activities adopted by civil resistance movements that seek to combat discrimination and exclusion within a nominally democratic political system, where the rights of certain sectors of society are significantly circumscribed and limited. The working hypothesis is

---

58 Rijke and van Teeffelen, 2014, p.90.
59 See A. Rigby, *The first Palestinian Intifada revisited,* Sparsnas, Sweden: Irene, 2015, p. 244.

that within regimes where there is a statutory *degree* of openness and respect for the rule of law and human rights, however flawed this might be in practice, then the prime function of constructive resistance within movements seeking to achieve full citizenship rights is the servicing of the needs of the movement's activists and participants. Invariably this is performed through various forms of political education and community organising, and the creation of 'safe spaces' for activists. The most apposite case study through which to illustrate this is the US civil rights movement.

Community mobilisation and community organization

Most of us know the story-line of the civil rights movement – here is the simplified orthodox version: 'One day a nice lady called Rosa Parks, sat down on a bus and got arrested. The next day Martin Luther King Jr. stood up and the Montgomery Bus Boycott followed. And sometime later King delivered his famous "I Have a Dream" speech and segregation was over.'[60] This is obviously a caricature of the dominant narrative of the movement, but in essence it is the version of which most people have been made aware through the various documentary and feature films available for viewing – one which can be labelled the community mobilisation paradigm. This involved the mobilisation of significant numbers of people to participate in large-scale contentious actions, that attracted media attention, and created significant dilemmas for policy-makers and those seeking to defend the status quo. This was the tradition best symbolised by Martin Luther King with his charismatic leadership, oratory that could inspire vast crowds, and the organizational resources to coordinate large-scale public protest actions such as the Birmingham bus boycott, the March on Washington, and the Selma-Montgomery Marches.

However, there was another tradition within the civil rights movement, although less well-known - what Bob Moses labelled the community organising tradition.[61] The most pre-eminent practitioners

60 E. Crosby, *A little taste of freedom: The Black freedom struggle in Clairborne County, Mississippi,* Chapel Hill: University of North Carolina Press, 2005, p. xiii.

61 R. Moses et al, 'The Algebra Project: Organising in the spirit of Ella', *Harvard*

and advocates of this approach were two women – Ella Baker (1903-1986) and Septima Clark (1898 – 1987).

Ella Baker: 'Strong people don't need strong leaders'

Ella Baker, 1964

Ella Baker's activist career spanned more than five decades, and she came to be regarded as 'the greatest organiser the civil rights movement ever knew.' [62] One of her most famous quotes was, 'You didn't see me on television, you didn't see news stories about me. The kind of role that I tried to play was to pick up pieces or put together pieces out of which I hoped organization might come.'[63]

She was an advocate of grass-roots action as a means of social change, believing that the strength of an organization grew from the bottom up, not the top down. The bedrock of any social change organization was not the oratorical power of its leaders so much as the commitment and hard work of the rank and file membership - especially young people and women. In 1956 Baker, along with two of Martin Luther King's closest confidantes, Stanley Levison and Bayard Rustin, formed *In Friendship*, a fundraising organization designed to aid victims of discrimination in the South. A year later the Southern Christian Leadership Conference (SCLC) was established in February 1957, with King as its first president. At the instigation of Rustin and Levison, King invited Baker to take up the position of executive director of SCLC. But over time she became critical of the manner in which its organizational culture seemed to be modelled on the patriarchal pattern of the black churches, where the majority of the congregation were women but the pastors were men.[64]

Educational Review, n. 59, Winter 1989, pp. 423-43.

62 D. Houck & D. Dixon, eds., *Women and the Civil Rights Movement, 1954–1965* , Jackson: University Press of Mississippi, Jackson, 2009, p. 245.

63 Houck & Dixon, eds., 2009, p. 246.

64 A comrade of Ella Baker, Medgar Evers (who was assassinated in 1963), was initially involved with the SLCC, but became critical of its approach. He

The pastors were the shepherds, the congregation (predominantly women) was the flock, to be guided. The women traditionally provided financial and emotional support, and were expected to keep on top of the day-to-day management of the church.[65]

It was Ella Baker who was most responsible for developing an alternative organizational culture within the civil rights movement, one based on the principle of collective leadership. Her mantra was 'strong people don't need strong leaders'. Her focus, she declared, was to cultivate leadership, not leaders.[66] In 1960 she was instrumental in the establishment of the Student Nonviolent Coordinating Committee (SNCC), which was composed mainly of young activists who had been involved in the lunch-counter sit-ins. Here she found people only too willing to take to heart her emphasis on the importance of developing a movement on the basis of vigorous and active local participation. Such an ethos was at the very heart of the new movement, as Charles Payne has remarked:

> The young people who formed SNCC were the product of a number of political influences, but Ella Baker's was among the most significant. In its organizational structure, its program, its ideology, early SNCC would be almost exactly the kind of organization Ella Baker had been trying to create for almost three decades.[67]

Baker was committed to the idea that everyone should be prepared to take on leadership to effect change in their lives. Consequently she was a great believer in the importance of adult education in preparing African Americans to fully exercise their rights in a democratic society.

---

thought they put too much emphasis on mobilising a community to create a crisis and win concessions, only to move on, leaving local organizations to collapse. C. Payne, *I've got the light of freedom: The organizing tradition and the Mississippi Freedom struggle* , Berkeley: University of California Press, 2007, p. 61.

65 A. Elliott, 'Ella Baker: Free agent in the Civil Rights Movement', *Journal of Black Studies* , v. 26, n. 5, May, 1996, pp. 593-603, p. 598.

66 Houck & Dixon, eds., 2009, p. 247.

67 Payne, 2007, p. 96.

This led quite naturally to her championing the citizenship schools, a constructive initiative led and directed by another pillar of the civil rights movement – Septima Clark.[68]

Septima Clark and the Citizenship Schools

Born in 1898, to a family that placed a high value on education, Septima Clark began her first teaching post in 1916 at a school for African-Americans on John's Island, one of the off-shore islands of South Carolina, just south of Charleston. During her time there local residents approached her for help in developing basic literacy and numeracy skills. So she began to spend her spare time teaching adults the same classes she was delivering to the children. In 1919 she left to take up another posting, and spent the next three decades bringing up a family and working as a teacher in a range of colleges. She had joined the National Association for the Advancement of Coloured People (NAACP) in 1919 and had become increasingly active in a range of issues relating to equal rights for African-Americans and women.

Septima Clark

In 1956 the state legislature of South Carolina passed into law a requirement prohibiting any state or municipal employee from belonging to a civil rights organization. Septima Clark refused to relinquish her membership of NAACP, and was dismissed. By this time, however, she had become attracted to the work of the Highlander Folk School, having attended her first workshop there in 1954. In 1956 the co-founder, Miles Horton, offered her the post of Director of Workshops. The Highlander had been established in 1932 in the Tennessee mountains as a school

---

68 Baker tried to get the SCLC to build a programme around the citizenship schools that had grown out of an initiative of Septime Clark at the Highlander Folk School. Only after she left in the summer of 1960 did the SCLC take the programme under its wing. (Payne, 2007, p. 94.)

for the poor of the region – a place where the 'learned helplessness' of the poor would be replaced by the capacity and the will to take more control of their lives. Horton's goal was not '*community* development in terms of organization and programs, but *people* development in terms of their ability to articulate their problems and the development of self-confidence that they could resolve these problems.'[69]   In the 1930s its students included coal miners, forestry workers, small farmers. Later it was heavily involved in training labour organisers, as unionisation spread to the South. Right from the start Highlander had been inter-racial, defying the state law that Blacks and Whites could neither eat together nor sleep in the same building. So it was that by the 1950s it had become an important meeting place and training centre for civil rights movement activists.[70]

It was at Highlander that Clark developed the pedagogy that informed the Citizenship Education programme which she directed. In an interview in 1976 she provided a taste of the methodology used to enable potential community leaders to develop their dormant capacities.

> We used the election laws of that particular state to teach the reading. We used the amount of fertilizer and the amount of seeds to teach the arithmetic, how much they would pay for it and the like. We did some political work by having them to find out about the kind of government that they had in their particular community. And these were the things that we taught them when they went back home. Each state had to have its own particular reading, because each state had different requirements for the election laws.[71]

The story of how the citizenship school network came into being is

---

69 Quoted in P. Ling, 'Local leadership in the early Civil Rights Movement: The South Carolina Citizenship Education Program of the Highlander Folk School', *Journal of American Studies,* v. 29, n. 3, 1995, pp. 399-422, p. 402.

70 Rosa Parkes attended her first workshop in 1955 and was struck by the novel experience of Black and White interacting together with mutual respect and tolerance.

71 Septima Clark, 30 July 1976. Oral history program at University of North Carolina at Chapel Hill. Accessible at https://tinyurl.com/yz5h85wv (23 May 2021).

interesting in itself, but it also illustrates the significance of friendship links and trust relationships, established and maintained over time by activists and local community members, in enabling movement organizations to respond to emergent issues. Highlander had experienced great difficulty in attracting people from the off-shore islands to their workshops. Septima Clark, however, had good contacts there from her time as a teacher, and was able to persuade Esau Jenkins, a community leader in John's Island, to start coming to the workshops.

In 1945 Jenkins had purchased a bus so local children could get to and from school in Charleston. He later transported adults to their jobs. During the daily commutes he would stress to the adults the importance of voting, and taught them to read and recite passages from the state constitution, which was one of the requirements to vote in South Carolina during that time. One of the regular passengers on this 'rolling school bus', who had memorised the relevant passages and registered successfully, still wanted to learn to read, and asked Jenkins about possible schools within their locality. After meeting with several people in the community about holding evening classes, Jenkins finally sought help from Highlander. Septima Clark and Miles Horton agreed to work with Jenkins on obtaining a location, teachers, and materials for the school. The first Citizenship School on Johns Island was held in the back-room of a cooperative store, purchased with the aid of a short-term loan from Highlander.

Clark and Horton were clear that they did not want a professional teacher to run the class, and prevailed upon a younger relative of Clark's, Bernice Robinson, to take up the challenge.[72] A beautician by profession, Bernice had worked with Jenkins on a voter-registration campaign, and so was trusted by the local people. The first cohort of 14 students

---

72 Robinson later recalled the pressure to which she was subjected: 'Well, they just laid the law down to me … "We don't want a certified teacher …. We need a community worker … who understands the people … and someone who has been to Highlander … So there's nobody to do it but you. Either you do it or we don't have the school." So I said OK.' Quoted in S. Lazar, 'Bernice Robinson and the Citizenship Education Schools', 2005, p. 11. Accessible at https://tinyurl.com/rdxxuefw (24 March 2021).

attended for four hours a week during the January-February period when they were free from their farming commitments. The class size and the number of schools snowballed from there – the initial group brought in others, another class commenced on a nearby island, and by 1961 thirty-seven schools had been established on the islands and the nearby mainland, with Black voting strength having increased significantly.[73]

In the summer of 1961 the Tennessee Supreme Court revoked Highlander's charter and ordered that the school be closed. The Citizen Education programme was taken over by the SCLC. Apparently there had been some initial reluctance on Martin Luther King's part about being directly involved in the education programme, allegedly because the Citizenship Schools had never associated themselves with offensive nonviolent resistance. According to Carl Tjerandsen, King was won over by the force of Clark's argument:

> ... after demonstrations in community after community, there was no tangible result. No oppressive laws were taken off the books; no power was gained by blacks. Citizenship classes, on the other hand, did lead to voter registration; potentially, they could do so on a large scale.[74]

Septima Clark was very clear that running the literacy classes so that people might successfully register for the right to vote was a first step on a longer road - enabling people within grassroots communities to discover and fulfil their potential as citizens and as community leaders.[75] For Clark, 'The basic purpose of the Citizenship Schools is discovering local community leaders. ... It is my belief that creative leadership is present in any community and only awaits discovery and development.'[76]

Under the auspices of the SCLC the work of the Citizenship

---

73 Payne, 2007, pp. 74-5.
74 C. Tjerandsen, *Education for citizenship: A Foundation's experience,* Santa Cruz, CA: Emil Schwartzhaupt Foundation, 1980, p.181.
75 Clark believed that 'along with learning how to read and write comes always this thing of becoming a responsible citizen.... One should know the laws and obey them for one's own protection as well as for the protection of others.' (S. Clark, *Echo in my soul,* New York: E. P. Dutton, 1962, p. 150).
76 S. Clark, 'Literacy and liberation', in J. Grant, ed., *Black protest,* New York: Fawcett, 1968, p. 297.

Education programme continued to expand. Eventually there were as many as 200 Citizenship Schools spread across the southern states of the USA, with nearly 10,000 people trained as teachers, and as many as 60,000 graduates, a large percentage of whom became registered voters.[77] Charles Payne provides a fascinating glimpse of one such school established in 1963 in the town of Greenwood, in the Mississippi Delta region.

> The classes had not changed much since their early development by Septima Clark and Bernice Robinson. Classes met twice a week for three months, concentrating on literacy, the state constitution, and local and state government, but supplementing that with Negro history and community problem-solving, by which they meant boycott, demonstrations and the like. The first fifteen classes started that spring, all taught by women, enrolled close to two hundred students, mostly older people, in their middle forties or older. Septima Clark, who believed firmly that social status has nothing to do with leadership ability, would have been delighted to know that the first class to get started, and the largest, was taught by Ida 'Cat' Holland, a former prostitute who had become interested in the movement.[78]

In an address that Ella Baker delivered in December 1963 to the SNCC Conference in Washington, DC she referred to her conviction that 'we have reached the point that the old line methods of just getting out in a demonstration just for the sake of demonstrating is far from being enough. And we've got to find ways in which to involve people at many different levels.'[79] The Citizenship Schools, that were at the heart of the community organising approach within the civil rights movement, were an important way of involving people in the movement, particularly those who felt uneasy and uncomfortable about engaging in some of the more confrontational and controversial modes of action favoured by some activists within the movement. Engagement with 'literacy classes' was a very non-threatening and relatively low-risk form of involvement

77 Payne, 2007, p. 75.
78 Payne, 2007, p. 166.
79 Houk & Dixon, eds., p. 247.

with the struggle for change.

Participation or cooptation?

The focus on community organization and voter registration was not without its critics within the ranks of the overall civil rights movement. There were those who saw it as draining energy and resources from the more offensive forms of direct action, particularly the marches, the sit-downs and the protest demonstrations. The issue was complicated by the well-grounded suspicion on the part of some activists that political elites in Washington were pressuring the movement towards the less publicly controversial activities, such as voter registration, and away from the more offensive modes of action that were causing great distress to their political allies in the south. Here is the context.

In the early summer of 1961, spurred on by a Supreme Court ruling outlawing segregation at inter-state bus terminals, a group of nonviolent activists associated with CORE (Congress of Racial Equality) decided to test the law by sending a team of riders, black and white, into the southern states. They met serious levels of white intimidation and violence, with coaches torched and vicious beatings inflicted on the riders.[80] Alarmed that the racists might claim a victory, members of SNCC decided to participate. Emboldened by the reinforcements the 'freedom riders' continued their journey, only to encounter new confrontations with the white supremacists. The Kennedy administration in Washington felt pressured to intervene, and authorised federal marshals to accompany the buses. But whilst they were wary of seeming to allow racists to flout the law with the world watching, interceding in support of the civil rights activists put the administration on a collision course with the southern political leaders upon whose support Kennedy depended in Washington. They tried to resolve their dilemma by encouraging CORE and SNCC to focus more on voter registration and not on the dramatic and confrontational direct action projects. The result was the formation of the Voter Education Project early in 1962, generously funded by foundations close to the Kennedy administration.[81]

---

80 For a personal account of the experience, see J. Peck, *Freedom ride*, New York: Grove Press, 1962.
81 Payne, 2007, p.108.

A significant proportion of SNCC members saw this as an attempt to buy off the movement and the issue came close to splitting the organization into two. According to Charles Payne,

> To some within the organization, the whole idea sounded like cooptation, which of course was fairly close to the truth. They were reluctant to see organizational resources directed away from the spiritually empowering nonviolent direct-action tactics, which, they had already shown, forced the powers-that-be to respond and to respond quickly. By comparison, voter registration seemed a long, slow road, a narrower form of politics.[82]

Concluding observations

The conflict within the ranks of the SNCC highlights the dilemma around constructive modes of action in civil resistance. In a nutshell, constructive action tends to be *worthy*, deserving of our respect and admiration; but it is not *newsworthy*, it does not grab our attention or move public opinion.[83] Herein lies its strength and its weakness. The strength of constructive modes of resistance, particularly when pursued under authoritarian and deeply repressive regimes, is that they can take place without attracting unwelcome attention and sanctions from the regime. They thereby provide a way for people living under repression to retain some relatively low-risk way of holding on to their identity and conviction; they enable people to create spaces within which they can 'live within the truth'. Moreover, as we have seen, by incurring a low level of risk and associated cost, constructive modes of resistance can appeal to a far wider range of people than high-risk offensive forms of unarmed resistance. It widens the boundaries of participation in the struggle to encompass constituencies of support far beyond the small minority of would-be martyrs for the cause, those prepared to pay the price for their

---

82 Payne, 2007, p.110.

83 Where I come from to describe someone as 'worthy' can be something of a barbed observation, implying that the person has admirable qualities but is also unremarkable, run-of-the-mill.

open and public resistance.

But, it has to be conceded that most forms of constructive action lack the newsworthiness of direct nonviolent confrontations with agents of repression. When I reflect back on those images that have moved me, emotionally and politically, what comes to mind are pictures of African-American women in the southern states of the USA being blasted by water-cannon, cowering in shop door-ways, whilst police dogs snapped at their limbs. Similar images come to mind from the South African townships during the years of the anti-apartheid struggle. More recently it has been the images of Palestinians being beaten and assaulted by Israeli conscripts and settler zealots. These are the types of images that generate outrage and demands that 'something must be done' amongst wide swathes of the public, nationally and globally. When faced with such brutal, and brutalising, experiences, community organising and associated forms of constructive action can come across as a tortuously slow road to change.

But herein also lies the strength of constructive modes of action. They can represent low-risk ways of holding on to valued identities and convictions, ways of being that can be integrated into everyday life and sustained over time. Whilst trying to figure out what points to make in this conclusion, the pilot-light in our gas boiler went out. No hot water and no central heating! But no big crisis – it was easily relit and all was well. I have found myself comparing constructive modes of action to that pilot-light in the gas boiler. Hopefully it stays alight and remains ready to heat the pipes as and when required, performing a crucial function without attracting attention to itself, except when it ceases to function properly! So with constructive modes of resistance, they can persist over time, without incurring unbearable cost. The very fact that they involve processes that are not in themselves dramatic and attention-grabbing is their strength. They have the capacity to keep the pilot-light of resistance alight during periods of dormancy until conditions and events coalesce to feed the flame of more offensive forms of resistance.

5

CONSTRUCTIVE ACTION AND RESISTANCE IN WARTIME

Personal preface

I grew up in a respectable working class environment just outside Liverpool. And one of the things that has stayed in my mind from my early days are the stories my mother used to tell of spending nights in the Mersey Tunnel or sleeping under the dining room table sheltering from German Luftwaffe raids during the Second World War. Then, growing up in the 1950s, I remember all the comics that I used to read. Robert Fisk, the well-known British journalist wrote about his love of comics as a boy growing up in the 1950s, an experience in which, to quote Fisk, 'a generation of schoolboys learned that Germans and Japanese were sub-humans, and that we, the Brits – and occasionally Frenchmen and Americans, even Soviets – were fighting courageously against these hordes'.[1] My personal view is that those stereotypes never disappear completely, but rather they get over-laden by new images and impressions. With me the source of those new images was, quite simply, human contacts – meetings with Germans and Japanese; and also the remonstrations of my children who pulled me up whenever I gave verbal expression to my prejudices. Alongside these negative stereotypes I have to confess that I also grew up admiring the courage and bravery of everyday citizens of the UK who risked their lives and their well-being in combat during the Second World War.

Overlaying these constructions has been my pacifist rejection of war, which left me with a niggling worry that maybe my pacifism had

---

1   R. Fisk, 'Battlefield stereotypes that were fed to young minds', *Dawn*, 28
    August 2010. Accessible at https://tinyurl.com/42derxra (13 March 2020).

something to do with cowardice, and a perennial puzzlement about what I would have done if I had been of conscription age during the Second World War. I believe this background has been part of the reason for my abiding interest in nonviolent resistance to state terror and occupation, alongside a fascination with the challenges faced by pacifists in creating a constructive role for themselves in the midst of war and violent conflict.

Types of constructive action in wartime

Reviewing the literature on unarmed resistance by those living under wartime conditions of large-scale violence and occupation, five main types of constructive action become apparent.[2]

i.   Humanitarian constructive action: Supporting and saving the victims of war, especially those targeted by the enemy/occupier.

ii.   Constructive living: Attempting to live in such a way as to embody (and thereby preserve) the values and ways of life threatened by the conditions of war.

iii.   Constructive work to meet basic needs: Creating the structures and practices necessary to meet the basic needs of those threatened by the violence of war and occupation.

iv.   Accompaniment in order to support and empower those most active and prominent in the struggle to defend human rights and associated values under wartime conditions.

v.   Creating zones of peace – spaces within which significant dimensions of life might be pursued without the direct intrusion of the violence of war.

---

2   The key sources drawn on in this chapter, in addition to sources cited elsewhere, include Jacques Semelin's invaluable study *Unarmed against Hitler: Civilian resistance in Europe, 1939-1943,* London: Praeger, 1993. Adam Roberts, *Civilian resistance as a national defence: Nonviolent action against aggression* (Harmondsworth: Penguin, 1967) remains a valuable source, as does Anders Boserup and Andrew Mack, *War without weapons*, (London: Frances Pinter, 1974). Howard Clark's edited volume on *People power: Unarmed resistance and global solidarity* (London: Pluto, 2009) remains a rich source of material. Other sources are identified in the footnotes throughout the text.

At the heart of each of these types of constructive action is the attempt to act in ways that embody the values, priorities and principles that run counter to those championed and practised by the enemy/occupier, and which the practitioners hope will flourish more widely once the war is over and the enemy/occupier is overcome. In the remainder of the chapter I will attempt to identify the key features of these five different types of constructive action, drawing on case study material with which I have a degree of familiarity. I should make clear that the illustrative material presented reflects my own predilections and interests – in no way is it intended to present a comprehensive coverage. The research field remains wide open!

Humanitarian constructive action: Supporting the victims of war

Humanitarian constructive action by third parties: Basque refugees and kindertransport

In Europe in the 1930s and 1940s, economic and political breakdown and the rise of extremist politics turned citizens into refugees. From 1933 onwards the flow of people leaving Germany and Austria to escape persecution escalated. Nazi persecution of Jews in Germany and the takeover of Austria (1938), Czechoslovakia (1938-39) and Poland (1939) increased the numbers of Jewish refugees – before the Holocaust itself commenced.

Adding to the flow of refugees in Europe was the civil war in Spain which started in July 1936 with an attempted military coup against the government. The official British response to the war was one of 'non-intervention', despite Germany's support for General Franco's right-wing rebel coalition. In the spring of 1937 the rebels launched an offensive in northern Spain, and on 26 April the German Condor Legion bombed the market town of Guernica. It is considered to have been the first deliberate aerial attack on a civilian population centre, and was one of the first crimes against humanity to grip the global imagination. As rebel troops advanced, the threat posed to women and children in the Basque country by food shortages and further bombing campaigns heightened.

An appeal went out for countries to accept Basque refugees, and by the end of 1937 nearly 20,000 Basque children had been evacuated. Many went to France and Belgium, with others finding refuge as far afield as Mexico and the Soviet Union.[3] Following intense lobbying the British government eventually agreed on 29 April to receive some of the children, and on 23 May 1937 a vessel carrying nearly 4000 Basque child refugees docked at Southampton.[4]

A Basque Children's Committee had been formed to take responsibility for their care and finding accommodation. The Salvation Army and the Catholic Church agreed to take almost half the children, but this still left over 2000 to be housed.[5] Over the ensuing months a network of children's committees came into existence responsible for the establishment of a number of hostels, mainly in the south of England. One of these was the site of a former commune in Langham, Essex where 64 of the children were housed under the auspices of the Peace Pledge Union.

A similar network of citizens' groups and organisations came together in the UK in the 1930s to raise funds to support Jewish refugees from Germany and Austria. These included the Religious Society of Friends (Quakers) who had set up a German Emergency Committee (GEC) to raise awareness of conditions in Germany and support refugees within the UK. The GEC, alongside Jewish relief agencies, also assisted in the evacuation of refugees to the free port of Shanghai which was the only city in the world where refugees could enter without a visa.

The violence of the November Pogrom (*Kristallnacht*) on 9-10 November 1938 in Germany highlighted the desperate plight of Jews in Germany and the urgency of doing something. The GEC decided that their best course of action was to arrange for unaccompanied Jewish children to be granted immediate visa-free access to the UK. A joint Jewish-Quaker delegation successfully lobbied the UK government

---

3   D. Legarreta, *The Guernica generation: Basque refugee children of the Spanish Civil War*, Reno, NV: University of Nevada Press, 1984, p. ix.

4   T. Buchanan, *Britain and the Spanish Civil War*, Cambridge: Cambridge University Press, 1997, p. 110.

5   A. Bell, *Only for three months: the Basque children in exile*, Norwich: Mousehold Press, 2007, p. 12.

to agree that it would permit an unspecified number of children to enter. A network of Quaker and refugee organisations proceeded to circulate information as widely as possible about how parents could register their children for the *kindertransport*, and offices were established to issue the travel documents. Within days of the announcement thousands of children had been signed up. The first trains left on 1 December 1938 with Quaker volunteers chaperoning each stage of the journey. When the trains began to arrive in London they were met by Quakers and other volunteers. They were found homes with Quaker families and other communities

Memorial to kindertransport, Liverpool Street Station, London.

throughout the country. In total ten thousand refugee children made the journey before the outbreak of war in September 1939.[6]

The provision of a safe-haven outside the main theatre of war for those at risk seems to be one of the most constructive forms of nonviolent action that can be undertaken in times of war and violent conflict. However, the risks and potential costs faced by those engaging in this form of activity escalate considerably when the activity of providing sanctuary is deemed illegal and illegitimate by an occupying power. This was the reality faced by those seeking to help Jews and other minorities escape from occupied Europe in the Second World War. For them humanitarian aid became a clear form of constructive *resistance*, insofar as it was in clear opposition to the dictates of the occupying power.[7]

---

6   See *Quakers and kindertransport*, accessible at https://tinyurl.com/y8lvourj (31 April 2020). Also *A bitter road: Britain and the refugee crisis of the 1930s and 1940s*, Wiener Holocaust Library, accessible at https://www.wienerlibrary.co.uk/a-bitter-road-online (30 April 2020).

7   This is where it seems appropriate to use the term constructive *resistance* insofar as the activity constituted a direct challenge to the regulations imposed by

Humanitarian constructive resistance by third parties: the Emergency Rescue Committee

For most people in Britain, the declaration of war brought little change. There was no sign of the expected bombing raids and gas attacks. During the first six or seven months, the period of the 'phoney war' as it became known, there seemed to be a possibility, however slight, that the war might be stopped and a negotiated peace achieved. But in April 1940 the Germans invaded Norway and Denmark, the next month Holland and Belgium were overrun, and British forces retreated towards Dunkirk, and France fell.

Under the terms of the armistice signed on 22 June 1940 France was divided into two zones. The larger zone, comprising the north and west of the country, was to be under German occupation. The southern 'free zone' was under nominal French sovereignty in the guise of Marshal Petain's regime, with its headquarters in the spa-town of Vichy in central France. The German invasion pushed nearly four million French and foreign refugees south to the relative safety of the unoccupied zone. Among them were thousands of German political exiles, many of whom headed to the Mediterranean port city of Marseilles, where they hoped to find passage out of France, knowing that they might be arrested at any time.[8]

In New York a group of concerned citizens, including representatives of Jewish groups, trade unions, faith communities, and European ex-patriates met together in June 1940 to establish the Emergency Rescue Committee.[9] Their intention was to send a representative to Marseilles to help the most desperately threatened refugees leave France before the Gestapo arrested them. The person who took up this role was a

---

the occupying power. By contrast, the provision of safe-haven in the UK for Basque and German Jewish children was not in any contravention of British regulations.

8 Article 19 of the Franco-German Armistice required the Vichy government to extradite any German nationals the Gestapo demanded, and made it clear to the refugees that France could only be a dangerous stop on the way to safer havens.

9 Eleanor Roosevelt had supported the initiative, and promised to help obtain emergency visas for the refugees.

committed anti-Nazi called Varian Fry. He had been in Berlin in 1935 as a journalist and had witnessed first-hand the abuses perpetrated against Jews, an experience which was the source of his commitment to the cause of saving the lives of those threatened by the regime of the Third Reich.

Fry arrived in Marseilles on 14 August 1940. He proceeded to assemble a small team to help forge documents, exchange money on the black-market and develop escape routes to Spain. Over the next thirteen months Fry and his colleagues managed to spirit over 2,000 people from France, among them politicians, artists, writers, scientists, and musicians. The majority of the escapees were taken across the border to Spain and then to the safety of neutral Portugal from where they made their way to the United States. Others escaped on ships leaving Marseille for the French colony of Martinique, where they could obtain visas for onward travel.[10] Especially instrumental in getting Fry the visas necessary for entry to the United States was the head of the visa service at the American consulate in Marseille, who fought against anti-Semitism in the State Department and was personally responsible for issuing thousands of visas, both legal and illegal. His views were not shared by the Consul General himself, who grew increasingly frustrated by Fry's covert activities. His antipathy was shared by the Vichy authorities, and in September 1941 Fry was expelled on the grounds that 'you have protected Jews and anti-Nazis.'[11]

Humanitarian constructive resistance: The Marcel Network

Shortly after Varian Fry was expelled the Vichy authorities began to escalate the arrest of foreign Jews in the Free Zone and hand them over to the Germans. Amongst those threatened by this new regime was an

---

10 One of my heroes, Victor Serge, passed through Fry's network, staying for several months at their hide-away just outside Marseilles, before he and his son voyaged to Martinique en route to Mexico.

11 Quoted in the guide to the United States Holocaust Museum exhibition, *Assignment, Rescue, The Story of Varian Fry and the Emergency Rescue Committee.* Accessible at https://tinyurl.com/y8622pot (3. May 2020). The guide also includes an extract from a letter to his mother written whilst en route across Spain for Lisbon, which I think is revealing about Fry's own nature, and which resonates strongly with me at a deeply personal level: 'I have to admit that I am proud to have stayed. I stayed because the refugees needed me. But it took courage, and courage is a quality I hadn't previously been sure I possessed.'

actor and student of theatre, Moussa Abadi, who had been born to a Jewish couple in Damascus. Abadi was one of those who had fled from the north as the German occupation was implemented. His partner, Odette Rosenstock, a medical doctor from a Parisian middle class Jewish family, joined Abadi on the Mediterranean coast at Nice in November 1941. Both equipped themselves with false identity documents to reduce the risk of capture.[12]

In April 1942 Abadi came across the shocking scene of a French police officer beating a young Jewish mother to death in the street, witnessed by her small son. Shocked and shamed, Abadi kept thinking about the young boy, 'What would happen to him? …. It was the day I decided I would not just sit idly by and watch the parade. … I was going to do something. I didn't know how, but Odette and I were going to help.'[13] With the assistance of some key people they created a clandestine operation that would ultimately save 527 Jewish children from deportation by placing them in Catholic institutions and with Protestant families.

Odette Rosenstock

One of Abadi's first contacts was with the bishop of Nice, who had made a number of public stands against the persecution of the Jews. He agreed to provide office space where the documentation necessary for the children (baptismal certificates, ration cards etc.) could be prepared. In addition he provided a list of catholic institutions in his

Abadi Moussa

diocese – schools, orphanages and convents – where the children might find shelter. Two local Protestant pastors also offered to help by finding families from their congregations to host children. Meantime Odette began working in Nice for the Children's Aid Society, a Jewish-French humanitarian agency (OSE), and used that network to inform people of

---

12 F. Coleman, *The Marcel Network: How one French couple saved 527 children from the Holocaust*, Lincoln NE: University of Nebraska Press, 2011, p. 10.
13 Quoted in Coleman, 2011, p.11.

the contact points through which children in need of sanctuary might be channelled.[14]

Funding for the network was organised through one of Moussa's friends from his days in Paris, Maurice Brenner, who had become a key liaison figure in the French resistance. Brenner had been closely involved in establishing a clandestine network for hiding Jewish children in the northern zone, and drew on this experience to advise and encourage Abadi (Monsieur Marcel) to set up a similar initiative in the south. Funds came from the American Jewish Joint Distribution Committee, through the OSE initially and later in the war via Swiss agencies in Geneva.

What is clear about this example of humanitarian constructive resistance is that whilst the courage and resourcefulness of the two main figures was a necessary factor in the relative success of the network, it also depended on a number of other factors.[15]

i.   The cooperation of local people in significant positions within established institutions, who could facilitate access to their infrastructure and resources – such as the bishop of Nice, who made it possible for the children to be hidden within the convents, orphanages, chaplaincies and schools within his diocese. A similar role was played by those Protestant pastors who found homes for children amongst their parishioners.

ii. The involvement of people in positions of influence within national networks – such as Maurice Brenner, who could draw on his experience to advise and encourage Monsieur Marcel in the establishment of his network.

iii. The support of international networks such as the American Jewish Joint Distribution Committee which sourced the bulk of the funding upon which the project relied.

iv. Finally, and crucially, none of the work could have been carried out without the resilience and steadfastness of those 'ordinary

---

14 OSE is the acronym of *Oeuvre de Secours aux Enfants* (*Society for Rescuing Children*). See *Centennial brochure: OSE: 100 years of History, 1912-2012*, accessible at https://tinyurl.com/y7jzk4yo (27 April 2020).

15 Odette Rosenstock was arrested in late April 1944 and sent to Auschwitz. She survived and the couple were reunited after the war.

people' who cared for the children, sometimes at considerable risk to their own well-being.

Humanitarian constructive resistance: community based safe-havens

Other initiatives, driven by a similar commitment to that which inspired the work of the Marcel Network – the felt need to protect and care for those most threatened by the Third Reich - were community-based, involving the inhabitants of towns and villages.

Nieuwlande is a small Dutch village originally established as a peat-colony some ten kilometres east of Hoogeveen in the north-eastern province of Denthe. During the Second World War its population was around 800. The provision of refuge started when hiding places were sought for men evading conscripted labour in Germany, but over time the locals began opening their homes to increasing numbers of Jews. At some farms as many as ten people were hiding out in barns, outhouses and other secret places. Between 1942 and 1944 around 250 Jews were provided with sanctuary.[16]

Le Chambon-sur-Lignon is located on a high plateau in the Auvergne region of central-eastern France, some 80 kilometres south of Saint Etienne. It was in the Vichy-controlled, free-zone of France. In the winter of 1940-41 a small number of Jews fleeing from the occupied zone in the north sought refuge, and when the

Commemorative plaque, Le Chambon

---

16 'Drenthe village awarded medal for large-scale WWII aid to hunted Jews', accessible at https://tinyurl.com/dcrn9ncd (7 May 2020). Nieuwlande, along with Le Chambon-sur-Lignon, are the two villages in the world that collectively received Righteous Among the Nations award from Yad Vashem Holocaust Memorial Centre in Israel.

local inhabitants helped them the word spread to other refugees. [17] From December 1940 to September 1944, the inhabitants of Le Chambon and the villages on the surrounding plateau provided refuge or assistance in escaping to Switzerland for an estimated 5,000 people, including about 3,000–3,500 Jews seeking to avoid the extermination camps.

When we try to analyse why these communities acted the way they did a number of factors appear to be significant.[18]

i. *Strong local leadership*:

In both communities the authority of local leaders was firmly entrenched before the outbreak of war. In Le Chambon there were some remarkable men and women. The pastor André Trocmé was a pacifist with a powerful intellect and huge charisma. Alongside him was his Italian wife Magda, more grounded and practical than her husband - they complemented each other. The mayor, Charles Guillon, had a career working with the international YMCA network, and as such had a range of international connections; whilst the headteacher of the local secondary school, Edouard Theis, was an invaluable colleague and co-conspirator who was also a dab-hand at forgery. The pastors of the surrounding villages also played a vital leadership role in organising the sheltering of the refugees.

In Nieuwlande the immediate cause of the villagers committing themselves to the shelter of the victims of the Third Reich can be traced to the influence of a combination of local secular and religious authority. A respected local municipal councillor, Johannes Post, invited a former minister at the village church, the Reverend Frits Slomp, to come and address a village meeting in the church in 1942. Slomp used the occasion to remind his former parishioners of the dangers of Nazism and to do their Christian duty of protecting

17 A number of books and other published sources have focused on the inspirational rescue mission carried out by the people of Le Chambon and its neighbouring parishes. I have found the most accessible to be by Peter Grose, *A good place to hide: How one community saved thousands of lives from the Nazis*, London: Nicholas Brealey Publishing, 2014.

18 This analysis draws heavily on Michael Gross, 'Jewish Rescue in Holland and France during the Second World War: Moral Cognition and Collective Action', *Social Forces*, v. 73, n. 2, December 1994, pp. 463-496.

those threatened by the occupying regime.[19] Post was one of the first people in the village to house Jews, and other villagers vouched that his direct appeal was sufficient reason for their involvement.[20]

ii.   *Supportive norms and value base*:

Although appeals from authoritative local leaders might have an impact on the actions of their community, the response will be all the stronger when such calls strike a chord with the norms and values of the locals – whether this be local pride and sense of identity, political values and commitments, or tenets of religious faith.

When André Trocmé appealed to the people of Le Chambon and its environs to offer shelter to those in need, he couched it in terms of the religious imperative to 'resist whenever our adversaries demand of us obedience contrary to the order of the gospel.' The Chambonnais were predominantly devout Christians who responded to the plight of the Jews as a test of faith. After all, they were enjoined in the New Testament (James 1:27) to 'reach out to the homeless and loveless in their plight'. Moreover, the local population had a long history of religious dissent with a high proportion of Protestant Huguenots whose collective memory went back to their own persecution following the religious strife in 17th century France. As a consequence many of them had the deep conviction that saving the persecuted Jews was a religious imperative. Furthermore, there was a strong tradition of hospitality on the plateau where the locals had been receiving tourists and visitors, especially children, for summer visits since the 19th century.[21]

In the village of Nieuwlande there is evidence that many of the local people had a firm Christian faith and a commitment to the ethic of reciprocity embodied in the Golden Rule of treating others as you would wish to be treated yourself, hence the appeal of Frits Stomp's

---

19 'Firebrand pastor criss-crossed country to coordinate resistance', https://tinyurl.com/y8uhnvxj (8 May 2020).

20 Gross, 1994, p. 469.

21 In 1935 some 3500 children spent their summer holidays in and around Le Chambon, either with their families or at children's summer camps. (Grose, 2014).

message. But in Holland rescuers also tapped into other deeply felt values and beliefs. For the nationalists there was the appeal to patriotism; for the liberal-democrats the appeal would be based on the sanctity of basic democratic principles and practices and to basic civic norms that emphasised the importance of protecting democratic values and practices, particularly in relation to safeguarding the rights of one's fellow citizens; and for the socialists the appeal could be pitched around the commitment to the international fellowship of working people.

iii. *Tapping into pre-existing organisational infrastructures and networks*:

In his analysis of the factors pertinent to understanding why some communities engaged in collective action to protect Jews in occupied Europe during the Second World Wars Michael Gross emphasised the importance of local leaders having an intimate knowledge of their constituencies and the pre-existing networks that could be utilised. They knew which people might be motivated by the promise of material reward as against those moved by religious conviction or socialist internationalism. He observed, 'In Nieuwlande, Le Chambon and the Cevennes local leaders were able to operate within the confines of their respective organizations and the framework of a small and tightly knit community.'[22]

These local leaders also had access to national (and international) networks of support and solidarity. In the case of Nieuwlande, both Frits Stomp and Johannes Post became members of the coordinating committee of the National Organization for Assistance to People in Hiding (known by the acronym LO in Holland) with access to its human and material resources. This underground network was established at the very beginning of the war to aid fleeing non-Jewish Dutch citizens conscripted by the Nazis for forced labour. In late-1942 its scope was widened to include Jews fleeing persecution.[23]

---

22 Gross, 1994, p. 470.

23 At the end of the war around 350,000 people, including 18,000 Jews, emerged from hiding in Holland. The bulk of this number were those evading conscripted labour in Germany. Accessible at https://tinyurl.com/eu3r6aee. (16

The rescue activities in Le Chambon were disconnected from the resistance, but the local leaders were well integrated into different national and international faith-based organisations such as the international YMCA and the Committee to Coordinate Activities for the Displaced, a Protestant refugee organization which was particularly active in finding escape routes to Switzerland.

iv. *Ability to minimise risks and defray costs*:

Very few people volunteered sanctuary to those in need, they had to be asked, and in making their decision a key factor would be the risk entailed and the accompanying cost, including the practical matters of how to feed extra mouths at a time of shortages and ration cards. In both locations there was the relatively high level of trust that can exist in small rural communities where people share similar life-experiences and world-view. In such circumstances the incidence of informers was minimised, and the identity of those suspected of being collaborators soon became common-knowledge. Moreover, in the case of Le Chambon in particular, its relative isolation on a high plateau, away from any major transport routes, rendered it a relatively safe haven for harbouring refugees, particularly during the winter months when the area was often snow-bound. Indeed, there is substantial evidence that the local German authorities knew that fugitives were being housed in and around Le Chambon, but for a range of possible reasons the number of surprise raids was kept to a minimum.[24] Nieuwlande did not enjoy the same degree of relative isolation, nor the 'sympathy' of the occupying power. Various precautions were taken to reduce the risk of surprise raids, which invariably took place at night. In addition to building elaborate hide-outs, house numbers were removed to sow confusion amongst strangers, whilst families would block access to their homes by turning sideways the bridges used to cross the drainage channels and waterways.

July 2020).

24 One possible reason was that the commitment of the leaders of the rescue operations to nonviolence meant that there was no suspicion of their involvement in violent resistance activities, which would have incurred retaliatory raids by the German military. In a way it could be said that Le Chambon practised 'non-provocative resistance'.

In both cases, Le Chambon and Nieuwlande, the ability to defray the material and financial costs was critical for sustaining rescue operations. The Dutch resistance had a well-developed fundraising organization (The National Assistance Fund) which made money and ration cards available to rescue leaders to set against the cost of housing refugees.[25] Raids by the underground resistance targeted supplies of ration cards that could then be used to obtain supplies for those in hiding, whilst in Le Chambon there were a number of very competent forgers who were able to produce the necessary documentation.

Humanitarian constructive resistance at a national level: The case of Denmark

One of the most impressive examples of constructive nonviolent resistance in wartime to save the lives of those under threat was the evacuation of over 7000 Jewish citizens of Denmark across the Kattegat straits to Sweden in early October 1943.[26] Denmark was occupied by German forces on 9 April 1940. Unable to defend itself militarily, the Danish government came to an agreement with Germany that the country's neutrality would be respected by Germany, thus saving the population from the ravages of war. The Germans did their utmost to convince the Danes that they would respect its government and judiciary, with the civil administration remaining in Danish hands along with the police force and a reduced army. It was agreed that parliament should continue and the King (Christian X) would remain head of state.

Whilst this arrangement allowed the Danish government a degree of relative autonomy (especially compared with the occupied countries to the east like Poland), it also made sense when viewed from Berlin. The Third Reich could present Denmark as a model German protectorate, it

---

25 See the 2018 film *The Resistance Banker* (*Bankier van het Verzet*) for a powerful and realistic portrayal of the origins and functioning of this underground banking system.

26 For an informed overview of the different narratives relating to the 'Danish story', see M. J. Sorensen, 'Glorifications and simplifications in case studies of Danish WWII nonviolent resistance', *Journal of Resistance Studies*, v. 3, no 1, 2017. pp. 99-137.

was good for public relations. Secondly, it was very efficient. At a time when Hitler's priority was the military advance of his army, the fewer German soldiers and administrators required to 'neutralise' Denmark the better. Four million Danes requiring the attention of just a couple of hundred German civil servants was a very good deal. So, there was a mutual interest in preserving the fiction of Denmark's neutrality. From the Danish perspective it meant that if the Germans wanted something done, they had to wait for the Danish government to give agreement. This meant that Danes could enjoy a screen of protection from the German regime and its representatives. The German military were given strict instructions to avoid provocation, treat women with respect, and avoid offending their 'hosts', bearing in mind at all times that Denmark was not an enemy country. It was not in Germany's interests to upset the Danes, and the Danish made it very clear that any attempt to deport the Jews would agitate them very much.

This accommodation lasted until late August 1943 when the Germans proclaimed a state of emergency after the Danish government refused to introduce the death penalty for sabotage. Parliament was dissolved, the government dismissed and the Danish military disarmed.[27] After the collapse of the cooperation policy the German plenipotentiary in Denmark came under pressure to rid Denmark of its Jews. By 1943, however, even some of the fiercest Nazi officials were becoming apprehensive about the consequences of what they were doing in the context of Germany's likely defeat. This could explain the fact that a German official at the embassy in Copenhagen forewarned the Danish authorities about the impending round-up of the Jews.

From the moment they knew it was coming, Danish government officials made it clear to their police that no help was to be given to the Germans. People stood up for neighbours and co-workers, Jews were hidden in hospitals, old people's homes and private houses and transported in taxis and ambulances to the coast, where fishermen ferried them across

---

27 This followed an upsurge of strikes and other forms of resistance in Denmark, linked to the growing awareness that Germany was losing the war, following the surrender of the Sixth Army at Stalingrad in February 1943 and the surrender of Italy to the Allies later that year.

to neutral Sweden.[28] An estimated 7,220 escaped to Sweden, along with 686 non-Jewish spouses. Thirty people died attempting to escape; some drowned, others committed suicide rather than risk capture. Up to 100 hid out in the countryside until the war ended. Only 464 Jews were

Danish Jews being transported to Sweden

taken prisoner and transported to Theresienstadt in Czechoslovakia, where their situation was closely monitored by the Danish authorities, thereby preventing them from being sent on to the extermination camps. Estimates of the number of non-Jewish Danes who helped in the massive escape to the coast range as high as 10,000, but the exact number is unknown.[29]

In his study of civil resistance in occupied Europe during the Second World War Jacques Semelin identified a number of factors that can act to mitigate the impact of genocidal policies.[30] From this we can understand some of the reasons for the success of the Danish Jews in escaping the 'final solution'.

i. *Degree of integration of Jewish communities*:   Most of the Danish Jewish population had lived in Denmark for generations and were well integrated into society.

---

28 The fishermen charged for their services, but as more fishermen became involved the price dropped. See M. Mogensen, 'The rescue of the Danish Jews', in M. Bastholm Jensen and S. L. B. Jensen, eds., *Denmark and the Holocaust*, Copenhagen: Department for Holocaust and Genocide Studies, Institute for International Studies, 2003, pp. 33-61, p.47.

29 D. Schulz, 'The kindness of strangers: Thousands of Danes and one brave German defy the Nazis to rescue Denmark's Jews', *World War II*, March-April 2011. Accessible at https://tinyurl.com/ycbagbt7   (12 May 2020). A personal note – a Danish student of mine once remarked sarcastically to me, 'Oh yes, everybody's grandfather participated in the rescue of the Jews!' A wry comment on the power of collective memory and the creation of myth.

30 Semelin, 1993, p. 130.

ii. *The distribution of the threatened population*: In Denmark the Jews lived throughout the country, not congregated into ghettoes.

iii. *The nature of the country's occupation*: The German-Danish accommodation that lasted until 1943 afforded Danish citizens, and Jews in particular, a degree of protection from the more heinous of Nazi policies and practices. The Danes enjoyed a degree of 'open space' that was unimaginable to Poles and other nationalities who experienced the full force of the Third Reich's genocidal project.

iv. *The amount of warning time*: As we have seen, the Danes were forewarned of the impending round-up, which enabled the Jewish citizens to prepare for escape and the non-Jewish citizens prepare to offer assistance.

v.   *Proximity of a welcoming country*: If you are trying to escape, you need somewhere to escape to, and Sweden was not only close-by but also prepared to welcome the refugees.

To these factors identified by Semelin we might also add some of those derived from the analysis of community-based initiatives to provide sanctuary.

vi. *The role of legitimate leaders* : In Denmark the acknowledged head of state, King Christian, became a rallying symbol for Danish national sentiment during the German occupation and made it clear, as he wrote in his diary, that he considered 'our own Jews to be Danish citizens'.

vii. *Supportive culture and civic norms*: In most cases of civil resistance against occupation the initial driver is likely to be a desire to defend or strengthen national and patriotic values. In Denmark there was a strong sense of social cohesion and a belief in democratic values and the rule of law. Consequently the threat to the Jews was seen as an attack on the very fabric of Danish society, such that the fate of the Jews became intertwined with the fate of the nation, and a symbol of resistance against the imposed regime of the Nazis.[31]

viii. Ability to minimise risks and defray costs: Without wishing to denigrate the moral courage displayed by thousands of people who participated in the rescue of the Danish Jews to Sweden, they did enjoy a degree of space within which their care for their neighbour might be manifested. Furthermore, many of the fishermen who ferried the refugees made a substantial financial profit from their 'good works'. In addition there is substantial evidence that by 1943 the German occupation forces in Denmark were not enthusiastic about rounding up the Jews, whilst the German navy made no attempt to intercept the vessels carrying the Jews to Sweden.[32] Furthermore, the refugees were assured of a welcome in Sweden, unlike many who were denied entry to Switzerland during the Second World War.

In this section our focus has been upon constructive action and resistance driven by a humanitarian concern for the well-being of those threatened by the lethal violence wielded by armed parties and occupation regimes. In the next section the focus turns to those whose prime motivation for constructive nonviolent action has been the desire to preserve the values, culture and way of life that they valued and which they believed to be threatened by an enemy regime and its occupation forces. Their main mode of resistance has involved the attempt to live significant dimensions of their everyday lives in such a way as to embody those values and ideals they wish to preserve into the future, to keep alive aspects of their culture so that they might flourish once again once they became free.

---

31 Gross,1994, p. 469.
32 Mogensen, 2003, p. 51.

Constructive living in wartime – preserving values and ways of life threatened by the conditions of war.

In his study of civilian-based resistance to occupation in Europe in the Second World War Jacques Semelin emphasised that those who engaged in such resistance did not think their activities would defeat the enemy and displace the occupation. They knew that liberation would have to come from outside. The significance of their resistance was that it symbolised their refusal to recognise the legitimacy of the occupier. Their oppressor might enjoy *de facto* power achieved through military might, but in the eyes of the oppressed their loyalty lay with the *de jure* authority that had been forcibly displaced by the enemy. He wrote:

> Civilian resistance was rarely directed against the occupation forces openly; it did not have the means to drive them from the territory. The goal … was instead to preserve the collective identity of the attacked societies; that is to say, their fundamental values. … When a society feels less and less submissive, it becomes more and more uncontrollable. Then, even if the occupier keeps its power, it loses its authority. This expresses how much civil resistance consisted primarily of a clash of wills, expressing above all a fight for values.[33]

Viewed from this perspective any form of civilian-based resistance activity might be seen to embody to some degree this clash of wills and the aim of preserving the collective identity of the subjugated. However, certain types of activity carried out by those living under occupation do seem to be driven primarily by the felt need to affirm certain values (and associated ways of life) directly threatened by the occupier. Sometimes these values might have their basis in the national culture, but they can also stem from adherence to what many would consider to be basic human values or be embodied in the organisational or vocational culture of particular professions. In this section we shall look at some examples of this form of constructive resistance carried out by those who chose to live certain aspects of their lives in such a way as to keep alive those values and aspects of their identity, including professional codes of conduct, that

---

33 Semelin, 1993, p. 3.

they held dear and which they believed to be threatened by the imposed regime of the occupier.

Constructive living by professional occupational groups: Norway, 1940-45

The German invasion of Norway commenced 9 April 1940. The Norwegian military fought a delaying action, relinquishing stretches of territory, but eventually an armistice was agreed on 10 June 1940. There then followed a confused period when the Germans were trying to establish a political regime with some claim to legitimacy by involving some of the pre-occupation political parties and institutions. In this they were unsuccessful. When the German reichskommissar Joseph Treborn issued an order to forbid the Supreme Court from discussing the constitutionality of his decisions in December 1940 the members of what was the highest judicial authority in the country resigned. According to Semelin this refusal to compromise their principles as members of the legal profession 'censured the illegitimacy of the new regime in a spectacular way and advanced the legitimation of a growing social opposition against the occupier.'[34]

One of the first instances of organised resistance in defence of core values was on the 'athletics front'. Terboven dissolved the established sports organisations and clubs and created a new central association under Nazi control to which all clubs were required to affiliate. The response was 'Boycott all sporting events of every kind so long as the Nazis are in control; don't participate in them, either as teams or as individuals, and don't patronize them as spectators.'[35] Throughout the period of occupation no public sporting events took place in Norway, although some were held in secret the Germans failed to break the 'sports strike' which lasted until liberation in 1945.

Continuing to pursue the Nazification of Norwegian society the occupation regime next came up against two other 'fronts' – the church

---

34 Semelin, 1993, p. 53.

35 Quoted in K. M. Johnson, 'An analysis of the Norwegian resistance during the Second World War', Air Command & Staff College, Maxwell Airbase, Montgomery, AL, March 1997, p.18.

and the school system. In February 1941 a notice or epistle was read out in churches throughout the country condemning the new regime affirming that 'When those who have authority in a community tolerate violence and injustice and oppress souls, the Church must be the guardian of people's consciences.'[36] In early February 1942 Vidkun Quisling, the founder of the Norwegian National Socialist Party (Nasjonal Samlin), was appointed chief minister, which seriously escalated the tension between civil society networks and the German occupation powers. He passed new laws requiring the Church to endorse certain Nazi principles, including a demand that an alteration be made in the Common Prayer of the service-book involving endorsement of the new regime. Bishops and priests refused to accede to this attempt at 'Nazification'. Many of them resigned from the state church, but continued to hold services outside the church buildings. On 5 April Norway's clergy finally broke all administrative ties with the state. In retaliation Quisling had several of their number arrested but to little avail. Of 699 clergymen of the Church of Norway, 645 resigned, and 151 out of 155 ordained priests followed suit, continuing to fulfil their priestly duties outside the confines of the church buildings.

Around the same time Quisling promulgated a law creating a new teachers union, and a national-socialist youth organisation that all youth were required to join. This move was challenged by 90 percent of the nation's teachers who signed individual letters sent to the Ministry of Education and Religious Affairs rejecting the instructions received. The Nazis believed that the key to control of both the teachers and the curriculum was the issue of union membership.[37] Consequently the regime announced that all those who failed to renounce their declaration would be dismissed, and proceeded to close all the schools on the pretext of lack of fuel. Over a thousand teachers were arrested and incarcerated at forced labour camps in the north of the country, but somewhere in excess of 100,000 parents each wrote individual letters of protest regarding the school closures to the Ministry.

---

36 Quoted in Semelin, 1993, p. 67.

37 T. Dunseath , 'Teachers at war: Norwegian teachers during the German Occupation of Norway 1940-45', *History of Education*, v. 31, n. 4, 2002, pp. 371-383, p. 381.

Confronted by such a level of mobilisation and in an effort to save face, the government announced that the dispute was all due to a misunderstanding and the schools would be reopened on 1 May, on the presumption that all teachers returning to take up their posts would be considered to have become members of the new union (*Norges Laerersamband*). On their return to the classroom each teacher made the following declaration, disassociating themselves from the new union:

> ... being a member of the *Norges Laerersamband* and teaching are incompatible. ....The teacher's vocation is not only to give children knowledge; teachers must also teach their pupils to believe in and uphold truth and justice. Therefore teachers cannot, without betraying their calling, teach anything that violates their consciences. ... That, I promise you, I shall not do.[38]

Those deported returned. The teachers had succeeded in mobilising society in their favour and in so doing frustrated Quisling's national socialist project.

In concluding this case study a few observations can be made regarding the conditions that enabled such a level of social mobilisation to take place.

i.   Of crucial significance is the degree of operating space the resisters were allowed by the Nazi occupation and its Norwegian collaborators. The Nazis viewed the Norwegians as racially pure, and their goal was to win them over rather than subjugate them. By contrast, in the Eastern European countries, including Poland, the Nazis had no intention of swaying hearts and minds of the *Untermenschen* (sub-humans) who faced the threat of racial annihilation. This explains the relative degree of restraint displayed by the regime in dealing with the teachers.

ii.   An important source of the legitimacy enjoyed by the resisters, and hence the level of mobilisation they helped inspire, was their determined attachment to the professional values and ethics deemed central to the practice of their chosen vocations.

---

38 Quoted in Semelin, 1993, p. 69.

iii. Strong social institutions and civil society networks: Apparently 96 percent of Norway's population belonged to the national (Lutheran) church in the early 1940s.[39] In addition there was a strong trade union system and a vibrant network of voluntary associations (such as sports clubs). All these played a role in the organisation of the protest actions and the social mobilisation.

iv. There was a strong degree of social solidarity at the local level in Norway, with small rural communities composed of people reliant on 'good neighbours' in everyday life.

v. Traditionally the vast majority of the working population of Norway were farmers or fishermen right up to the beginning of the 20th century. Without a strong landed gentry and a solid urban bourgeoisie, Norwegian society was not so fractured as other European states, and this undoubtedly helped create a relatively strong sense of national identity, which was one of the key drivers of the mobilisation. As was noted by Tessa Dunseath in her study of the teachers' resistance:

> The attempts of the Nazis to uproot traditions of Norwegian education that were deeply embedded in national culture had little possibility of succeeding as those traditions were guarded with enormous pride. The intervention of an alien ideology was seen by the majority of Norwegians as an act of political and cultural trespass. It was in their failure to recognize the natural and profound hostility of Norwegians to ideological tyranny, a hostility exemplified in the resistance activities of the teachers, that the grossest error of judgement was made by Hitler and his lieutenants.[40]

---

39 Semelin, 1993, p. 66.
40 Dunseath, 2002, p. 382.

Constructive work to meet the basic needs of those threatened by the violence of war and occupation.

Education in Poland under German occupation

On 1 September 1939 German forces invaded Poland. Under the terms of the Ribbentrop-Molotov Pact the USSR advanced on Polish territory on 17 September. Within a few weeks Poland was split in two, divided between the two occupying forces. Germany annexed territory in the west, whilst the eastern territories were incorporated into the USSR. The remaining territory in-between was formally occupied by Germany and termed the 'General Governorate'.

In the western territories annexed to the Third Reich the Polish education system was completely eliminated. Teachers, professors, and the whole intelligentsia were displaced or arrested as part of mass deportation of its Polish residents In the central region only primary and vocational schools with significantly limited curricula stripped of all Polish content was permitted. All secondary and higher schools were closed to Poles, following the directives contained in a policy document on the 'Germanisation of Poland':

> Universities and other institutions of higher education, as well as secondary and trade schools, have always provided a means for the cultivation of Polish nationalism; therefore, for these very fundamental reasons, such institutions must be closed. The only permissible institutions are those that teach the most elementary skills: reading, writing and arithmetic.[41]

On 6 November 1939 the academic staff at Cracow University in the General Governate were called to a meeting, where they were arrested and sent to camps. That same month the Polish underground determined that whilst the attempt to repel the invaders had failed, the resistance would continue. This resistance would include the attempt to defend and preserve as much of Polish culture as possible, including the setting up of underground educational courses at all levels. Accordingly an extensive

---

41 Quoted by A. Redzik, 'Polish universities during the Second World War'. Accessible at https://tinyurl.com/pfxxbpfp (28 May 2020).

underground teaching movement developed under the leadership of the Polish Teachers' Association, which had been established in December 1939. In 1940 an underground Department of Education and Culture was established to represent the Polish government-in-exile.

Initially covert teaching only took place at the primary school level. No one attempted to conduct courses at the secondary or higher education tiers due to the lethal consequences that teachers would face on discovery. Also in those first weeks of occupation no-one knew how long the war would last. There was still hope that the war would come to a speedy conclusion, and that higher institutions would therefore recommence their usual work in the near future. By the early months of 1940, however, university teachers began meeting up with individuals and small groups of students (never more than seven in number) in unofficial settings such as private residences and church properties.

Polish underground education, 1941

High school courses took place on a large scale, using church premises and other locations, including technical and trade schools which had remained open - classes nominally devoted to developing skills such as typing or basic mechanics were used to teach Polish history and the like. It is estimated that somewhere in the region of 90,000 students participated in some form of higher education during the war years, including some 6,300 students who were awarded their degrees.[42] There was some geographical unevenness. In the west, where the territory had been annexed by Germany, academics and intellectuals had been either arrested or deported, there was little space or opportunity to develop any significant level of underground education, and there were comparable constraints in the east under Soviet occupation. But overall it was an amazing achievement, and a number of factors seem to have played a part in making this possible:

---

42 Figures sourced from Redzik.

i.   There was a strong sense of identity and solidarity amongst the Polish population.

ii.   This sense of unity was strengthened by the nature of the enemy they faced in the Third Reich. It became clear very early on that nothing could be expected from the occupier other than lethal violence, cruelty, abuse and contempt. As Semelin observed, 'The unbelievable brutality of Nazi repression created a new unity in this country.'[43]

iii. There was strong and clear leadership from both the underground leaders within Poland and the government-in-exile outside. There was a conviction that military defeat did not mean the end of the struggle and that collaboration with the occupier was not a possibility.

iv.   Poles had a history of occupation and partition by the major powers on their borders, and accordingly they possessed a tradition of creating their own parallel institutions whilst under occupation as a means of preserving their culture and identity.

v.   Finally, mention must be made of the courage of those who made the underground educational system possible – the students and the teachers in particular. According to Redzik around 8000 school teachers lost their lives alongside about a thousand academics.

To set against the cost, however, it is important to herald the significance of their constructive resistance. As one of the organisers concluded:

> Underground teaching on all levels of schooling was the most admirable work accomplished by Polish society. Neither tracts, nor violence, nor sabotages were as productive as this last manifestation of the national consciousness. It saved our society from a catastrophe equal at least to the destruction of Warsaw: the loss of five graduating classes of engineers, architects, doctors, teachers, and students who passed their baccalaureate exam.[44]

---

43 Semelin, 1993, p. 77
44 Quoted in Semelin, 1993, p. 80.

Constructive unarmed civilian intervention in violent conflict zones – accompaniment

Moving now from occupied Europe during the Second World War, it is time to examine some of the ways in which third-party civilians in more recent times have intervened nonviolently in violent conflict zones in order to protect other civilians from the threat of violence as well as to support local efforts to build peace. Humanitarian aid agencies, journalists, solidarity movements are just some of the 'external' civilian actors playing roles in violent conflict situations, but the focus of this section is upon volunteers who enter such zones with the express purpose of supporting the work of local peace activists by enabling them and the members of the communities and neighbourhoods in which they work to fulfil their chosen role – whether this be that of a human rights lawyer and monitor, a local peace worker and community organiser, or a primary school pupil. The most frequent method by which such volunteers seek to pursue this goal is generally described as accompaniment.

Perhaps the best known agency involved in this kind of work is Peace Brigades International (PBI). PBI was founded in 1981, and over the years has developed its methodology of 'international protective accompaniment' as a way of protecting human rights defenders and communities whose lives and work are threatened by political violence. At its core this involves the physical accompaniment, by international personnel, of activists, organisations and communities threatened with politically motivated violence. Accompaniment can take many forms, with some threatened individuals getting round-the-clock accompaniment, whilst for others the presence is more intermittent, as required. Sometimes the international volunteers spend their days in the offices of threatened organisations, others might spend the bulk of their time living amidst rural villagers enduring uncertain conditions in the midst of a conflict zone.[45] The intention behind such accompaniment is that by their presence the international accompaniers can help open the political space for threatened activists to carry out their work, whilst also

---

45 Much of this section draws upon Peace Brigades International, *Human rights defenders under attack: Twenty five years of safeguarding the right to defend human rights.* Accessible at https://tinyurl.com/yad3slnu (11 June 2020).

providing moral support and encouragement to those who continue to struggle despite the very real threat of repression and violence.[46]

Central to the effectiveness of accompaniment as a means of protecting people from politically motivated threats is the international dimension. Indeed, according to two of the founding members of PBI, accompaniment without international support is a facade with no real protective value.[47] The leverage exercised by the accompanier resides in their status as a representative and symbol of international human rights concern, a visible reminder to potential perpetrators that their use of violence will not go unnoticed by significant actors and agencies in the outside world. The threat is that there will be an international response to whatever violence is targeted at those the international volunteer is accompanying. Of course threats can only exercise leverage if they are credible and significant. The likelihood of a potential assailant being deterred from inflicting violence on a target would depend on them perceiving the threat to be credible (their actions would result in diplomatic and economic pressure and similar sanctions) and significant (international sanctions would impose significant cost on the perpetrators and those responsible for the violence). It follows from this that the stronger the international interest in a particular country or conflict zone, the more effective will be the protection and space offered by the accompaniers.

My own encounters with protective accompaniment have been primarily in the occupied West Bank where different groups including Israeli solidarity activists, international volunteers and Palestinian activists have adopted the practice as part of their methodology. For example, in the South Hebron Hills activists from the Israeli solidarity group *Ta'ayush* and from *Rabbis for Human Rights* have acted as a protective presence in the area since 2000. They were then joined by international volunteers

---

46 It is relevant to note that PBI always seeks permission for their intervention from the host government. Some other accompaniment programmes do not seek permission, which changes the dynamics. See Pat Coy's observations, accessible at https://tinyurl.com/u4wdmcj5 (2 July 2021).

47 L. Mahoney & L. E. Eguren, *Unarmed bodyguards: International accompaniment for the protection of human rights*, West Hartford, Ct.: Kumarian Press, 1997, p. 84.

with the Italian project *Operation Dove* whose volunteers have been accompanying local children on their route to school that passes close to an Israeli settlement since 2004. Within the city of Hebron members of *Youth Against Settlements* (YAS) have attempted to act as a protective presence for those Palestinians living adjacent to Israeli settlements in the city. As one of the movement's members explained in an interview in 2014,

> We observe the settlers … We have 50 people ready to mobilise if any house is threatened … We are not afraid to confront the settlers. Our aim is to empower the local people – they are not alone – so that they can hold on to their property.[48]

As part of their activities the YAS runs training programmes in film-making for young people. Whenever violations happen they film as much as possible and then upload it to YouTube. Indeed, it has become increasingly common for accompaniers to be equipped with camcorders, cameras and, of course, smart-phones in order to record and subsequently document any assaults perpetrated against local people by Israeli settlers and occupation forces. Frequently footage of human rights violations have been uploaded to websites such as YouTube within an hour of them taking place. Using electronic media in this manner has opened up a significant international dimension to accompaniment on the ground – international audiences can now bear witness to the violations perpetrated by settlers and others. A Palestinian activist interviewed by Marwan Darweish and myself back in 2014 smiled as he observed, 'The Israeli soldiers have changed. They are more scared of us, or actually they are scared of our cameras. When they shoot at us we can record all of that now.' International accompaniers with such organisations as the Ecumenical Accompaniment Programme in Palestine and Israel (EAPPI) also carry cameras with them to record incidents. Such images become part of the advocacy and lobbying campaigns in their countries of origin.

Such use of electronic media heightens the effectiveness of protective accompaniment insofar as it helps nullify the attempts by the Israeli state to frame its occupation policies and practices through a benign lens of legality and legitimacy. There is an old adage that 'a picture is

---

48 Quoted in Darweish & Rigby, 2015, p. 85.

worth a thousand words', meaning that complex concepts and ideas can be conveyed by a single image – to see a fully-armed soldier or Israeli settler knock an elderly Palestinian to the ground with the butt of a rifle conveys the essence of occupation and what it means to those whose land is occupied and what it does to those involved in the occupation itself.[49] The guarantee that 'someone is watching' can be empowering for activists, and act as a restraint on those with the means to physically intimidate them.

Creating zones of peace

We saw towards the beginning of this chapter how one significant form of constructive action in wartime has been the provision of sanctuary to those whose lives and well-being have been threatened by occupiers and hostile forces.[50] A variant of this form of constructive action has been the creation of peace zones in the midst of violent conflict – when residents living within a specific geographical area declare their space to be 'off-limits' to war and other forms of armed hostility taking place around them.

The origins of the contemporary wave of peace zones is often traced to the Philippines in the 1980s during a period of protracted violent conflict between the guerrilla forces of the New Peoples Army (NPA) and the Philippine military (AFP). In the aftermath of the nonviolent overthrow of the Marcos dictatorship in 1986 the spirit of 'people power' energised civil society agencies in the Philippines (and beyond). In 1986 the residents of Hungduan, in Ifugao Province, seeking to shield themselves from the ongoing violence, managed to persuade the insurgent NPA to withdraw, whilst also succeeding in preventing the government forcers of the AFP from establishing a base in the area. The example set by Hungduan inspired a network of peace NGOs called Coalitions for

49 Brian Martin's writings on 'backfire' are very pertinent to understanding the deterrence dimension of accompaniment. See in particular B. Martin, 'Making accompaniment effective', in Clark, ed., 2009, pp. 93-97.

50 For an interesting overview of the history of the institution of sanctuary, see C. Mitchell, 'The theory and practice of sanctuary', in L. E. Hancock & C. Mitchell, eds., *Zones of peace*, Bloomfield, CT: Kumarian Press, 2007, pp. 1–28.

Peace to develop the concept and parameters of peace zones, leading to a series of formal declaration of peace zones throughout the Philippines.[51]

The history of peace zones in the Philippines and other areas of protracted violent conflict such as Colombia reveals a series of challenges that can frustrate their claims for inviolability. If a community seeking to establish itself as a peace zone is in an area considered by combatants to be of significant strategic significance, then claims of sanctuary are unlikely to be respected. Another problem, and one of the most enduring challenges, is the ongoing need to reassure the armed forces engaged in combat that the residents of the peace zone do not represent a threat to the interests of the antagonists. In particular it is vital that the community representatives can provide credible assurances that they are not shielding any informers, spies, deserters, saboteurs or collaborators in their midst. And, of course, there is always the risk that a peace zone might simply be engulfed by the tide of war flowing over their territory. This was the experience of one of the earliest peace zones to be established in northern Philippines, Sagada in Mount Province, which was established in 1988. In 2013 fighting flared up with the Philippines Airforce launching airstrikes against the NPA, which had become more active in the region, prompting the military to threaten to end their recognition of the area's status as a peace zone because it had become, in their eyes, a staging area for rebel attacks.[52] In such cases it becomes imperative that the residents within the peace zone can convince the armed parties of their absolute neutrality – that they are neither a launch-pad for rebel raids nor a party to state-sponsored counter-insurgency programmes.[53] The bottom-line would seem to be that there has to be shared interest among the armed forces not to target the civilian peace zone.

Oliver Kaplan, in his study of peace zones established during the decades-long Colombian civil war, presents an insightful analysis of one such peace zone where, in paradoxical fashion, the success of the initiative created challenges that threatened its very existence as a zone

---

51 K. Avruch & R.S. Jose, 'Peace zones in the Philippines', in Hancock & Mitchell, eds., 2007, p. 54.

52 'Sagada no longer peace zone', *Philippine Daily Inquirer*, 15 September 2013. Accessible at https://tinyurl.com/7dsntb7r (1 July 2020).

53 Avrich & Jose, in Hancock & Mitchell, eds., 2007, p. 60.

of peace.[54] In 1987 village leaders from communities scattered along the Carare River in the Middle Magdalena Region, a day's drive north of Bogota, met to consider how to respond to the threat of violence facing them. Various armed groups in the region had threatened them with attack unless they evacuated their communities or aligned with the rebels. Rather than seeking weapons with which to protect themselves they decided to appeal to the armed groups to respect the neutrality of their villages. They made contact with the different armed groups which, over time, came to respect the decision.

The village councils proceeded to establish themselves as the Peasant Workers Association of the Carare River (ATCC), taking upon itself the responsibility of managing the delicate ongoing negotiation process that was required in order to maintain the villages as safe-havens for their residents. Over time the ATCC took a lead role in community development as well as providing advance warnings of impending armed activities in the region. Most crucially they developed institutional procedures for addressing allegations made by the militias against particular civilian community members.

According to Kaplan the ensuing decades saw very few instances of militia-related violence involving residents. But around the turn of the century instances of armed violence began to occur. Kaplan explains this by reference to the demographic changes within the territory of the ATCC. The peace and development nurtured during the 1990s attracted migrants to the region, some of them fleeing their home communities after allegations of anti-social behaviour. These newcomers did not share the same collective memory of the older residents and did not manifest the same commitment to the norms that informed the protective work of the ATCC founders. They had not absorbed the ways of life necessary to sustain the neutrality of the villages. Some of them, perhaps more opportunistic than the locals, began to grow coca as a cash crop, which inevitably ensured their entanglement in the web of the illegal drug trade upon which the paramilitaries thrived. When these individuals, having become parties to the conflict, became targets of violence, there was little the ATCC could do to protect them. Another factor was the growing

---

54 See O. Kaplan, *Resisting war: How communities protect themselves*, Cambridge: Cambridge University Press, 2017. Espec. pp. 183-218.

population of youths who had been born around the time of the founding of the ATCC and who reached their early teens at the turn of the century. They were less influenced by the community's neutrality norms and were often paid by armed actors to be informants. As such they became parties to the conflict and consequently potential targets, about which there was little that the ATCC network could do. Kaplan concludes his analysis with the cautionary observation that establishing a zone of peace is not a panacea:

> Along with successes, communities face challenges and
> failures. The ATCC suffered continued pressure and, at times,
> outbursts of violence. As the ATCC and other communities
> have realized, stability requires continuing collective action
> and active management to counteract the self-undermining
> processes triggered by their successes.[55]

Concluding observations

In emphasising the significance of 'continuing collective action and active management' Kaplan identifies two of the key factors that have kept cropping up throughout this chapter in the attempt to identify those conditions necessary for sustained constructive action of different types during wartime. The most significant seem to be:

i.   The existence of clear and legitimate leadership to inspire, set an example and help organise the resistance.

ii. A strong sense of community, social solidarity and collective identity.

iii. Supportive linkages between different institutional levels – local, national and international.

iv. These three factors help underpin a fourth factor - the courage of those people who are prepared to risk their well-being and indeed their lives in the process of combatting nonviolently some of the worst horrors of war and occupation.

At the start of this chapter I referred to my self-doubts about my

---

55   O. Kaplan, 'Protecting civilians in civil war: The institution of the ATCC in Colombia', *Journal of Peace Research*, v. 50, n. 3, 2013, pp. 351-367, p. 366.

level of courage in the face of potentially lethal threats, and how this fed my interest in unarmed resistance in the context of war. It was only later in life that I recognised that fear of lethal violence is a completely normal emotion. Those who have no fear are a bit like those who feel no pain, they can suffer the most hideous injury and trauma. I also learned from a professional soldier in the British army that soldiers perform acts of heroism not for the big issues of 'Queen and country' or 'democracy and freedom' – they do it for their mates, their comrades in arms. As Jacques Semelin observed,

> In a group, and because of it, individuals can accept risks
> that they would not take alone, both because their feelings
> are shared and because belonging to a group usually fosters a
> feeling of solidarity.[56]

Repeatedly as I researched this chapter I was struck by the manner in which so many acts of individual and collective courage emerged out of communities and networks with a strong sense of shared identity and social solidarity. Often this reflected a shared moral stance and value-commitment, whether this was based on religious faith or secular ideological conviction. Whatever the roots of the courage displayed, we need to recognise that for such people fear did not disappear, but it was overcome by more powerful emotions – moral courage and loyalty to one's community and its basic values, the shame of being seen to have failed in one's responsibilities as a moral being. Of course, such emotions are not confined to war-time – most of us have experienced them in aspects of our everyday life. Concluding with a personal note – I am always strengthened by recalling an observation made by an Iranian research student in Peace Studies at Bradford University who had been imprisoned by the Shah's security apparatus. I had asked him how he coped with the threat of torture – he replied: 'You never know what you can withstand until you actually face it!'

---

56 Semelin, 1993, p. 64.

6

CONSTRUCTIVE RESISTANCE TO
ORGANISED CRIME:
THE ANTI-MAFIA STRUGGLE IN SICILY

Introduction

During the 1960s when my interest in radical pacifism was developing I was very dependent on the weekly pacifist publication *Peace News* as an invaluable source of analysis and critique. It was through the pages of *Peace News* that I was introduced to the work and the ideas of such figures as Vinoba Bhave, Cesar Chavez, Lanza Del Vasto, Jayaprakash Narayan, and Danilo Dolci. It was through my reading about Dolci that the seeds of my interest in nonviolent resistance to organised crime were sown. As with the other chapters of this book I make no claims to be presenting anything remotely resembling a comprehensive survey of the field. Rather, my aim is to focus on case studies that have caught my interest, and which I believe can act as a fruitful source of ideas and insight for others.

Before embarking on the case study material I think it is worth reminding ourselves at this juncture about what is actually being referred to when using the term constructive nonviolent direct action. There are two dimensions to be emphasised. Firstly, the term nonviolent direct action refers to nonviolent action against violence that is carried out by activists themselves, rather than delegating or petitioning others to act on their behalf. Secondly, constructive modes of nonviolent direct action generally involve some attempt to create a change in the here-and-now that embodies or prefigures the kind of changes that activists aspire to bring about on a wider scale in the future. We have seen how this approach to creating the future in the here-and-now was a core element of Gandhi's approach to social transformation, and Dolci adapted elements of Gandhi's approach as he sought to address the related challenges he encountered in Sicily – desperate poverty and material hardship, the erosion of any sense of agency on the part of the local population, and the pernicious all-pervading presence of organised crime families and clans in the form of the Mafia.

Dolci's work in Sicily took place in the 1950s and 1960s, after which his influence and public profile faded significantly. But over recent years a nonviolent movement has emerged in Sicily that has sought to challenge and undermine the power of the Mafia by various nonviolent methods, with a particular focus on persuading people to embody in their everyday lives the desired changes necessary to weaken the power of organised crime – *Addiopizzo*.

But before tracing the continuity between Dolci's work and the constructive initiatives of the present day we should first of all attempt to identify the manner in which the tentacles of organised crime contributed to and helped reproduce the social, economic and moral underdevelopment of significant sectors of the island of Sicily over the years.

The nature of the Mafia in Sicily

For the majority of its recorded history the island of Sicily, just across from the toe of Italy, has been ruled by a series of foreign conquerors – the Phoenicians, Romans, Arabs, French and Spanish. In 1861 Sicily became a province of the newly unified Italian state. By the 19th century Sicilian society, particularly in the western regions of the island, was marked by a feudal type social structure with a largely absentee land-owning aristocracy and an impoverished peasantry. Most of the landowners spent their time in Palermo or other urban centres, leasing their properties to middle-men, who filled the power-vacuum left by the absentee landowners and the distant locus of weak state power in Rome. They in turn leased the land to share-cropping peasants, using hired guards to keep everybody in step. One of the outcomes of these processes was a condition of endemic banditry and brigandage, made up of desperate men with nothing to lose, and occasional peasant revolts quashed by the hired gangs of armed men. It was these gangs that were the seed-beds of the Mafia network.

By the latter part of the 19th century the basic framework of the Sicilian Mafia had been established: a loose association of local groups or 'families', each claiming control of criminal activities within a particular village, town or neighbourhood. The Italian sociologist Diego Gambetta likened the Mafia (or *Cosa Nostra*) to a cartel of private protection firms, a network of gangs carrying out their criminal activities under a 'common brand'. Their core activity has been the selling of extra-legal protection to willing or unwilling clients within their territory. The fact that their influence became so deep and long-lasting reflects the weakness of the state in Sicily and the manner in which the Mafia groups influenced and controlled politicians – offering them the 'protection' that came from the Mafia's capacity to force people to vote for candidates they favoured.[1]

In the mid-1920s Mussolini launched a campaign to quash the Sicilian Mafia. Special police units were charged with rounding up suspected members resulting in the incarceration of over 1200. Many fled to the USA. However, with the allied invasion and occupation of Sicily in 1943 the opportunity arose for the Mafia to restore its strength and influence. In the chaos that followed the invasion of Sicily and the collapse of the Fascist regime, the US army command was desperate to find local leaders, who were not communists, upon whom they could rely to take the place of the deposed Fascists. They relied on senior churchmen for advice, and one of those recommended to them was Calogero Vizzini (known as Don Calo) who had been a generous donor to church charities. Accordingly he was appointed mayor of the southern town of Villalba and an Honorary Colonel of the US Army. One of his first actions was to compile a list of suitable candidates for the office of mayor throughout western Sicily. As Norman Lewis has recounted:

> No one seems to have had time to investigate his claim that
> his nominees had suffered for their political ideals, rather
> than for crimes ranging from armed train-robbery to multiple
> homicides. In a matter of days, half the towns in Sicily had

---

1   L. Paoli, *Mafia brotherhoods: Organized crime, Italian style*, Oxford: Oxford University Press, 2003, p.8.

mayors who were either members of the Mafia or were at
least closely associated with it. ... Thus for the first time,
due to the military authorities' complete incomprehension
of the situation in which they found themselves, the Mafia
ruled directly, instead of, as in the past, exerting its influence
indirectly through the control of corrupt pubic officials.[2]

This was the situation that Dolci encountered when he moved to live on
the island in 1952.

Danilo Dolci (1924 – 1997)

Dolci was born near Trieste in 1924. His father was a station-master with
the Italian railways, and so the family moved frequently from one posting
to the next. Driven by what he depicted as 'an instinctive repugnance in
reaction to Fascism', he evaded conscription when he became of age for
military service, eluding the state authorities whilst living in Rome.[3]

After the war he resumed his architectural studies in Milan, but in
1948 he fell under the influence of Don Zeno Saltini, a Catholic priest
and founder of a Christian community caring for orphans and abandoned
children. Dolci spent almost two years living in the community before
leaving in late 1951. His decision was based on his conviction that
working within the community was akin to living 'in a warm nest that was
on the verge of complacency', and he felt compelled to widen his focus
to challenge the wider social injustices and structural inequalities within
Italy.[4] He decided to head for the poorest place he had ever witnessed –
the small Sicilian town of Trappeto, some 40 kilometres west of Palermo,
where his father had once been the station-master.

He arrived in Trappeto late January 1952. Asked by locals why he
had decided to settle amongst them he explained that he wanted to learn
how they managed to endure the grinding poverty of their lives and
thereby help them to change their circumstances. He began by studying

---

2   N. Lewis, *The honoured society: The Sicilian Mafia observed,* London: Eland,
    2003, p. 22.

3   E. R. Chaudhuri, *Planning with the poor: The nonviolent experiment of Danilo
    Dolci in Sicily,* New Delhi: Gandhi Peace Foundation, 1998, p. 6.

4   Chaudhuri, 1998, p. 8.

the nature and the causes of their atrocious conditions. He then borrowed some money, bought a plot of land, and proceeded to erect a refuge for the destitute and homeless – using the labour of locals who volunteered in return for food.

Danilo Dolci

His initiative is reminiscent of the settlement movement that began in the UK and elsewhere in the 1880s, when well-intentioned middle class people established settlement houses in poor urban areas.[5] Their aim was to share the lives of the poor and alleviate the poverty of their living conditions by providing basic community services such as adult education, health care, and cultural activities. In part their interventions were informed by an analysis that later sociologists termed the 'culture of poverty' – a culture which contributed to the perpetuation of the cycle of poverty.[6]

What set Dolci apart from the earlier generation of community development practitioners of the settlement houses was the extent to which he would go in pressing the case for justice for the dispossessed and to generate hope amongst those in despair. Like Gandhi, he prefaced campaigns with detailed first-hand research, talking with people, listening to their stories, detailing their economic conditions, their customs and their superstitions. Much of this material he published – an important means of engaging the interest and the support of networks of people beyond the north-west of Sicily. He used his findings to attempt to shame the authorities into action. When this failed to produce substantive

5   See R. C. Reinders, 'Toynbee Hall and the American Settlement Movement', *Social Service Review*, v. 56, n. 1, March 1982, pp. 39-54.

6   See N. Duvoux, 'The culture of poverty reconsidered', *Books & Ideas*, 6 October 2010. Accessible at https://booksandideas.net/The-Culture-of-Poverty. html (27 September 2021).

changes he was prepared to go further – embarking on numerous fasts as a way to ratchet up the pressure. The effectiveness of the fasts grew as his national and international reputation spread.

He launched his first public fast in October 1952 in the dwelling where a child had died from malnutrition. The intention was to spur the local authorities into action on public works that they had promised to implement in response to representations from Dolci and his associates. The main public work Dolci was concerned with was the construction of a dam on the Jato River which would provide irrigation for 25,000 acres of land around Trappeto and Partinico, thereby providing the local people with the means to live. 'I am going to fast until something is done' Dolci declared. After a week his health deteriorated dramatically and there were fears for his life, with the result that representatives came from Palermo to promise the funds and materials necessary for irrigation work and road repairs to begin.[7]

Campaign for Jato River dam

It was in this campaign for the Jato River dam that Dolci came up against the power of the local Mafia, whose members controlled the existing water sources, a monopoly that was threatened by the dam project. At the time there was still in certain quarters a distorted view of the Mafia as some kind of rural self-help protection service. Dolci, in his writing and public statements, radically challenged such a 'romanticised' vision. For him they were 'parasites by nature … they live on the blood of those who do not belong to their group.'[8] He condemned the unholy alliance that existed between the Mafia and politicians, writing that 'All over Sicily the Mafia exercises an intimidating influence on politics. … They side with those in power, and those in power protect them in their turn.'[9]

Dolci never gave up on his campaign for a dam. In November 1955, as he commenced another fast, he pledged to fast each year for a week until the dam was constructed. Eventually, in 1960, funds for the dam were promised, but once again the Mafia frustrated progress. Engineers

7   D. Dolci, *The outlaws of Partinico*, London: MacGibbon & Kee, 1960, pp. 51-54.
8   Dolci, 1960, p. 36.
9   Dolci, 1960, p. 41.

and contractors were scared off, machinery sabotaged, and local landowners whose land would be submerged were 'advised' to demand crazy levels of compensation. So, in September 1962, Dolci launched another fast, in response to which a cabinet minister in Rome agreed to take responsibility for getting the project moving, the landowners agreed to accept the compensation being offered, and construction work finally began. The dam eventually approached completion in 1968. A cooperative of farmers was organized to manage it, keeping it out of the control of the Mafia, and to this day the dam still provides 'democratic water' to the inhabitants of the surrounding countryside, including the local cultivators.

This practice of Dolci's to launch fasts on behalf of those whose cause he sought to champion reminds me of when I was researching the work of radical young Gandhian activists in Bihar, *Chhatra Yuva Sangharsh Vahini*, in the 1980s.[10] They shared the commitment of Jayaprakash Narayan to 'total revolution', and one of their criticisms of the old-guard Gandhians was their predilection to start fasting on behalf of oppressed groups, rather than organising the oppressed for self-directed activity.

Strike in reverse

Whatever egotism there might have been in Dolci's make-up, as evidenced by his frequent fasting, it was this self-same sense of the importance of the causes that he embraced – and his role in their pursuance – that also led him to initiate a number of constructive modes of activity involving those whose cause he championed. The best known of these was the 'strike in reverse'. An issue would be identified as in need of change in order to improve the living conditions of the oppressed. Volunteers drawn from the ranks of the potential beneficiaries would then be mobilised to carry out the work necessary to bring about the desired change – thereby creating real change on the ground but also drawing public attention to the cause itself, not least by shaming the authorities for their failure to meet their legal and moral responsibilities to its citizens.

---

10 For a report of the work of the Vahini with the landless in Bihar in the 1980s, particularly around Bodghaya, see https://tinyurl.com/y2gxslu7 (24 September 2020). See also A. Rigby in D. Hardiman, ed., 2017, p. 204.

On 30 January 1956 several hundred people gathered together on a beach near Trappeto. They spent the day together fasting, denouncing the illegal fishing practices of the Mafia-controlled trawlers in local waters, and finalising plans for their first strike-in-reverse due to commence 2 February – to repair a country lane near Partinico that had become impassable due to municipal neglect. In a public statement addressed to the President and the Prime Minister of Italy and the political leadership within Sicily the assembled gathering proclaimed:

> We are fasting today not out of despair, but in the hope that we can help make Italy a civilized country. We know that by working in the spirit of generosity, we are on the side of life. Whoever stops us is a murderer. We pay taxes so that we are responsible human beings who can work to make our earth and sea productive for all citizens of this country.
>
> *Signed, 1000 citizens who believe in Article 4 of the Italian Constitution.*[11]

On the day the work to repair the road was due to commence Dolci posted a leaflet articulating the constructive nature of the work upon which they were about to embark:

> Yesterday, fasting and meditating together, we prepared ourselves in conscience for Thursday's celebration of work. No one can stop us from working together in peace. Anyone who tries commits a crime against humanity.
>
> We must be responsible to our families and our laws; so we are initiating a public works project. Using the human and natural resources now wasted in this area, we can make it one of the most beautiful places on earth, a place where we can live together as human beings should.
>
> We are searching in peace for more perfect structural relationships for ourselves and everybody. [12]

In more contemporary parlance we might describe this as a classic, yet constructive, dilemma action.[13] The police, who had been forewarned

---

11 Quoted in Chaudhuri, 1998, pp. 46-47.
12 Quoted in Chaudhuri,1998, pp. 49-50.
13 See M. Sorensen & B. Martin, 'The dilemma action: Analysis of an activist

the day before the reverse strike was due to take place, arrived to arrest the unemployed who were exercising their constitutional right to work by repairing a public road. By their action they highlighted the hypocrisy of a regime that recognised the right to strike but denied the unemployed the right to work, a right enshrined in the Italian constitution. Dolci himself was arrested and charged with causing a public disturbance, trespassing and damaging public property, refusal to disperse when ordered to do so, and resisting arrest. The action and the police response became headline news in Italy and beyond. At the trial on 24 March 1956 a range of luminaries testified on behalf of Dolci and his fellow-accused.[14] As Salvatore Coluccello has observed:

> The 'Dolci case' became a national phenomenon, and intellectuals, writers, journalists and poets came to Palermo in March to witness the trial. Dolci's commitment to the Sicilian cause had attracted the attention of those who were interested in the fate of that part of Italy, which, unlike the Italy of the economic miracle, had experienced a boom of desperation. From then on, the Mafia would no longer be simply an aspect of the centuries-old Southern problem, but became a subject for national political debate ...[15]

Despite the public attention and support generated by the case, the majority of the defendants, including Dolci, were sentenced to 50 days in jail for criminal trespass and disturbance of the peace. Moreover, back in Partinico and Trappeto, away from the public gaze, retribution was swift. Dolci and several of his co-workers were 'advised' to leave whilst the children staying at his centre were rounded up and dispersed to other institutions and the refuge itself closed down on the pretext of insanitary conditions.

---

technique', *Peace and Change*, v. 39, n. 1, January 2014, pp. 73-100.

14 Amongst those who expressed their solidarity were such figures as Alberto Moravia, Ignacio Silone and Carlo Levi. One of the main reasons for the public interest in the case was the impact of Dolci's publications profiling the people amongst whom he lived, their living conditions and the challenges they faced from an unresponsive state and the Mafia crime network.

15 R. Coluccello, *Challenging the Mafia mystique: Cosa Nostra from legitimisation to denunciation*, Basingstoke: Palgrave MacMillan, 2016, p. 151.

Educational work and cultural development

Undeterred Dolci continued to study the lives of those around him, becoming increasingly aware of the dead-hand of a world-view informed by the conviction that misery was inevitable. Consequently he came to the conclusion that one of the most important resources required for local people to start making a difference in their lives was literacy. Hence the decision to establish a library and cultural centre in Partinico where he and his associates developed their own teaching techniques and pedagogy. The centre at Partinico had a wider-ranging remit besides sowing the seeds of democratic action amongst those touched by its activities, it was also to be a study-centre for constructive work - exploring and developing more productive forms of livelihood. It was also a research centre for documenting the realities of Mafia power and the block it placed on constructive socio-economic and cultural change.

Challenging the Sicilian Mafia

Through his own publications Dolci did much to challenge the prevailing view of the Mafia as a problem peculiar to Sicily and its 'southern mentality'. According to Coluccello ,

> Dolci's studies revealed that it was not to a backward mentality that one had to look in order to understand Mafia and banditry. Human degradation depends not only on precise structural conditions – high unemployment and illiteracy levels, economic dependency, or geographic isolation – but, above all, on an unjust and violent state. The image of the Mafia was radically changed by Dolci's studies – it was a 'business' phenomenon, a civic reality, a force which *managed statutory powers*, a consortium which cohabited with the forces of law and order. But it was a force which could and must be weakened.[16]

The rapacious nature of the Mafia businesses in Sicily was highlighted by the protests Dolci helped instigate against the illegal fishing practices of trawlers they controlled and which threatened the livelihood of the local

---

16 Coluccello, 2016, p. 153. (Emphasis in original).

168

fishermen. In his published journals he recorded the incidence of trawlers using illegal nets and explosives in shallow waters within the three-mile limit and drew attention to the manner in which the authorities failed to act and indeed 'condoned the abuse by their inaction'.[17] In a petition signed by 300 locals dated 25 January 1956 it was noted:

> For years now, we have provided the responsible authorities and public opinion with ample evidence of the serious damage done to us, the fishermen of the area, and to the economy of the nation, by the illegal fishing practices of trawlers within the three-mile limit.
>
> It is with sadness and repugnance that we are forced to note the apparent inability of the state to enforce respect for the most elementary and just of its laws. The normal channels of information and pressure, which would have their effect in any civilized state would here seem to be totally powerless.
>
> In our determination to see that the laws are respected we propose to launch a movement that will not be halted until we have ensured the triumph of good sense and honesty. On Monday 30th January we shall begin by fasting for twenty-four hours.[18]

Whilst Dolci's over-riding focus remained the uplift of the citizens of western Sicily, his awareness that most pathways to development were blocked by the Mafia and their political partners led to a growing public stance identifying and challenging their corrosive and pernicious influence. The research and evidence-gathering carried out by Dolci and his close associate Franco Alasia intensified after the establishment in 1963 of the first Italian Anti-Mafia Commission. Indeed, by the mid-1960s they had begun publicly identifying leaders of the governing Christian Democratic Party and accusing them of collusion with organized crime. In 1967 Dolci led an unprecedented six-day march of several hundred people from Partanna to Palermo, a distance of 145 kilometres through some of the main Mafia strongholds on the island. The marchers carried placards calling for the implementation of long-promised irrigation

---

17 Dolci,1960, p. 148.
18 Dolci,1960, p. 247.

dams, re-afforestation plans, geological surveys, new schools, various agricultural projects - and the exclusion of the Mafia from public life.[19]

The fact that Dolci was able to take such a public stance and avoid assassination was due in strong measure to his burgeoning international reputation. Some commentators even referred to him as the 'Gandhi of Sicily', and comparisons were made between him and Martin Luther King and Cesar Chavez. He was the recipient of several prestigious international peace prizes, with support groups formed in a number of countries to help raise funds and spread awareness of his work.

Likening Dolci to Gandhi was not completely fanciful. Like Gandhi the *leitmotif* of Dolci's activities was the uplift of his fellow-citizens by nonviolent means. In pursuing this goal Dolci, like Gandhi, embraced a number of different types of action for change, with a symbiotic relationship between each of them. His documentation of the living conditions and the abuses to which his fellow-citizens were exposed helped inform his protest activities, whilst his constructive work for community development strengthened his standing and legitimacy amongst the impoverished citizens he was seeking to mobilise. There is a further parallel that can be drawn. Gandhi was a firm believer in what can be termed the voluntary servitude theory of power: unjust and repressive regimes and institutional structures depend, in the final analysis, upon the more or less voluntary submission, co-operation and obedience of the subordinate group. This submission was, for Gandhi, the root cause of tyranny. In similar vein Dolci came to the realisation that whilst the persistence of the feudal-like relationships and conditions was bolstered by the octopus-like tentacles of Mafia power that infiltrated so many aspects of life, the power of the Mafia in its turn depended to a significant degree on the complicity of those who bore the burden of this oppressive system. It was the everyday citizens who bolstered the power of the Mafia by participating in the asymmetric protector/patron – client relationship that lay at the heart of the Mafia phenomenon. The Mafia network offered their services in return for support and solidarity from their clients who, amongst other things, were required to promise their political fidelity. This enduring asymmetric relationship was also

---

19 For news-footage of the march, see ScreenOcean, record id. 636086. Accessible at https://reuters.screenocean.com/record/636086 (3 September 2021).

sustained by the Mafia's capacity to inflict violence and instil terror in a cultural milieu that valued *omerta* and failed to acknowledge any degree of social solidarity beyond the parameters of one's family.[20]

In the latter years of his life Dolci's public denunciation of the web of collusion that helped sustain the 'many-tentacled octopus of organised crime' in Sicily faded. One probable reason was exhaustion and 'burn-out', aligned to a declining sense of his own agency in facing the multi-faceted struggle in which he had been engaged. But whilst he might have become dispirited at the enduring strength of the Mafia network in Sicily, there can be little doubt about the significance of his work. In the conclusion to his study of Dolci's work Coluccello has emphasised:

> … his work and studies on the Mafia were fundamental
> despite being hampered at all levels. The results of his
> campaigns and his writings contributed to a change in the idea
> of the Mafia in popular imagination in Italy and elsewhere.
> He courageously revealed the links between the Mafia and
> business interests which dominated Sicily in the 1950s and
> 1960s, and he illustrated how the institutions often protected
> and collaborated with the criminal organisation, leaving Sicily,
> in particular in the area around Palermo, in a condition of near
> feudalism.[21]

Interestingly his legacy is now being rediscovered by a new generation of anti-Mafia campaigners in Sicily, particularly those in the Addiopizzo movement. Addiopizzo means 'goodbye to the 'pizzo' or protection money paid to the Mafia. Businesses such as restaurants and hotels openly display a symbol indicating they are refusing to pay the pizzo to the Mafia, and they are working with local police to apprehend Mafia figures who try to coerce them into paying. The Addiopizzo movement is growing so quickly that it is now mentioned in major guide books on Sicily, and anti-Mafia tours organized by Addiopizzo are becoming increasingly popular. Part of the story told in the tours of Palermo and

---

20 *Omerta* refers to a code of honour that places importance on silence in the face of questioning by authorities. The failure to recognise bonds of solidarity beyond the family is best expressed by the saying *Chi gioca solo non perde mai - Those who play alone never lose* .

21 Coluccello, 2016, p. 177.

the surrounding countryside of western Sicily is the rediscovery of what Danilo Dolci accomplished there in his lifetime.

The Falcone generation

In order to understand the emergence of the Addiopizzo movement in 2004 it is necessary to go back a few years to 1992 and the murder of the two most prominent anti-Mafia prosecutors – Giovanni Falcone and Paulo Borsellino. They had been childhood friends, growing up in a middle class neighbourhood of Palermo. Both qualified as lawyers and eventually became the foremost anti-Mafia prosecutors in Italy. During their formative years the struggle against the Mafia in Italy had taken on a pattern of inertia punctuated by periods of frenzied activity in response to particularly outrageous Mafia atrocities. Thus, in 1963, the Italian public was horrified when seven police and military personnel were killed whilst trying to defuse a car bomb in the Ciaculli suburb of Palermo.[22] Responding to the public outcry the Italian authorities embarked on the first concerted anti-Mafia efforts of the post-war period. Within a matter of weeks over a thousand mafiosi had been arrested and a new Anti-Mafia Commission established.[23] However, such was the level of impunity enjoyed by the Mafia during the 1960s and 1970s, due to its penetration of public institutions and political life, that it was rare for mafiosi to pass more than a few years in prison, after which they would return to their former activities and position in the hierarchy with their financial investments within the legal economy substantially intact.[24]

In the four years between 1979 and 1982 the Sicilian Mafia systematically assassinated the most committed political, institutional and judicial representatives of state power in Sicily – two judges, three politicians, and two police officers.[25] In 1982, however, public feeling was aroused once again by the murder in April of Pio La Torre, the Sicilian secretary of the Italian Communist Party and a life-long opponent of

---

22 The car bomb was targeted at the head of the Ciaculli Mafia family. An anonymous caller had alerted the bomb squad to its presence.

23 This was the fourth such commission established by the Italian state.

24 A. Jamieson, *The anti-Mafia: Italy's fight against organized crime*, NY: St. Martin's Press, 2000, p. 2.

25 Jamieson, 2000, p. 25.

organised crime, and the assassination, a few weeks later, of the newly appointed Prefect of Palermo, General Carlo Dalla Chiesa, his wife and bodyguard on 3 May 1982.[26] Spurred once again into action the anti-Mafia legislation that La Torre had been drafting was passed into law. Known as the Rognoni-La Torre Law which defined the Mafia in the penal code for the first time, it introduced the new crime of 'Mafia conspiracy', and also extended the power of the courts to seize and to confiscate the goods of those belonging to the Mafia conspiracy. [27]

The killings of 1982 took place in the midst of a bloody and murderous struggle for power between competing Mafia families in Sicily, that resulted in over a thousand homicides. One outcome of this unprecedented level of violence was the decision of a small number of senior mafiosi to break with the code of silence (omerta) and collaborate with the state authorities. It was their testimony that was central to the arrest and prosecution of nearly 500 members of the Cosa Nostra. In the 'maxi-trial' which opened in Palermo in February 1986 338 people were found guilty and sentenced, convictions which were finally upheld by the Italian Supreme Court at the end of January 1992. Falcone and Borsellino had taken a prominent part in the proceedings as leading members of the pool of investigating magistrates, and accordingly they became key targets of the vengeful Mafia 'boss of bosses' in Sicily, Toto Riina.[28]

The brutal murders of Falcone and Borsellino triggered an unprecedented outpouring of shock, anger, grief and shame amongst the Italian public. Once again the Italian state had proven its inability (or unwillingness) to protect two of its finest citizens. The fact that Falcone and Borsellino had devoted a significant portion of their time to public education – giving talks at schools and local community groups as well as international seminars and conferences – meant that many Italians experienced their murder as a deep personal loss. There was an immediate upsurge of public

---

26 Dalla Chiesa had been in charge of Italian anti-terrorist activities focused on the Red Brigade. He was appointed to the position in Sicily to strengthen anti-Mafia efforts.

27 Jamieson, 2000, p. 2.

28 Riina was the head of the Corleone clan of the Mafia that had initiated the violence against other Mafia families in order to establish their dominance. See S. Lupo, *History of the Mafia*, NY: Columbia University Press, 2011, p. 257.

Poster in Palermo ('A south abandoned to the mafia'), with image of Falcone & Borsellino

expressions of protest and remorse. In Palermo women hung sheets with anti-Mafia slogans from their balconies. The Association of Sicilian Women against the Mafia, founded in 1982 by the widow of a murdered judge, organised a three-day vigil and fast in one of Palermo's central squares, proclaiming 'We are fasting because we are hungry for justice'.[29] Throughout the country, and especially in the south, new civic and community associations sprang up, driven by a determination to challenge the manner in which so many sectors of Italian society were prepared to cohabit with gross criminality, violence and corruption. Such a level of popular mobilisation against organised crime was unprecedented in Italy, and marked an important break with tradition – particularly in the south.

In February 1993 Luigi Ciotti, a Roman Catholic priest from Turin, collaborated with the Palermo-based Sicilian Documentation Centre and two other centres in publishing the first issue of a monthly magazine -*Narcomafie*.[30] The aim of the publication, according to Father Ciotti,

29 Jamieson, 2000, p. 152.

30 The Sicilian Documentation Centre was established in 1977 as the first anti-Mafia research centre. It played a key role in bringing to justice the murderers of Giuseppe 'Peppino' Impastato, an anti-Mafia activist assassinated by the Mafia in May 1978. In April 2002 Gaetano Badalamenti, the head of the local Mafia family, was given a life sentence for ordering Impastato's murder.

was to challenge the culture of mafiosity which tolerates and connives with criminality, the psychology of dependence whereby what would normally be considered basic human and civil rights come to be viewed as favours to be granted or withheld, according to the dictates of criminal gangs and their corrupt associates.[31]

Constructive resistance against the Mafia – agricultural cooperatives

In 1995 Father Ciotti established the non-governmental organisation *Libera* to empower and help coordinate the activities of the hundreds of anti-Mafia groups and associations that had come into existence.[32] *Libera*'s first major initiative was to launch a petition calling on the Italian parliament to pass a law allowing properties confiscated from people associated with organised crime to be made available for socially useful purposes, demanding 'the Mafia restitute what was unjustly usurped'. *Libera*'s activism was successful and the law passed through parliament in March 1996. One consequence has been that in the past few years, not-for-profit organisations and other groups have taken over villas, office accommodation, and agricultural land.

In Italy non-profit associations and cooperatives have a long history, but in 1991 a new type of cooperative was authorised – social cooperatives. By 2005 it has been estimated there were 7,400 social cooperatives, with more than 260,000 members, nearly 250,000 paid workers and over 34,000 volunteers.[33] This growth can be attributed to the erosion of the welfare state under the neoliberal regimes pursued by European states (and beyond) that has left huge gaps in the provision of basic social services that free-market capitalism has had minimal interest in filling. As a result there has been a growth in what might be called the not-for-profit third sector – voluntary associations and different forms of social

31 Jamieson, 2000, p. 143.
32 See https://www.*Libera*terra.it/en/world-*Libera*-terra/ (30 October 2020). *Libera* claims to be involved in helping coordinate the activities of more than 1600 civil society groups (including schools).
33 'Fears for future of social cooperatives in Italy', *Pioneers Post*, 31 March 2020. Accessible at https://tinyurl.com/y2ghtzx6 (3 September 2021).

enterprise that have emerged to provide the services necessary to meet citizens' basic needs. In Italy this growth has taken the institutional form of social cooperatives.[34] Many of the social cooperatives are involved in caring provision for the elderly and vulnerable sections of the population, but a significant number are also engaged in social entrepreneurship - pursuing social, cultural or environmental change through some kind of business activity intended to be of benefit to the wider society.

A number of these have been the recipients of confiscated Mafia land which they have begun to develop as agricultural cooperatives. The process represents an interesting collaboration between the state, civil society organisations and local communities. Once a mafioso is convicted, their assets, including property rights, are handed over to the Ministry for Internal Affairs. Having identified the location of the properties the Ministry transfers them to the relevant municipalities. They are then offered for tender to not-for-profit cooperatives and similar organisations. The properties are leased under renewable contracts valid for twenty years or more at a 'pepper-corn rent'. In this way the new lease-holders have full rights to use the properties whilst the formal ownership continues to reside with the state. *Libera*, through its agricultural development arm *Libera Terra* (Freed land) has played an important role in this process, acting as a consultant helping local people form a cooperative to take over the lease of confiscated land and associated assets such as tractors and farm equipment. In other cases *Libera Terra* can take a more hands-on role by providing the start-up funding, specialist advice and logistical support. According to Theodoros Rakopoulos the resultant social enterprises have come to be viewed throughout Italy as the most significant symbol of the anti-Mafia movement.[35] The first cooperative set up in Sicily near San Guiseppe Jato in 2001 was named after Placido Rizzotto, the socialist trade union leader from Corleone who was assassinated by the Mafia in 1948. Other victims of Mafia violence have been memorialised in the names of other cooperatives, such as Coop. Pio La Torre in San Guiseppe

---

34 A. Thomas, 'The rise of social cooperatives in Italy', *Voluntas: International journal of voluntary and non-profit organizations*, v.15, n. 3, September 2004, pp. 243-263.

35 T. Rakopoulos, *From clans to co-ops: Confiscated Mafia land in Sicily*, New York: Berghahn, 2018, p. 9.

Jato and Coop. Rosario Livatino near Naro in the Agrigento Province of Sicily.[36]

By 2010 Libera Terra was involved in the reclamation of over 2000 acres of confiscated land in western Sicily. Restoring citrus groves, using organic methods to cultivate olives, wheat, grapes and other crops. In 2008 *Libera Terra Mediterraneo* was established to work with the anti-Mafia agricultural cooperatives in the marketing of their produce. By 2015 cooperative products distributed to shops throughout Italy and beyond were generating a turnover in excess of £6 million.[37] Some of the products bear the name of a Mafia victim, helping to create a story behind the food and possibly even an occasion for moral reflection.

Historically agriculture has been the life-blood of the Sicilian Mafia and it continues to be a major channel of criminal activity. According to a recent report the organised crime syndicates have strengthened their claws in the production, transport, distribution and sale of food and related agricultural products – generating around 24.5 billion euros in business in the Italian agriculture sector in 2018.[38] This has meant not only higher prices for consumers but increased health risks due to tampering with ingredients and the consequent adulteration of products. In the development of cooperatives that seek to respect not only the dignity of the workers but also the sustainability of the environment and the well-being of consumers, agricultural cooperatives and associated social enterprises are presenting a small yet significant alternative to the models perpetuated by the organised crime networks. In the process they are feeding into a wider citizens' socio-cultural movement that is questioning not only the historic collaboration between corrupt officials and organised crime, but also the complicity of everyday folk who have for generations accepted the moral corruption and perversion of so many aspects of mundane life occasioned by their own acceptance of the Mafia.

---

36 Rosario Livatino was an Italian magistrate who was killed by the Cosa Nostra on 21 September 1990.

37 'Libera Terra: Sicily's anti-Mafia farms', *BBC Food Programme*, 7 September 2015. Accessible at https://www.bbc.co.uk/programmes/b068s4qs (17 November 2020).

38 Figures from *Coldiretti* (National Confederation of Growers), 19 February 2019. Accessible at https://tinyurl.com/328huax9 (17 November 2020).

Logo of Libera

In this sense the reclamation of confiscated agricultural land has entailed a type of purificatory constructive action, a cleansing of impurities to create something new. As one of the people working with *Libera Terra* expressed it, 'To be organic is a form of respect. The idea is being kind to the soil itself, to start anew – to take symbolic and real poisons from the soil itself.'[39]

One of the poisons that has been integral to the way of life permeated by organised crime in Sicily and elsewhere has been 'pizzo' – extortion, the payment of protection money demanded from shopkeepers and business owners.

Addiopizzo

Addiopizzo is a grassroots movement set up by a group of friends in 2004. Having graduated from Palermo University, they decided to set up a bar as a place where young people of their generation could enjoy themselves. Working on their business plan they realised that if they were successful in establishing their enterprise they would face the dilemma of whether or

not to pay the local Cosa Nostra clans the *pizzo* - the 'protection tax' levied on local businesses by the Mafia.

Pizzo in Sicilian dialect refers to the beak of a bird, and in Mafia usage draws on the imagery of a bird getting its beak wet as it moves from one source of water and nectar to another, analogous to the manner the Mafia has

39 'The pizza connection: Fighting the Mafia through food', *NPR*, 6. May 2014. Accessible at https://tinyurl.com/y29y9jrl (20 November 2020).

satisfied its need for cash by dipping its beak into the pockets of all kinds of businesses, demanding regular payments of 'protection money'. An authoritative survey in 2008 calculated that the pizzo racket was generating 15 billion euros a year, while some 80 percent of all businesses in Palermo habitually paid up to avoid trouble.[40] From the Mafia's point of view such racketeering provides a regular flow of cash to pay salaries and cover associated costs such as medical treatment and vehicles, and providing economic support for imprisoned Mafia members'

Libera retail outlet in Palermo

families. Individual monthly payments from small retailers and street-vendors might seem quite modest for protection against theft and property damage. [41] But there is always the likelihood that the monthly demands are raised over time as the Mafia tightens its grip, with businesses required to purchase products and services from Mafia-controlled suppliers and culminating in some cases with the Mafia taking over a legal company that is then used for money laundering. However, according to students of the Cosa Nostra, in Sicily the financial returns relating to the pizzo are not the Mafia's principal interest. It is more important to make everybody within a specific territory pay as a sign of subordination to the Mafia family and to establish a territorial dominance.[42] As one factory-owner

40 P. Jacobson, 'Addiopizzo: The grassroots campaign making life hell for the Sicilian Mafia', *Newsweek*, 17 September 2014.

41 In 2008 it was estimated that the average monthly pizzo payment in Palermo was 600 euros, with street vendors paying from 50 to 100 euros a month, a neighbourhood bread store 150-250 euros, a simple clothing store 250 euros and a local mini-mart 500 euros. (Figures taken from F. D'Emilio, 'Sicilians decide Mafia protection an offer they can refuse', *Lawrence Journal-World*, 14 January 2008).

42 C. Gunnarson, 'Changing the game: Addiopizzo's mobilisation against

observed, 'In their system, it's not important how much you pay. It's important that you pay. It's a form of submission.'[43]

Facing up to the reality of extortion the young friends abandoned their business venture and agreed to turn their undoubted entrepreneurial flair to combatting the pizzo. As one of their number recalled, 'We budgeted for rent, utilities and insurance, but then somebody said, "What about the pizzo?" That tells you how deeply the culture of acquiescence to extortion had become embedded in Sicily. …. We Sicilians place a high value on personal dignity … but how could we square that with ignoring the Mafia's grip on our island?'[44]

They set about designing and printing stickers, designed to look like traditional black Sicilian obituary notices, carrying the message: 'An entire people that pays pizzo is a people without dignity.' On the night of 28 June 2004 they fly-posted the stickers all over central Palermo. People awoke to see the slogan questioning their moral worth. The provocative message struck some responsive chords – apparently on the second night of fly-posting a police squad car pulled up, 'Keep up the good work' was their encouraging observation![45]

The symbolic protest evolved into a campaign to persuade businesses to declare publicly that they refused to pay pizzo. But take-up was slow. People in Palermo were familiar with the fate of Libero Grassi, the clothing manufacturer who, in 1991, publicly declared that he refused to pay the pizzo that was being demanded, and reported his would-be extortioners to the police. Far from being supported by the Palermo business community he was ostracised and accused of damaging the image of the Palermo business world.[46] Despite increasing threats Grassi

racketeering in Palermo', *European Review of Organised Crime* v.1, n.1, 2014 , pp. 39-77, p. 44.

43 Quoted in J. Hammer, 'In Sicily defying the Mafia', *Smithsonian Magazine,* October 2010.

44 Quoted in Jacobson, 2014.

45 A. Humphries, 'Beating the Mafia at their own game', *National Post*, 24. January 2013. Accessible at https://tinyurl.com/y5lpbegs (20 November 2020).

46 In April 1991 a Sicilian judge acquitted some prominent businessmen of collusion with the Mafia through the payment of pizzo on the grounds that they had no choice if they were to continue to function without harassment.

continued to appear in the media condemning the complicity of those who acceded to the demands of the extortioners. He stated:

> My colleagues have begun to attack me, saying that one should not wash dirty clothes in public. But in the meantime they continue to put up with it, because I know they all pay. In my opinion being intimidated and being collusive is the same thing. ... I think that if everyone was ready to collaborate with the police and *carabinieri*, to report and to name names, this racketeering would not last long. I myself have had eight people arrested. If 200 businessmen talked, 1600 mafiosi would be in handcuffs. Don't you think we would have won?[47]

On the morning of 29 August 1991 Grassi was shot three times in the head as he walked from his home to his car.[48] A plaque now marks the spot where he was killed, installed by his family it reads, 'Here was murdered Libero Grassi, entrepreneur, brave man, killed by the Mafia, by the *omertà* of the associations of industrialists, by the indifference of parties and absence of the state.' Grassi's widow, Pina, was one of the first to actively support Addiopizzo. Others whose lives had been scarred by Mafia violence joined her, including the brother of the murdered anti-Mafia activist Peppino Impastato and the younger sister of the murdered prosecutor Paulo Borsellino.

One of the lessons anti-Mafia activists have to take to heart is that there is safety in numbers – it is the isolated resisters such as Libero Grassi who are more likely to be picked off. So, in order to encourage businesses to come on board, in 2005 the group published the names of 3500 people who pledged to support Mafia-free shops. Then, in 2006, possibly emboldened by the arrest in April 2006 of the Mafia leader Bernado Provenzano, who had been a fugitive for over thirty years, Addiopizzo held its first public rally at which a hundred shop-owners affirmed their refusal to pay protection money.[49] The movement received a boost the

---

See Jamieson, 2000, p. 36.

47 Interview, 4 April 1991. Quoted in Jamieson, 2000, p. 36.

48 It was not until October 2006 that the head of the local Mafia family and his son were charged with Grassi's murder and sentenced.

49 In 2006 a parallel network, Addiopizzo Catania, was established in Sicily's second largest city.

following year when *Confindustria*, Italy's industrialists' confederation, threatened to expel members who paid protection money.

The participation of a business in Addiopizzo's campaign entails a very public declaration of the stance being taken, a radical departure from the traditional silence that has been a fundamental part of the culture of mafiosity. The details of businesses who have joined are publicised in leaflets, tourist maps, the internet and on an Addiopizzo app. They are asked to display the Addiopizzo symbol in a prominent position on their shop-front, as a way of attracting customers and publicising the movement with which the business is aligned.

In 2008 the movement took another step forward with the opening of the first store in Palermo devoted entirely to products and produce from pizzo-free businesses. The initiative was supported by *Libero Futuro*, an association formed in 2007 to support businesses in Palermo refusing to pay protection money to the Mafia.[50] At the formal opening of the store one of the founders of *Libero Futuro* remarked, 'The idea of opening this shop is as delicious as it is simple. All you need to do is introduce consumers to producers, neither of whom want to pay the pizzo, and bring about a common bond, a more ethical consumption and a client loyalty which is absolutely guaranteed,'[51]

But refusing to pay protection money to local Mafia families still incurs risks. In the summer of 2007 the warehouse of Rodolfo Guajana's company, a wholesaler for hardware stores across Sicily since 1875, was torched after he had ignored various threats designed to pressure him into paying the pizzo. However, in contrast to the isolation experienced by Libero Grassi in 1991, Addiopizzo mobilised a campaign of public solidarity, the trade associations stood by him and the local municipality found him a new warehouse. It was evidence of a new and more resilient stance by the public and institutions against the extortion rackets run by the local Mafia.

---

50 *Libero Futuro* was established by Addiopizzo, its name commemorates Libero Grassi.

51 Quoted in AFP report, 'To the Mafia's horror pizzo-free shop opens Palermo doors', 14 March 2008. Accessible at https://tinyurl.com/y6s7dqlj (27 November 2020).

As part of their efforts to undermine the culture of mafiosity, the acceptance of co-existence with illegality in all its forms, and promote a culture of legality, Addiopizzo has placed great emphasis on education, working with schools, universities and other groups. This work has embraced not just classroom-based presentations but more participatory educational tools such as tours of significant sites in the history of the anti-Mafia struggle in Sicily, including visits to agricultural cooperatives working on confiscated Mafia land and summer camps. In 2009 Addiopizzo set up its own travel agency to offer pizzo-free excursions, study trips and holidays to visitors – 'ethical tourism for those who say NO to the Mafia' as their website proclaims.[52] Amongst the core features of the tours are escorted visits to agricultural cooperatives and other social enterprises associated with the broader anti-Mafia movement. The profits from the enterprise in ethical tourism go to support the Addiopizzo campaigns and other centres established over the years to strengthen the anti-Mafia struggle.

One of the main initiatives that receives financial support from the ethical tourism enterprise is the community development work that Addiopizzo commenced in 2017 with the children of the Piazza Magione neighbourhood of Palermo.[53] The square is located in the Kalsa district of the city, a quarter where the presence of the Mafia is particularly marked. The local population is of mixed ethnicity with high rates of poverty, unemployment and other indices of socio-economic marginalisation. It also happens to be close to the neighbourhood where Giovanni Falcone and Paulo Borsellino grew up. Launched by Addiopizzo in association with the municipality and local community organisations the initiative focuses primarily on local children, using the medium of sporting activities as a means to engender socio-cultural change. It is based on the premise that in order to undermine the power of the Mafia it is not sufficient to accompany and encourage traders and entrepreneurs to refuse to accede to the extortion demands of the Mafia clans. Of equal significance is the need to work to transform the socio-economic and cultural conditions

---

52 Accessible at https://www.addiopizzotravel.it/?sort=0 (27 November 2020).

53 For information about the symbolic significance of the Piazza Magione, see https://tinyurl.com/y4vwenwg (30 November 2020).

prevalent in neighbourhoods where the poverty and social decay feeds into a culture of illegality upon which the power of the Mafia feeds.[54]

Addiopizzo and Dolci – the linkage

There is something about the trajectory along which the focus of Addiopizzo's activities has developed that invites comparison with the work of Danilo Dolci. First off, their original sticker accusing the citizens of Palermo of lacking in dignity due to their preparedness to tolerate the payment of pizzo – this resonates with Dolci's conviction that it was the complicity of everyday folk which ensured the persistence of the Mafia's pernicious influence. It is also relevant to note that Dolci started his work trying to organise the local peasants and fishermen for collective action to change the conditions under which they lived. After appeals and petitions to state authorities proved futile he launched the 'reverse strike', mobilising local people to effect the change they sought by means of their own direct action – the municipality, under the domination of the Mafia, will not repair the road, so we must do it ourselves! In comparable fashion Addiopizzo's initial campaign focused on getting traders to resist extortion demands – persuading shop-owners and other businesses to refuse to pay the pizzo, thereby effecting by their own actions changes in the here-and-now which prefigure the hoped-for future when all business life can take place without extortion. A third parallel relates to the manner in which Addiopizzo has broadened its scope to encompass constructive work in a neglected neighbourhood of Palermo, seeking to transform the prevailing culture of mafiosity, particularly amongst the young, by means of sport and other activities as a vehicle for the participants to appreciate values such as respect, solidarity, friendship and integration. In similar vein Dolci came to focus much of his energy on educational activities at his centre in Partinico, having come to the realisation that if change was to be realised it required a change in the outlook of the local people with their fatalistic acceptance that 'nothing can be done'.

Despite the clear continuity between the work of Dolci and the contemporary movements of Addiopizzo and Libera there are some

---

54 'Street education: Social inclusion in Piazza Magione', *Addiopizzo Committee*. Accessible at https://tinyurl.com/y69fhskp (29 November 2020).

manifest contrasts. Dolci's initiatives were to a significant degree dependent on his leadership, his charisma, his reputation and international standing. Furthermore, as noted earlier in this chapter, many of the initiatives revolved around Dolci. Although he depended heavily on a number of close associates it was he who would launch the individual fasts intended to sway public opinion and influence the stance of the authorities. By contrast Addiopizzo is typical of contemporary leaderless social movements, captured perhaps by the slogan 'No leaders but a leading idea', as evidenced by its self-portrayal on its website:

> Addiopizzo is an open, fluid and dynamic movement, that acts from below and presents itself as a spokesman of a 'cultural revolution' against the mafia. It is constituted by all the women and men, the girls and the boys, the shopkeepers and the customers who recognize themselves in the sentence 'A whole people that pays the pizzo is a people without dignity'. ... Addiopizzo is also an association of volunteers.[55]

Both have been initiatives of their time. In the 1950s when Dolci started his work there was an intimate linkage between the Mafia, politicians and associated state institutions and law-enforcement agencies. But over recent decades there has been a significant shift in government behaviour and the overall civic culture in Italy, and Addiopizzo enjoys healthy collaborative relationships with civic and non-governmental institutions.

Concluding observations

Building to some extent on the example of Dolci and others, the contemporary generation of anti-Mafia activists have made some remarkable progress. The growth in agricultural cooperatives and other social enterprises has been noteworthy, as has the campaign initiated by Addiopizzo which has received considerable global coverage. Yet, despite the undoubted significance of their achievements, it has to be recognised that their impact on the functioning of organised crime in Italy has been limited. According to a report presented by the interior

---

55 Accessed at https://www.addiopizzo.org/index.php/who-we-are/ (28 November 2020). The movement in Palermo has a number of recognised spokespersons, a secretariat and a 'committee' or assembly of around 30 activists.

minister to the Italian parliament's Anti-Mafia Commission in October 2019 the organised crime networks might have become less high-profile, but they continued to infiltrate almost every area of business, including healthcare, renewable energy, waste management and tourism, while maintaining a hand in their more traditional construction sector. Gangs have also penetrated the food chain, seizing control of farms, controlling distribution and counterfeiting food products, including cheese, wine and olive oil. Their growth beyond Italy has also remained strong, especially in Europe and South America.[56]

Furthermore, research by Carina Gunnarson would seem to indicate that the impact of Addiopizzo within Palermo itself is uneven. According to Gunnarson, writing in 2014, the majority of members of the campaign, firms and consumers, are located in the central commercial areas of Palermo, with significantly lower participation outside the main tourist areas. In the more peripheral areas, where unemployment rates are higher and educational attainments lower, it is reportedly more risky to refuse to pay, in part at least because there are fewer members and active supporters of Addiopizzo.[57] Despite this, Gunnarson concludes that the real significance of Addiopizzo's mobilisation against protection money is as a manifestation of 'a long-term cultural change involving increased demands from citizens in Palermo to restrain the influence of organised crime'.[58] Furthermore there is evidence that the constructive resistance and related activities of Addiopizzo in Sicily has resonated further afield. Similar movements have emerged in other regions of Italy blighted by the presence of organised crime networks such as the 'Ndrangheta in Calabria and the Camorra in the region of Campania. In addition researchers and policy-makers in other parts of the world have drawn inspiration and insight from the work of Addiopizzo.

Guillermo Vazquez, a senior analyst with the Global Initiative Against Transnational Organized Crime, whilst acknowledging the particularities of the Sicilian context within which Addiopizzo has grown,

---

56 A. Giuffrida, 'Italy mafia networks are more complex and powerful, says minister', *The Guardian*, 30 October 2019. Accessed at https://tinyurl.com/y5acgkl4 (30 November 2020).

57 Gunnarson, 2014, p.45.

58 Gunnarson, 2014, p. 68.

has argued that there are lessons to be drawn which are relevant to those taking a stance against extortion in Central American countries such as Guatemala, El Salvador and Honduras.[59] From his studies Vazquez has compiled a list of nine recommendations relevant to those seeking to build resilience to organised crime gangs in Central America.

1. *Break the silence*: As Addiopizzo did with its stickers back in 2004 – bring the issue out into the open.

2. *Change the perspective*: Whilst businesses and their customers can be an integral component in the extortion problem, with changes of awareness and culture they can become part of the solution.

3. *Create a network:* Addiopizzo has created a network of businesses supported by thousands of people committed to 'critical consumption', a network that can ensure a level of mutual solidarity and support.

4. *Overcome victim isolation:* Drawing on the lessons from the fate of Libero Grassi, Addiopizzo has been able to generate a level of community support that can act as a protective shield for those facing retaliation from organised crime.

5. *Declare your membership*: Addiopizzo stickers and logos displayed prominently on shop-fronts can be a defensive tool against extortion.[60]

6. *Boost trust:* Establish good working relationships with law-enforcement agencies so that you can present credible assurances to those threatened by the gangs that they will be supported.

7. *Leverage economic impact:* Try to increase the social and economic impact of the ethical consumerism campaigns, in the

---

59 G. Vazquez, 'Saying no to extortion in Central America: Lessons learnt from Italy', *Global Initiative Network Against Transnational Organized Crime*, 2020. Accessible at https://tinyurl.com/yybv2wdu (29 November 2020).

60 There is evidence that Mafia families in Palermo do not demand pizzo from Addiopizzo stores because they are sure they will not be paid and they fear being arrested. (Humphreys, 2014)

same manner as Addiopizzo expanded its activities to encompass ethical tourism

8. *Develop a social approach:* Economic and socially depressed neighbourhoods are fertile ground for mafia recruitment, hence the involvement of Addiopizzo in constructive social inclusion activities in the Piazza Magone neighbourhood.

9. *Educate for change*: Before it developed its informal educational activities in Piazza Magone Addiopizzo had developed a significant outreach into schools and colleges in the Palermo region, educating the younger generations about extortion and its costs.

Interesting and insightful as such recommendations are, they do fail to convey what I feel to be one of the key drivers of Addiopizzo's growth – the energy, vitality and enthusiasm of its predominantly young activists and volunteers. What comes across strongly talking with Addiopizzo activists is their deep sense that the penetration of so many dimensions of life in Sicily by the Mafia robs them of their dignity as citizens and human beings, which they are determined to reclaim – despite the risks of retaliation they might face as a consequence.[61] This impression is informed by my own experiences in 2014 when I accompanied my partner Carol Rank and her colleague Rino Coluccello on a study tour to Sicily organised by Rino. During the visit I kept thinking about these young people, active in a movement for change, facing significant risk of violent and costly retaliation by those whose power they sought to undermine. And yet they were so full of the joy of life – and the joy of the struggle. And here, I believe, is one of the fundamental strengths of constructive forms of resistance. Activities such as reverse strikes, establishing social cooperatives, community development, and establishing extortion-free networks are ways of undermining the power of organised crime gangs without provoking them into violent modes of retaliation. The focus is

---

61 It is interesting to note that the uprisings across much of North Africa and the Middle East in 2011, collectively referred to as the 'Arab Spring', were driven to a significant degree by the shared desire of dispossessed citizens seeking respect, asserting their dignity. See F. Fukuyama, 'The drive for dignity', *Foreign Policy*, 12 January 2012.

on changing patterns of action and relationships amongst those bearing the cost of the extortionists, rather than a direct show of strength in direct challenges to the dominance of the gangs. More like the erosive power of drips of water rather than dramatic combat, it is a form of resistance that people can integrate into their daily lives at levels of risk with which they can feel comfortable, and as such can develop the degree of sustainability necessary for significant cultural change.

7

CONSTRUCTIVE ACTION
IN THE SPHERE OF PRODUCTION

Introduction

The aim of this chapter is to introduce the reader to some different modes of constructive action for change within the sphere of production. As with the previous chapters no claim is made to the comprehensiveness of the coverage – the aim is to provide a 'taster' of the range of initiatives that I have come across over the years.

Most of us are familiar with the standard critiques of conventional market economies – the well-being of employees and other local stakeholders are subordinated to the drive to maximise financial returns for shareholders, wealth created in one locality is expropriated to benefit remote shareholders and financial institutions, whilst social and environmental costs are subordinated to the over-riding search for financial profit. Furthermore, the model spreads from private industry to infiltrate our public institutions and even our consciousness – prioritising private gain over the common good becomes the accepted norm, creating fractures and division instead of cooperative endeavour.

For Marxists the sphere of production has always been seen as the epicentre of the forces of societal transformation. In their view it is the mode of production, and the relationship to the means of production, that determines the class structure within society, and hence the dynamics of class conflict – the motor of societal transformation. The problem with this type of scientific socialist paradigm is that the agents of change are forewarned that they will have to wait until after the 'Revolution' before they will get to experience the utopian society that is promised. This is the chasm which can only be bridged by a special form of what Martin Buber termed 'Marxist utopics':

> ... a chasm between, on the one side, the transformation to
> be consummated sometime in the future – no one knows how
> long after the final victory in the Revolution – and, on the
> other, the road to the Revolution and beyond it, which road is
> characterized by a far-reaching centralization that permits no
> individual features and no individual initiative. Uniformity as
> a means is to change miraculously into multiplicity as an end;
> compulsion into freedom.[1]

Buber contrasted this approach with those who believe in a revolutionary
continuity between means and end, sowing seeds in the here and now
that might come to fulfilment in the future. This is the approach that has
been characterised in this book as constructive nonviolent direct action
for change. The most typical form this mode of action has taken in the
economic sphere of production and distribution of goods and services
has been some form of cooperative activity.

The peak periods for such initiatives always take place within a wider
context of social unrest, disquiet and aspirations for change. There seem
to be four main types of situations within which cooperative modes of
production and distribution emerge. One category involves the creation
of cooperative approaches to generating employment as one of a broader
range of activities pursued by a social movement for change. The example
that comes to mind is the establishment of social cooperatives in Sicily
(and other areas of Italy) by Libera Terra, utilising the properties and
resources confiscated from Mafiosi. This material has been covered in the
previous chapter, so the focus in this chapter will be on the other contexts
within which cooperative modes of production have been created.

i.   *Developing cooperative modes of production in the midst of
      politically driven civil strife and armed conflict.*
      In such circumstances certain groups may seek to use the space
      available to them to create cooperatives as 'advance posts' of the
      new society for which they are struggling. The workers councils
      and agricultural cooperatives created in certain areas of Spain
      during the period of the Civil War (1936-9) is an example

---

1   M. Buber, 1949, p.13.

of this type of constructive action in the midst of collective violence.

ii. *Initiatives to create employment in order to relieve economic hardship and create new patterns of working relationships.*
During periods of unemployment, poverty and associated socio-economic hardship there can be a growth of interest in developing workers cooperatives as a means of generating employment opportunities and sources of income for affected populations. The best known of this type of initiative is the Spanish network of workers cooperatives centred on Mondragon in the Basque region of Spain.

iii. *Initiatives that take place as part of a wider vision of societal and cultural transformation.*
It was this type of wider context that informed the growth of interest in the conversion of arms manufacturing to the production of socially-useful products during the 1970s. It was also a period when there was an upsurge in the number of worker cooperatives established in the UK and elsewhere as part of a broader concern with exploring alternatives to the established order.

iv. *A residual category relates to the conversion of established companies into some form of cooperative enterprise as a consequence of the value-commitment of the owners.*
An example of this type of process is the chemical company Scott Bader founded in England in 1920 by Ernest Bader who, in 1951, made the radical decision to place the business on a more ethical footing by creating the Scott Bader Commonwealth, based on the principle of common-ownership.

Cooperation in the midst of war:
Workers collectives in the Spanish Civil War

In February 1936 the left-leaning Popular Front won the general election in Spain that took place during a period of mounting tension and conflict between the supporters of the government and the conservative and Falangist opposition groupings. In July 1936 a group of military generals declared their opposition to the government, thereby initiating a civil war between the Republicans and the insurgent Nationalists. By 1 April 1939 General Franco entered Madrid and declared victory. The war aroused fierce passions around the world, symbolising the conflict between democracy and fascism that was becoming more intense throughout the 1930s, culminating in the Second World War. Within the Republican camp itself there developed a disastrous conflict between the different leftist factions, with the Communist Party of Spain (PCE) engaging in an intense struggle to undermine the position of its more libertarian leftist rivals. This partisanship permeated the historical treatment of the Civil War – particularly in the analysis of the processes of collectivisation that took place within Republican-held territory. Contemporaries who were sympathetic to anarchism and hostile to Communism authored the first accounts of workers' and peasants' collectives, which were dismissed as deeply biased by those more sympathetic to the communists.

My brother-in-law grew up in Girona, in the Catalan region of north-eastern Spain. His father had been a printer and active in the Republican struggle of the Civil War as a member of the POUM, a revolutionary communist party that was strongly critical of the Stalinist PCE. With the defeat of the Republicans he was one of those who crossed the border to France as a political refugee, he did not return to Spain for 14 years. Enric, my brother-in-law, told me of how his mother would take him on a north-bound train from Girona, at the last stop before the border she would leave the young boy on the train, and his father would meet him at the first station in France. Hearing such family stories aroused my fascination with this period of Spanish history. In particular I was intrigued by the efforts of the Spanish anarchists and libertarian socialists to implement workers control, particularly in Catalonia, and the creation of agricultural collectives in parts of Aragon and elsewhere.

At that time, during the 1970s, I was reading publications from *Freedom Press*, the London-based anarchist publishers. I recall reading sources like Gaston Leval's *Collectives in the Spanish revolution* and sections of Noam Chomsky's *American power and the new mandarins*.[2] The impression I formed back then was that the anarchists had actively sought to construct nuclei of a new libertarian social order within the Republican controlled territory. These examples of propaganda by the deed writ large, creating the new society by making it happen in the here-and-now – constructive revolutionary activity if you like – had been fatally weakened by the republican government's prioritisation of fighting the war over societal transformation. The final blow to the revolutionary activities was dealt by the Soviet-backed Spanish communists who consolidated their power within the government and proceeded to liquidate their political rivals and dismantle the collectives. Since then I have come across research that has produced a rather more nuanced overview of this thread of constructive initiatives during the Civil War.[3]

In Barcelona the military revolt of July 1936 was quickly dealt with through the combined actions of the anarcho-syndicalist trade union CNT (Confederation National de Trabajo), the socialist trade union UGT (Union General Trabajodores) and other Republican forces. Many factory owners and managers fled for their lives, abandoning their firms, which were quickly taken over by militants from the CNT and UGT. Where the owners remained, the enterprises were managed by the owner and a factory council. They faced significant challenges. There was a commitment to level wages and improve working conditions, especially with regard to health and safety, and to enhance insurance cover and welfare benefits. At the same time there was pressure to clothe and equip the militias fighting on the war-front. To achieve these goals there was

---

2 G. Leval, *Collectives in the Spanish Revolution*, tr. Vernon Richards, London: Freedom Press, 1975; N. Chomsky, *American power and the new mandarins*, New York: Pantheon Books, 1969, pp. 72-126.

3 In this section I have drawn heavily on the work of Michael Siedman. In particular see M. Siedman, 'Work and revolution: Workers' control in Barcelona in the Spanish Civil War, 1936-38', *Journal of Contemporary History*, v.17, n.3, 1982, pp. 409-433. See also M. Siedman, 'Agrarian Collectives during the Spanish Revolution and Civil War', *European History Quarterly*, v.30, n.2, 2000, pp. 209–235.

clear recognition that productivity levels needed to be improved. One way was to merge many of the small factories in the city in order to achieve economies of scale. There was also considerable interest in applying the approach of scientific management (Taylorism) that had been developed in the USA. This was the vision – all working together for the common good, drawing on modern management techniques and the latest machine technology to raise productivity and improve the work environment. Oh – if only lived experience conformed to our dreams!

The commitment to levelling wages was soon brought into question. Experience showed that a flat wage-rate discouraged initiative.[4] Furthermore, the quest to modernise outmoded production methods meant there was a need for qualified engineers and technicians with the relevant knowledge and skill-set. Some identified with the transformational project and the ideals upon which it was based, but others required a financial incentive if they were to consider working under the new conditions.

The factory councils and trade unions then faced the demand for the abolition of piece-work, payment by results, which the workers felt to have been a prime cause of their miserable working conditions. But when these demands were acceded to and piece-work was eliminated, productivity dropped.[5] The factory councils also found that, with the improvement of welfare benefits for workers, levels of absenteeism shot-up: the suspicion being that workers were using any means to take advantage of the availability of more generous levels of support

On top of all this, it was found that sabotage and theft continued to be a problem, whilst the unions and councils were faced with repeated wage demands from the rank-and-file workers. They responded with intensive propaganda campaigns against wage demands, absenteeism, sabotage and indiscipline – but to little avail. It seemed as if appeals to workers' sense of solidarity that extended beyond their immediate work-mates fell on deaf-ears. The rank-and-file seemed reluctant to sacrifice themselves (and their own narrowly defined interests) for the sake of the militants' vision, which they did not necessarily share.[6] I am reminded of

---

4   Siedman, 1982, p. 424.
5   Siedman, 1982, p. 423.
6   Siedman, 1982, p. 430.

the very old English proverb that apparently dates from the 12th century: 'You can lead a horse to water, but you can't make it drink'. If you want people to work alongside you, without the need for coercion, you need them to share your vision.

The history of the attempts to create sustainable agricultural collectives in the Aragon region during the Spanish Civil War reveals a similar theme – militants with a vision seeking to create institutions of their ideal society, but dependent on other people to realise their project, people who did not necessarily share the vision or the values of the militants. Immediately after the outbreak of the Civil War peasants throughout the Republican zone confiscated the land of local property-holders for redistribution. Most peasants opted for individual holdings, but in areas where anarchist militants were particularly strong agrarian collectives were formed.[7] The evidence would seem to indicate that collectives were not formed unless there was significant local support for the initiative, especially from the landless peasantry, but a number felt coerced into participating, out of fear of what might happen if they refused. As such they were more akin to reluctant conscripts than willing volunteers.[8] Eventually many of the village councils realised that it was counter-productive to force such unwilling members to remain within the collective, and allowed them to return to their traditional family-based subsistence farming. Other challenges reflected the age-old tension between the rural and the urban interests, divisions that were heightened by the disproportionate increase in the price of manufactured goods compared to agricultural produce. There was a widespread feeling amongst collectives that they were not receiving fair compensation for all their hard work, a reading of the situation that contributed to the erosion of the cooperative spirit of popular solidarity that was the founding ideal of the collective. This weakening of commitment to the national cause was reflected in the phenomenon of 'collective selfishness' – the prioritisation of the local above any broader sense of solidarity. This was manifested in the practice of hoarding which, of course, hindered efforts

---

7   More than 300,000 peasants acquired land during the Civil War period, Only 18.5% of land in the Republican zone was collectivised. (Siedman, 2000, p. 210).

8   Siedman, 2000, p. 211.

to feed other regions, particularly the urban centres with their growing numbers of refugees from the war.

The vision that inspired the collectivisation process was that of equality and the cooperative ethos – from each according to their ability, to each according to their need. But the lived experience showed that in many cases they were not bee-hives of solidarity. There were the usual problems of motivation and discipline, including the perennial problem of how to deal with the 'free-riders', those who did not work as hard as others felt they should, those who arrived late for work and left early. Then there was the resentment against those delegated by the village councils to manage the collectives, and who, in the eyes of some of the rank-and-file, proved themselves to be as authoritarian and unfeeling in their demands as the former owners they had displaced.

By the summer of 1937, with the Communists solidifying their grip on political power within the Republic, units of the Popular Army used force to dissolve the cooperatives in the anarchist heartland of Aragon. But, according to Siedman, the end of the experiment in village-level cooperation and collectivisation was also attributable to internal weaknesses.

> Certainly, without the support of an efficient and united government, it is difficult to see how collectives could have prospered. However, internal divisions amongst the workers themselves compounded political tensions and economic deficiencies. Many, if not most, members gave priority to their own needs first and then considered those of communities larger than themselves and their families. Activists devoted to a cause had to confront a relatively selfish rank-and-file. Village requirements provoked more solidarity than region, Republic, or revolution. The degree of commitment declined as the group became bigger or the cause more abstract. [9]

Comment

A few observations can be made on the basis of the brief overview of the attempts to reconstruct the pattern of working relationships during the years of the Spanish Civil War.

9   Siedman, 2000, pp. 229-30.

i. Any attempt at the large-scale reordering of significant spheres of life imposed from above will necessarily involve significant levels of coercion. The coercion can range from the mass killings that accompanied the collectivisation programme in the USSR (and the genocidal slaughter perpetrated by the Khmer Rouge in Cambodia in the 1970s), by which standards the coercion employed in Spain to force people to participate in the agricultural collectives was relatively mild.

ii. Any attempt to reorder significant spheres of life without the whole-hearted support and participation of those most affected will encounter severe problems. Reluctant conscripts are not the best people for pursuing a vision of reconstruction.

iii. An alternative, and more nonviolent approach, to such re-ordering would have involved the creation of working models that could act as examples for others to emulate once they were convinced of the merits of the project. But this presumes the luxury of time, which was not available to Republican idealists and visionaries during the Spanish Civil War.

Constructing cooperative modes of production to relieve socio-economic suffering

In chapter two we encountered Robert Owen and his ideas about the transformational potential of socialist communities as exemplars of a new age. Most of those experiments were relatively short-lived, but the cooperative values and vision upon which they were based continued to resonate with those seeking to forge an alternative to the capitalist factory system that was spreading so ubiquitously during the 19th century in the UK and elsewhere. Reference was also made to the manner in which Owen's ideas and practice influenced his contemporaries to pursue their visions of a more humane, just and fair mode of production.

Although the contemporary cooperative movement in Europe and elsewhere is comprised of a whole range of different types of cooperative ventures, the utopian vision of creating a society based on the principle of mutual aid was integral to its origins. One of the early advocates, the

Irish socialist William Thompson, enthused in 1830 about the spread of cooperative associations, 'all with the intention of ultimately forming themselves into complete Cooperative Communities as soon as they shall all have saved out of the profits of their trading fund ...' A contemporary of Thompson, the London-based printer George Mudie, established a small community at Spa Fields in London, and in 1821 launched a journal to spread Owenite ideas and report on cooperative schemes. In the August 1821 issue he wrote:

> ... the object sought to be obtained is not equality in rank or possessions, is not community of goods, but full, complete, unrestrained cooperation, on the part of all the members, for every purpose of social life, whether as regards the means of subsistence, or of promoting the intellectual and moral improvement and happiness of the whole body.[10]

However, it has to be acknowledged that over time many of the consumer cooperatives based on the pattern developed by the 'Rochdale Pioneers' lost their radical edge as their organisations grew in size and scope. A major issue they faced was the need to address increasingly efficient competition from other retail chains and producers. But to judge such ventures in terms of a Manichean distinction between success and failure is far too harsh and crude. There are so many lessons to be learned from the history of cooperatives – not least the very real challenges faced by those seeking to grow a business based on an ethic of solidarity and cooperative endeavour within an economic system dominated by a completely different set of values. But we should also acknowledge the significance of such cooperative initiatives of the past. As Bryan Henderson has noted, we should keep in mind

> ... a sense of the lived experience of people who tried to create a form of democracy which did not yet exist in society, and who continually revised their practices in light of their experience. They were not in the business of forming a true concept of co-operative life, they were trying to live a co-operative life. Their message to us is to do the same.[11]

---

10 Quoted in D. Hardy, *Alternative communities in nineteenth century England*, London: Longman, 1979, pp. 35-6.
11 B. Henderson, quoted in Fairbairn, 1994, p. 49.

It was this message that informed the work of a remarkable Roman Catholic priest in the Basque region of Spain in the years after the Spanish Civil War.

Mondragon Cooperatives

In the 1980s when I was teaching Peace Studies at Bradford University I was one of those who welcomed the introduction of videos as a teaching aid. It saved me hours of preparation, and I could never have matched the quality of the visual material communicated via the new medium.[12] One of the courses I taught, at undergraduate and postgraduate level, was entitled 'Social Alternatives' – examining the history of attempts to change the world by creating alternatives to the status-quo in different spheres of life. Anyway – one of the videos that I would show every year was a production by the BBC from November 1980 called 'The Mondragon Experiment'.[13] This was during the heyday of the 'Thatcher years' in Britain, when the Prime Minister Margaret Thatcher pushed through an assault on the welfare state and trade union power, whilst unemployment rocketed. They were years of great social tension and unrest, that reached its peak of bitterness in the miners' strike of 1984-5 and its aftermath. In 1987 Thatcher proudly proclaimed 'There is no such thing as society. There are individual men and women and there are families.' The appeal of the documentary programme on Mondragon was that it showed an alternative to this lauding of competitive materialism and 'devil take the hindmost'. Here was a sector of Spanish society that seemed to be practising and extending the values of mutual aid, cooperation, and promotion of the common good. So, here is the story of the Mondragon workers cooperatives.

In 1941 a Basque priest, Father Jose Maria Arizmendiarrieta, a veteran of the Republican side in the Civil War, was assigned to a parish

---

12 This was in the days before power-point, and if you wanted to display visual material to a class you had to use OHPs – overhead projectors: a light box with a flat, transparent top on which you would place an A4-sized transparency with the image to be projected via an overhead mirror on to the screen in the classroom.

13 A copy of the video is accessible at https://vimeo.com/180391126 (20 May 2021).

in the area of Arrasete-Mondragon.[14] At that time, in the aftermath of the violence, there was high unemployment in the locality and the Basque region in general. He determined to do what he could to improve conditions. He had been influenced by Catholic social doctrine, with its emphasis on the dignity of the human person and the importance of creating the conditions necessary for that dignity to thrive in community – not least by prioritising the needs of the poor and vulnerable. He had also studied Marxist texts and was familiar with the ideas and the cooperative initiatives of Robert Owen and his followers. Accordingly, one of his earliest steps was to establish a small technical college with funds raised through a local credit union, which he had encouraged local people to establish. Some years later, in 1956, he and five graduates from the college, started a small cooperative workshop making single-burner kerosene stoves that were much in demand at the time. Once again funds came from the credit union and other local sources. The enterprise thrived and became the first building-block of what has grown into a federation of almost one hundred worker-owned cooperatives with a combined workforce of over 81,000.[15] As Carl Davidson has pointed out, this small start-up contained the seeds of Mondragon's success: the three-in-one combination of school, credit union and factory, all owned and controlled by the workers and the community. A cooperative on its own would not thrive without a reliable source of credit and access to a source of skills and innovation.[16]

Mondragon cooperatives are autonomous enterprises owned by its workers, each of whom can purchase a single share which allows them a single vote in the annual assembly. As such the work-force are worker-owners, with their salary drawn from the firm's annual profit. The cooperatives have a relatively flat income spread, agreed at the annual assembly, with differentials according to seniority and skills.[17] New

14 Arrasete is the Basque name for the town, Mondragon the Spanish name.

15 See https://www.mondragon-corporation.com/en/about-us/ (25 May 2021).

16 C. Davidson, 'The Mondragon Cooperatives and 21st century socialism: A review of five books with radical critiques and new ideas', *Perspectives on global development and technology* , v.11, n.1, Jan. 2012, pp. 229-243, p. 231.

17 The highest paid can never make 6.5 times more than the lowest paid. V. Navarro, 'What about cooperatives as a solution? The case of Mondragon', *CounterPunch*, 30 April 2014. Accessible at https://tinyurl.com/yaptn2p2 (26

recruits start with a six-month probationary period, after which they can purchase a share in the enterprise. If they do not have the funds to purchase the share (several thousand euros), they can borrow from the cooperative bank and repay over time.[18] The cooperatives have a relatively flat hierarchy of positions, with the assembly electing a governing council, which in turn hires the management team. Managers, unlike worker-owners, can be dismissed from their post.

The various enterprises are encouraged to cooperate with each other, both in terms of broad production and marketing strategy, but also providing support when other cooperatives within the federation are in trouble. One of the mutual-support mechanisms is retraining workers in struggling companies and their transfer to stronger businesses. For example, in late 2013 one of the original cooperatives, Fagor, filed for bankruptcy due to the mountain of debt accrued, largely attributable to the collapse of the Spanish housing market in Spain and the consequent shrinking of the domestic market for the 'white goods' (fridges, washing machines etc.) the cooperative manufactured. Fagor had not made a profit since 2008, and over the years the other Mondragon cooperatives extended considerable loans to help it overcome its difficulties, but eventually the decision was made that there was no reasonable chance of recovery, and over five thousand jobs were put at risk. However, 600 of Fagor's worker-owners were relocated to other cooperatives within the Mondragon network, others were taken on by the private company that took over the assets of Fagor, others took early retirement. As Vincent Navarro observed, 'solidarity among worker-owners made the collapse of Fagor more bearable than it would have been otherwise'.[19] However, Navarro has noted one matter of concern – over recent years the proportion of employees (workers who are not worker-owners) has increased compared with those who are workers and co-owners. In fact, quoting figures from 2014, he noted that in the supermarket chains that

---

May 2021).

18 One of the stipulations of Arizmendiarrieta was that shares were not transferable. On retirement a worker-owner can 'cash-in' their share by handing it back to the cooperative. In this way the Mondragon model guards against external financial interests taking control of any of the cooperatives.

19 Navarro, 2014.

are owned by Mondragon in Spain and southern France, less than a third of the workforce of over 38,000 were worker-owners.[20]

The clear fact is that despite their internal cooperative practice, the Mondragon cooperatives must compete against other corporations in a capitalist market system. As one observers noted – for Mondragon 'large is beautiful', because it is the scale of their operations that allows them to compete successfully in the global markets.[21] However large the Mondragon federation of cooperatives is, they cannot survive outside the demands of the market. But, they do provide substantial evidence that another way is possible, an economy organised on the basis of human need rather than the pursuit of private profit. Indeed, so convincing has that evidence been that the example of Mondragon has inspired new models elsewhere in the world, particularly in the USA.

Mondragon's impact in the USA and beyond

There is a long history of cooperatives in the USA, albeit not particularly well-known. Today, according to the U.S. Federation of Worker Cooperatives, the United States has more than 300 worker cooperatives employing approximately 7,000 people and generating over $400 million in annual revenues. They operate in fields ranging from engineering, architecture and computer technology to taxi driving, house cleaning and construction.[22]

In 2009 the growing interest in alternatives to the established capitalist model was evidenced by the United Steel Workers (USW), one of the stronger trade unions in the USA, sending a delegation to Spain to learn more about the Mondragon model.[23] In March 2012 the USW

---

20 Mondragon has established manufacturing plants outside of Spain. In such factories the workforce remain employees of the cooperative, rather than worker-owners.

21 J. Bamburg, 'Mondragon through a critical lens', *Fifty by fifty: Employee ownership news,* 3 October 2017. Accessible at https://tinyurl.com/cccx7v5y (26 May 2021).

22 See https://institute.coop/worker-cooperative-faq#Q4 (18 May 2021).

23 This represented a marked change in the attitude of the union towards workers coops. In the late 1970s the union had opposed proposals to develop employee-owned factories, seeing such initiatives as a threat to their role and

presented the results of its consultations in a document which addressed the question: 'If we were to create an economy that worked for everyone, an economy that creates good, sustainable jobs and is accountable to the communities that drive it, what would that look like?'[24] The document went on to propose the creation of unionised worker-owned cooperatives based on the values and the principles of Mondragon. The only difference envisaged was the replacement of Mondragon's Social Councils by an elected Union Committee to represent the interests of the worker-owners in their role as workers over issues such as wages, benefits and working conditions.

The USW initiative was not the first example of Mondragon's impact in the USA. In 1995 a member of a worker-owned pizzeria in Berkeley decided to set up a new bakery-pizzeria, and two years later the venture was launched in Oakland. The founders named it 'Arizmendi', after the founder of Mondragon, Father Arizmendiarrieta. Today the Arizmendi Association of Coops encompasses six bakery-pizzerias across the San Francisco Bay area – a cooperative of cooperatives.[25]   Furthermore, in September 2010 the mayor of Richmond, a city in the eastern San Francisco Bay Area, signed a letter of intent with a representative from Mondragon – 'to explore how the Mondragon model of worker-owned cooperatives can be applied in Richmond, California and to initiate conversations and facilitate collaboration among potential worker owners, labor unions, community organizations, local funders and City officials in Richmond.'[26]

The Cleveland Model

One of the most significant developments to be seeded, in part, by the example of Mondragon took place in October 2009 with the

---

function as a trade union.

24 *Sustainable jobs, sustainable communities: The Union Co-op model,* Accessible at https://tinyurl.com/ek2drhc (25 May 2021).

25 R. Cima, 'The cheese-board collective', *Priceonomics*. Accessible at https://tinyurl.com/yufauy8k (3 June 2021).

26 The Network of Bay Area Worker Cooperatives estimates there are over 50 worker cooperatives in the San Francisco Bay Area. See https://tinyurl.com/2uk6eps   (6 September 2021).

launch of the Evergreen Cooperative Laundry, the first of a number of worker cooperatives to be established in a run-down area of Cleveland, Ohio. The initiative came about after a 'community wealth-building roundtable' held in December 2006 involving a range of local stake-holders. Their focus was how to address community development issues such as inadequate housing, lack of local facilities, unemployment and associated impoverishment in some of Cleveland's most deprived neighbourhoods. It was at this symposium that the idea was raised of linking the requirements of several 'anchor institutions', such as hospitals and colleges, to the need to generate employment in the neighbourhoods where the institutions were located.[27]

The basic premise was disarmingly simple. The large institutions had a stake in the well-being of the neighbourhoods where they were located. They also needed to be supplied with goods and services. Why shouldn't the procurement needs of the anchor institutions be met by cooperatives staffed by worker-owners from the local neighbourhoods? In this way wealth generated by the ventures would remain in the community, and not be siphoned off by external share-holders. Furthermore, the worker-owners would benefit from decent living wages and associated healthcare benefits, whilst also acquiring transferable skills in administration and management. It was also recognised that by providing 'green' services with low carbon-footprint the community-based cooperatives would be in a position to assist the anchor institutions meet their sustainability commitments.[28]

In October 2008, many of the people involved in the original roundtable in 2006 visited the Mondragon Cooperatives in Spain. Two subsequent trips to Mondragon have taken place involving a wider number of stake-holders from Cleveland in the learning process and trust-building necessary for successful involvement in the creation of sustainable worker cooperatives. The Mondragon model is readily apparent in the structuring of the cooperatives, each focusing on providing competitively priced services and products to the anchor institutions. The Evergreen Cooperative Laundry was established in 2009, with the aid of a long-term, low-interest federal loan and support

27 See https://tinyurl.com/nksbbrb4   (26 May 2021).
28   See https://www.evgoh.com/mission-vision/ (3 June 2021).

from the municipal Economic Development Department. The next to be launched was Evergreen Energy Cooperative specialising in the installation of solar power systems.[29] The third venture was the Green City Growers Cooperative, launched in October 2011, and the largest urban hydroponic vegetable growing venture in the USA.[30] In the 10 years since then, Evergreen Cooperatives has added three more cooperatives to its ranks, growing from two companies with a total of 18 workers in 2010 to five companies with approximately 320 workers.

As with the Mondragon network each cooperative is separately incorporated with its own business line, but formal ownership is vested in a non-profit umbrella organisation – the Evergreen Cooperative Corporation (ECC). The ECC holds a 20 percent equity role in each of the cooperatives, while the employee-owners own the remaining 80 percent. Ten percent of the profits of each of the cooperatives is paid to the ECC's fund for creating new cooperatives. In addition the ECC provides various administrative and support functions for each of the individual cooperatives. [31]

Throughout the early years the cooperatives had to deal with the significant challenges of starting and growing new businesses. In addition to ensuring the businesses had the operational know-how and skills necessary to become profitable enterprises, as cooperatives they needed added support to nurture and develop a cooperative culture within the businesses. By 2018 Evergreen had come to the conclusion that establishing new worker-cooperatives from the ground-up was not a particularly speedy pathway to multiplying employee ownership jobs. They decided to pursue a new strategy of 'acquire-convert-support'. They created a Fund for Employee Ownership and began raising capital to buy out existing businesses from their owners and convert the enterprise to

---

29 Evergreen Energy Cooperative started with 6 employees in 2010 and peaked at 40 employee-owners, but by 2020 was in the process of winding down operations and transferring its employees to other co-ops. Cooperatives are not immune to the challenges faced by all small start-up companies.

30 See http://www.evgoh.com/feature/green-city-growers/ (20 May 2021).

31 B. Duong, 'Despite a rocky start Cleveland model for worker coops stands test of time', *Shelterforce,* 9 March 2021. Accessible at https://tinyurl.com/4p9yr7ma (4 June 2021).

worker cooperatives.[32] Over recent years they have been able to finance the expansion of the laundry business and brought three additional businesses into the Evergreen network.[33]

Just as Mondragon helped inspire the Evergreen Cooperatives, the 'Cleveland model' has seeded other efforts around the USA and further afield. There are various factors that have contributed to their relative success, including the commitment of the partners such as the anchor institutions themselves, the city's Department of Economic Development, and various philanthropic funders. It shows that with the right support worker cooperatives can grow and thrive, helping workers and their families achieve a level of financial security that would otherwise have been beyond their reach. Such initiatives help put new ideas on the public agenda, like prioritising the welfare of workers and local communities rather than profit margins for shareholders, and showing the way in which city councils and associated agencies can create employment opportunities for those left impoverished and bereft of dignity by the workings of the current orthodox economic model.

Worker buyouts in Italy – the significance of the Marcora Law

I have lived the bulk of my life in the UK, and apart from a period in the 1970s when senior figures within the Labour Government were supportive of worker buyouts as a means of maintaining employment levels, there has been a noticeable lack of state interest in the creation of worker cooperatives. The priorities over past decades of 'New Labour' and Conservative governments have been the privatisation of public services and the privileging of private profit rather than promoting cooperative innovation in the production sphere.

This stance contrasts strongly with that taken by other governments in Europe and elsewhere. Italy, for example, has a thriving common-ownership sector. In the Emilio Romagna region, which has the lowest unemployment rate in Italy, a third of the GDP is generated by worker

---

32 The Kendeda Foundation was a major backer of this new fund. See https://tinyurl.com/u9rknjk2 (4 June 2021).

33 K. Kahn, 'Evergreen cooperatives adapt and grow', *Fifty by Fifty*, 31 March 2021. Accessible at https://tinyurl.com/rsrd8j85 (5 June 2021).

owned firms.[34] A crucial factor in this development has been the Marcora Law. It is named after the Italian Minister of Trade and Industry, Giovanni Marcora who was responsible for passing the law in 1985 that aimed to support worker buyouts. Thirty years after its introduction the law had helped to create 257 new employee owned firms, saving or creating 9,300 jobs.[35] When a business is close to shutting down, with the workers facing redundancy, the law allows them to claim their anticipated unemployment benefits as a lump sum in advance, to use as capital to buy out the business. The law also provides them with access to support and guidance to help them make a success of the venture. This action on the part of the Italian state not only allows people to keep their jobs and ensure the businesses continue to function, but overtime it also allows the economy to shift to a fairer, more democratic structure where employees can have a say and a stake in their workplaces.[36]

Alternative approaches to production as part of a wider vision

Alternative economic plans: Lucas Aerospace

In the earlier chapter on constructive action in the context of civil resistance movements I made reference to my involvement in Aberdeen Peoples Press (APP), which some of us saw as part of a much wider movement and culture of dissent, concerned with transforming a world based on competitive materialism and possessive individualism in the direction of cooperation, mutual aid and non-exploitation. At times we felt a utopian confidence that nothing was impossible, that by creating

---

34 E. Paczkowski, 'The Marcora Law: An innovative way to promote entrepreneurship', *Medium*, 24 December 2020.

35 'The Marcora Law supporting worker buyouts for thirty years', *International Cooperative Alliance*, 11 September 2015. Accessible at https://tinyurl.com/h8y8rrbm (31 May 2021).

36 For discussion regarding the importance of the enabling environment created by the Marcora Law and the evident resilience of the worker buyouts, see M. Vieta et al, *The Italian road to recuperating enterprises and the Legge Marcora framework*, Trento: European Research Institute on Cooperative and Social Enterprises, Research report n. 15/17, 2015.

alternative ways of working and living we would act as a kind of yeast – energising those around us by our 'propaganda of the deed', creating institutions and relationships as exemplars for others to follow. Amongst the rich variety of social experiments and initiatives that took place in that period were those concerned with transforming the world of work and production.

I stopped volunteering full-time with APP in 1976, which was the same year that the Shop Stewards Committee at the Lucas Aerospace Company came up with an alternative corporate plan (ACP) to 'demilitarise' the company and retain jobs by proposing alternative, socially-useful applications of the company's technology and their own skills. Lucas Aerospace was a major arms manufacturer, employing 13,000 workers at 17 sites. The workers were faced with clear indications from both the government and management that reduced orders for military equipment made a restructuring of the company necessary, with accompanying redundancies. The Shop Stewards Committee argued that it would be far more beneficial for all if state support was put to developing products society needed rather than paying out welfare benefits when the workers were laid off.[37]

Amongst the specific proposals there was a recommendation that the production of kidney dialysis machines, already being manufactured at one of the plants, should be expanded, whilst a number of proposals related to renewable energy initiatives such as heat pumps, solar cell technology, wind-turbines and hybrid power-packs for public transport.[38] The company rejected the proposals, but the ACP attracted world-wide interest. Nowadays some of the products proposed in the ACP have become mainstream, whilst Lucas Aerospace has ceased to exist. But the initiative spawned a number of kindred projects that sought to draw upon the technical skills and creativity of workers to develop alternative plans to produce socially-useful products rather than weapons of war.

---

37 H. Wainwright, 'When the workers nearly took control: Five lessons from the Lucas Plan', *Open Democracy*, 29 November 2016. Accessible at https://tinyurl.com/88xn8p5e (08 June 2021).

38 B. Salisbury, *The story of the Lucas Plan*, http://lucasplan.org.uk/story-of-the-lucas-plan/ (4 June 2021).

One of the off-shoots in the UK was an attempt to develop an alternative production plan for the Barrow shipyards where the Vickers Company built the nuclear-power submarines required for the Trident nuclear missiles. The Barrow Alternative Employment Committee (BAEC) was established in the mid-1980s, tasked with producing proposals for alternatives to Trident. Its report, *Oceans of Work*, was published in 1987. It highlighted the over-dependency of the company and the local economy on arms production, making the case for the pursuit of new, civil engineering opportunities in the marine sector, particularly offshore renewable energy systems like wind and wave power. By this time the Barrow yards were owned by British Aerospace, who rejected the proposals, even though the report argued strongly that conversion from arms production would result in enhanced prospects for skilled manufacturing jobs over the medium to long term.

One of the core researchers with BAEC was my friend Steve Schofield, who was a doctoral research student in Peace Studies at Bradford University and – more significantly for me – was one of the two friends I ran alongside to complete my first marathon in 1983.[39] In 2007, twenty years after the original publication, Steve authored a report published by the British-American Security Information Council (BASIC) entitled *Oceans of work: Arms conversion revisited*.[40] Reviewing his experience as the lead researcher with BAEC and the manner in which the original report was dismissed out-of-hand by the chief executive of the company, seemingly fixated on the company's involvement with armaments work and its specialist niche of nuclear submarines, Steve observed:

> Here, again, we meet the fundamental dilemma facing arms
> conversion; that of a mismatch between the prospects for
> new civil employment in associated areas and the reality
> of military production at specialist arms manufacturers,
> hamstrung by industrial and cultural barriers that made even
> the more modest ambition of product diversification on site,

---

39 Steve was always faster than me, but on this first occasion three of us who had trained together finished together - in a time of 3 hours 54 minutes. It remains one of my proudest achievements.

40 S. Schofield, *Oceans of work: Arms conversion revisited*, London: BASIC, 2007.

with both military and civil work, look highly unlikely, if not impossible.[41]

This sense of the limitations of site-based approaches to industrial conversion from armaments to socially-useful production is a thread that runs through the 2007 report, with Steve pointing to the array of vested interests and conservative mind-sets that mobilise to resist any suggestion of change that might be construed as a threat to the continuation of weapons-related-business-as-usual. The UK's defence policy remains fixated on maintaining a military-industrial base for the research, development and production of high-tech weaponry – immune to the visionary proposals advocated by those seeking a saner and more sustainable world. Perhaps the growing public awareness of the threat posed to our common security by the climate crisis might bring about a change in the political will and a greater degree of receptiveness to alternative security paradigms, one involving a root-and-branch revaluation of the state's defence policy and associated industrial strategy.[42] A significant dimension of such an alternative paradigm is the advocacy of a 'green new deal' – seeds of which can be found in the Lucas Plan and associated initiatives from the mid-1970s onwards.[43]

Collectives and cooperatives – the wave of the 1970s

In 1976 I took up a research post in the Department of Social Work at Aberdeen University, after two years spent volunteering with APP supplemented by various part-time jobs. By that time APP had moved into new basement premises in the city centre. The building was shared with two other alternative enterprises – Boomtown Books and Ambrosia Wholefoods. One of the key people involved with APP subsequently reflected on how the new premises at 163 King Street became a hub for activists of one sort or another.

> 163 King Street quickly became a central meeting point for people from a variety of backgrounds with a variety of political

---

41 Schofield, 2007, p. 5.

42 Of particular significance is the Rethinking Security network. See https://rethinkingsecurity.org.uk/about/ (22 May 2021).

43 N. Chomsky et al, *Climate crisis and the Global Green New Deal: The political economy of saving the planet*, London: Verso, 2020.

(and sometimes non-political) backgrounds who probably only agreed on one thing: that they wanted to change society. It was where community activists crossed paths with back-to-the-landers, Trotskyists with Labour Party stalwarts, dope smokers with academics, feminists with anarchists, students with trade unionists and Marxists with budding ecologists. 163 King Street was where you came to get stuff printed, buy books and pamphlets, stock up on healthy food, discuss, dispute and, more often than you might expect, end up agreeing with people you didn't normally agree with.[44]

Sometime in 1978 I applied for a position as a lecturer at what was then called the School of Peace Studies at Bradford University in West Yorkshire, UK. There were about six of us on the short-list and we spent the day meeting staff and students, and then facing an interview panel. I remember that one of the other applicants worked with a wholefood wholesale enterprise called SUMA, that was organised as a workers cooperative. Fortunately for my employment prospects she determined to commit her future to SUMA rather than to academia.[45] At that time, in the UK, it seemed as if every small town and city had its own 'alternative' shops, usually set up as workers cooperatives or collectives In Bradford I remember the Fourth Idea bookshop and not far away was a wholefood shop.[46] When I went over the Pennines from West Yorkshire to Merseyside to see my parents I would drop in to the News from Nowhere bookshop in Liverpool – which is still in existence as a women's cooperative forty-odd years later![47]

The growth of workers cooperatives during this period had different roots which, for a while, fed and complemented each other. On the one hand there were the radical roots of those seeking more convivial, people-centred and socially-useful modes of making a living. In this they

---

44 A. Marshall, 'Boomtown properties: property owning for freedom !', https://tinyurl.com/2bfu8czf (13 June 2021).

45 SUMA remains in existence as the largest equal pay workers cooperative in Europe. See https://www.suma.coop/about/our-co-op/ (12 June 2021).

46 Roland Rance has recalled some of his experiences working at Fourth Idea in the early 1980s. See https://tinyurl.com/2hut69je (13 June 2021).

47 See http://www.newsfromnowhere.org.uk/ (13 June 2021).

were encouraged and supported by the Industrial Common Ownership Movement (ICOM) which had been set up in 1971 to promote cooperatives.[48] There were also those facing redundancy as the established manufacturing units succumbed to intensifying global competition, and who were desperate to find ways of holding on to their jobs, such as by a workers' buyout. Thirdly, and crucially, was the coming to power in 1974 of a Labour Government with Tony Benn heading up the Department for Trade and Industry. He was committed to creating a supportive infrastructure for the formation of worker cooperatives as a source of employment.[49] In 1976 the Industrial Common Ownership Act came into being, creating a capital fund to support the setting up of common-ownership cooperatives. This was followed in 1978 by the establishment of a national Cooperative Development Agency, which enabled municipalities and other local and regional authorities to access central funds to establish their own cooperative development units, charged with promoting common ownership as a model to create employment.[50] Funding was also allocated to cooperatives through the job creation schemes of what was then called the Manpower Services Commission.

As a consequence of these various initiatives and inputs the number of worker cooperatives in the UK grew from about a hundred in the mid-1970s to over a thousand by the mid-1980s, employing close to 7000 people.[51] Since then the changes in government policy, the loss

---

48 In 2001 ICOM merged with the Cooperative Union to become Co-operatives UK.

49 In 1975 Benn was instrumental in providing funds to support the creation of a worker cooperative at the Triumph Motorcycle factory in Meriden. This followed an 18-month occupation of the factory by the workers to prevent its closure. I used to own a Triumph Bonneville made by the cooperative. The business eventually declared itself bankrupt in 1983.

50 The occupational trajectory of one of my comrades from APP provides an illustration of this process. Ian Baird was a volunteer with APP, then was instrumental in establishing the project as a formal worker cooperative. He subsequently was employed as the Cooperative Development officer for Aberdeen.

51 L. Sammallahti & I. Doherty, 'Why has the number of worker co-ops increased 20-fold in the UK since 1970?', *Mutual Interest Media*, 31 March

of funding to promote common ownership, aligned with the politics of austerity and the globalisation of the capitalist economy has resulted in the number dropping to under 500.[52]

Value-driven conversion of production to forms of common ownership – the case of Scott Bader

Sometime in the mid-1980s I started writing a biography of Wilfred Wellock (1879-1972), who Martin Ceadel once described as 'the most remarkable Christian socialist pacifist of the inter-war period'.[53] At that time I was actively involved in the resurgence of the nuclear disarmament movement as treasurer of the local group in Bradford, but I was also invited to give talks to different peace groups around the north of England in my capacity as a lecturer at Bradford University's School of Peace Studies, where much of the research focused on the new generation of nuclear weapons (particularly Cruise and Pershing II missiles) and the changes in strategic thinking that had accompanied their development. Whilst I did not dispute the significance of so much of this applied research, it did seem to me that we were in danger of losing sight of the more positive, utopian aspects of peace thinking that, for me, had always been central to my understanding of Peace Studies. It began to seem that in our response to the ever-present threat of nuclear annihilation that loomed so large in the 1980s there was no room or time for such questions as 'What would a nonviolent society look like?' It was very clear what we were struggling against, but we were far from clear about what was necessary to create a world without war. This was the background to my decision to explore the life of Wellock, a life-long advocate of a politics of creative living who had consistently urged pacifists 'to envisage the future and to seek ways and means of saving and introducing those values without which human existence ceases to have any meaning.'[54]

2021. Accessible at https://tinyurl.com/jxa34yhx   (20 September 2021)

52 Pat Conaty, New Economics Foundation, https://www.lowimpact.org/the-commons-pat-conaty/ (22 May 2021).

53 M. Ceadel, *Pacifism in Britain, 1914-1945: The defining of a faith*, Oxford: Clarendon Press, 1980, p. 50.

54 W. Wellock, *Peace News*, 14 June 1940. Quoted in A. Rigby, *A life in peace: A biography of Wilfred Wellock*, Bridport: Prism Press, 1988, p. 75.

During the 1940s Wellock became associated with an industrialist who shared a similar sense of moral purpose. This was Ernest Bader, a Swiss emigre who had founded the Scott Bader Company in 1920 in London and quickly established it as a leading chemical and resin manufacturing concern. Although successful as judged by normal capitalist standards Bader, who had joined the Society of Friends (Quakers) in 1944, remained dissatisfied with the disjunction between Christian morality and the ethics of competitive capitalism in general, and with the employer-employee power relationship in particular. He began to cast around for a nonviolent basis on which to order industrial life, leading him to think seriously about turning his company into some form of cooperative fellowship. In 1945 he shared his ideas with his seventy-odd employees in a document that had strong echoes of Wellock's ideas, quoting him in the conclusion, and referring to the need to restructure society 'by establishing responsible common ownership'.[55]

In 1951 Bader finally formed the Scott Bader Commonwealth and handed over 90 percent of the shares held by the Bader family to a newly constituted body, the Commonwealth, made up of all those members of the workforce who wished to belong to what was, on paper at least, the legal owner and ultimate authority in the enterprise. In the preamble to the 1951 constitution of the Scott Bader Commonwealth Bader appealed to those engaged in business activities to ask themselves 'to what extent violence resides in the demands we make upon the earth's resources and the available raw materials by reason of our self-indulgent existence, and what is to be our personal contribution to peace.' [56]

In 1963 the remaining ten percent of the family's shares was handed over to the Commonwealth. By this time Bader increasingly referred to Gandhi as the source of his ideas on communal ownership and trusteeship – that the Commonwealth should act to ensure that the enterprise was run in such a manner as to contribute to the well-being of people and planet. Thus, in the preamble to the 1963 constitution he wrote:

> The ultimate criteria in the organisation of work should be
> human dignity and service to others instead of solely economic

---

55   S. Hoe, *The man who gave his company away*, London: Heinemann, 1978, p. 80.
56   Quoted in Rigby, 1988, p. 103.

performance. We feel mutual responsibility must permeate the whole community of work and be upheld by democratic participation and the principle of trusteeship.[57]

When Scott Bader became a Common Trusteeship Company, it only operated in the UK. Since that time the company has continued to expand, and now has manufacturing companies in France, South Africa, Dubai, Croatia and Canada, along with distribution outlets in the Czech Republic, France, Sweden, Spain, USA, China and Eire. Over 600 people are employed worldwide, and there are more than 500 Commonwealth Members across the globe. The expansion has necessitated some organisational changes from time to time but the commitment to the values and principles that informed Bader's original initiative remains. In the introduction to the 2014 constitution Goderic Bader affirmed that their fundamental purpose was to generate social change: 'The goal is to create an industrial society that delivers social benefits to the world, as opposed to what we have at present – an economy based on private profit.'[58]

Concluding observation

No one living on this planet can escape the impact of the climate emergency. Wherever we live or whatever our station, it affects us all. Facing a common challenge it should be clear that we can no longer continue to live our lives in a socio-economic and cultural environment dominated by the narrow pursuit of private interest and a 'devil-take-the-hindmost' morality. We are all part of the human family living in a shared home – planet Earth. However reluctantly, we are having to realise that we all have a common responsibility for the welfare of our home and the future generations who will share it.

---

57 Quoted in Rigby, 1988, p.103.

58 *Scott Bader Constitution*, May 2014, p. 5. Accessible at https://tinyurl.com/whjemwtm (24 June 2021). It is relevant to note that there is a fundamental difference between the Scott Bader Commonwealth and those enterprises modelled on the example of Mondragon. In the Mondragon model individual workers own shares in the company. At Scott Bader all shares are held by the Commonwealth.

Who owns business enterprises determines their purpose and how the wealth generated is distributed. The dominant neo-liberal model of private ownership and profit-maximisation is broken, and lies at the root of the crises we face – the climate emergency, economic inequality, loss of biodiversity and global and intergenerational inequality. Creating an economy that produces goods and services designed to meet the real-world challenges we face is unlikely to happen so long as control lies with shareholding conglomerates committed to the pursuit of profit-maximisation. A new economic order requires a transformative increase in the political and economic agency of communities through the spread of forms of shared, democratic ownership. [59]

The seeds of such a change lie in some of the ventures reviewed in this chapter, embodying as so many of them do a concern for economic justice, social solidarity, community resilience and democratic practice. As Richard Bickle argued some years ago, 'If we are to have a future as individual people, as communities, and as the whole world, we must recognise the value of the cooperative model of doing business in building a more just and sustainable economy and society for everyone.'[60]

---

59 *Cooperatives unleashed: Doubling the size of the UK's cooperative sector*, New Economics Foundation, 3 July 2018.
60 R. Bickle, 'An atmosphere of cooperation', *The Ecologist*, 22 March 2007. Accessible at https://tinyurl.com/cfzcatm3 (20 July 2021).

8

CONCLUDING OBSERVATIONS

There is a simple purpose to this final chapter – I am going to try and extract what I think are the key features and dimensions of constructive modes of nonviolent action for change that have been touched upon in the analyses and case studies covered in the different chapters.

1. *Constructive action is a necessary counter to the statist fallacy that informs many civil resistance movements against authoritarian regimes.*

   Too narrow a focus on 'seizing state power' can weaken the transformatory potential of a civil resistance movement against authoritarian regimes. 'Success' too often leads to little more than a widening of political participation at election times and in some cases an erosion of social equality and human well-being. Chabot and Sharifi have argued persuasively that those seeking a more compassionate and caring society should prioritise constructive work to change ways of life in communities and neighbourhoods rather than focus solely on mobilising people for protest.[1]

2. *Constructive action is necessary to widen the base of a civil resistance movement.*

   Constructive modes of resistance constitute crucial avenues for broadening the participatory base of any movement for change. As Chenoweth and Stephan have argued, 'a critical source of the success of nonviolent resistance is mass participation'.[2]

   In chapter four it was argued that in the US civil rights movement' it was the community organising of those associated with the

---

1   Chabot & Sharifi, 2013, pp. 22-3.
2   Chenoweth & Stephan, 2011, p. 30.

Citizenship Schools, and similar programmes of voter education and registration, that involved people in the movement for change, particularly those who felt wary of engaging in the more confrontational modes of public action such as participating in marches and rallies. Engagement with 'literacy classes' was a very non-threatening and relatively low-risk form of involvement with the struggle, but it lay the groundwork upon which the community mobilisation initiatives of Martin Luther King and his associates depended.

3.   *Constructive action can enhance the legitimacy of movements for change.*

Furthermore, there is evidence from various sources that sustained involvement in constructive action, to bring about change 'on the ground' in neighbourhoods and communities, enhances the legitimacy (and hence the efficacy) of those same activists when they seek to mobilise people for more confrontational forms of action. As Charles Payne noted, in the Black community of Greenwood of Mississippi it was the example set by young organizers who had earned the respect of the local community that had the most powerful effect on the mobilisation of local people:

> The first factor in the transformation of Black Greenwood has to be the sheer courage and persistence of the young organisers, awakening a like response in some local residents, the more so as the organizers became deeply rooted into the Black community. The Sam Block the police roughed up in July 1962 was, in most eyes, at best a foolhardy young stranger. The Sam Block they arrested in February 1963 was someone who had patiently earned the respect and admiration of a great many people.[3]

In chapter six we saw how Danilo Dolci, following the methodology of Gandhi, was able to mobilise people because of the respect he had earned through his focus on community development. In the popular movements in India, figures such as Baba Amte, one of the leaders of

---

3   Payne, 2007, pp. 175-6.

the struggle against the Narmada Dams, drew upon the legitimacy he had gained through the years he had devoted to working with villagers to help them meet their basic needs. The ability of Ekta Parishad to recruit participants for its large-scale padyatras (foot marches) can be attributed in large part to the trust of villagers, built up over the years of constructive work.

4. *Constructive action can help sustain and reproduce oppositional cultures and identities*

We have seen how, in the unarmed struggle by Palestinians for basic human rights and the end to the Israeli occupation, forms of constructive resistance have broadened the participations of everyday people in the struggle, by offering them the opportunity to commit to the cause without incurring too high a cost. But more generally the practice of *sumud* in different walks of life has enabled Palestinians to integrate into their everyday lives ways to affirm and reproduce a culture and way of life integral to the maintenance of an oppositional identity.

I confess that for me this is perhaps the greatest strength of constructive modes of action and resistance. They can constitute low-risk ways of holding on to valued identities and convictions, ways of being that can be integrated into everyday life and sustained over time.

5. *Constructive action is a necessary dimension of any prolonged resistance struggle*

Where offensive modes of resistance are likely to be met by severe repression and associated sanctions, there is a strong likelihood that many resisters will choose 'quieter' and less contentious modes of action, such as constructive forms of resistance, that do not cause significant friction with the regime, and hence carry a lower risk of incurring costly sanctions. In the review of different civil resistance movements against authoritarian regimes it became apparent that the political mobilisation and offensive modes of resistance that were vital levers in pressuring the regimes to relinquish power in Poland, Czechoslovakia, the GDR, Serbia, and elsewhere, grew out of the constructive work of individuals seeking to maintain their oppositional identity. Under the radar, camouflaged, such people committed themselves to creating support networks, human rights monitoring groups, educational and information services, underground media outlets. In so doing they not only kept the democratic impulse alive, but they developed the levels of trust and camaraderie, the communication networks and the skill-sets necessary to support and sustain the mobilisation of large swathes of the population when the political opportunity arose for offensive resistance.

6. *Constructive action can contribute to the well-being of activists*

A key factor in any protracted struggle is the well-being of those engaged in the resistance. Personally, I am very aware that I have a very low tolerance of discomfort, and if you want folk like me to accompany you on a long journey to the promised land, then we need some rest-stops and recuperation points on the way, some 'time-out'. During the Indian independence struggle, phases of mass mobilisation and confrontation were interspersed by periods of relative quiescence.[4] There were times during the liberation struggle that Gandhi called a halt to confrontations and redirected collective energies towards the constructive programme. This reflected his awareness that in a movement based on mass participation, there were limits to the commitment and endurance that could be expected from participants who were not 'professional', full-time freedom-fighters.

However dedicated activists might be, no movement can sustain extended periods of mass mobilisation without exhausting its followers and 'burning out' its cadres. So, given the prolonged nature of the Indian freedom struggle, periods of intense mobilisation and contestation were interspersed with longer 'passive' periods when ideological work was carried out. The constructive programme helped fill the political space left vacant by the withdrawal from civil disobedience, thereby enabling people to sustain a sense of activism

---

4   Chandra characterised this aspect of the nationalist strategy as 'Struggle-Truce-Struggle'. Chandra, 1989, p. 509.

and provide a medium for continued involvement in the movement during the relatively quiet phases, whilst at the same time providing something of a 'safe haven' for the cadres where they could withdraw from the front-line struggle in order to recuperate and recharge their batteries.[5]

7. *Constructive work can act as a training ground for movement cadres*

Gandhi was convinced that any attempt to launch a large-scale civil disobedience campaign would be likely to deteriorate into violent confrontations once people's passions were aroused, unless the bulk of the participants had been trained and disciplined for nonviolent resistance. The key medium for this training was involvement in different forms of constructive action. As he wrote in *Constructive Programme*, 'Training for military revolt means learning the use of arms ending perhaps in the atomic bomb. For civil disobedience it means the constructive programme.'[6] Hence it was from the ranks of the constructive workers, those schooled and disciplined in the work for the uplift of the poorest sections of society, that Gandhi recruited the cadres of the movement. Likewise, in the analysis of the prawn satyagraha campaign led by Jagannathanji, my research indicated that a crucial factor in the organisation of the movement was the level of trust that existed between villagers and the village-level workers who had devoted significant periods of time to community development work. It was through the village committees that the mobilisation of local people for collective action during the campaign was organised, and it was from the ranks of the experienced constructive workers that the cadres of the movement against the prawn fisheries were drawn.

8. *Constructive action as propaganda of the deed – prefiguring the future*

As I noted in the introductory chapter, one of the factors that led to my long-term interest in constructive action as a means of change

---

5   Chandra, 1989, p. 510.
6   M. Gandhi, 1941, p. 4.

was my anarcho-pacifist convictions, and the consequent search for non-coercive methods of radically transforming relationships. This led to an abiding interest in forms of exemplary action, seeking to bring about change by the power of example. It was this that led to my early research into intentional communities, centres of alternative living that I viewed as forms of propaganda of the deed, seeking to sway others by the power of one's own actions. In reviewing the main points to emerge from my re-reading of the chapters in this book I have come to realise that so many forms of constructive action are variants of this political method.

In the study of constructive action in times of war and occupation reference was made to the attempts of people to incorporate into their everyday lives some of the values and practices they felt were threatened by the conditions of war. Through the medium of their own everyday lives they were seeking to preserve some of these threatened values and practices for the sake of the future. In the study of civil resistance movements we can see how significant the attempts were to create spaces where people might live in the truth, to use Vaclav Havel's terminology, as a counter to the public spaces where people were obliged to 'live within the lie' if they were to avoid serious sanctions. It was also noted how such efforts, by those seeking to retain some semblance of their human dignity as moral beings, fed into and strengthened the associated efforts to create alternative institutions and structures. The importance of such structures lay in their creation of a space where a different life might be lived, where people might seek to negate the system within themselves and reclaim their own identity, as against that required of them by the regime.

These are all forms of prefigurative action – attempting to create in the here-and-now modes of life and relationships that are intended to be examples of how life might be organised, on a far-wider scale, sometime in the future.

9. Constructive action – servicing the needs of activists and citizens

As I sit here at my desk in Coventry, in mid-July 2021, a few hundred miles north at a gallery in Aberdeen a new exhibition has opened, entitled 'Another world is possible – Aberdeen People's Press and radical media in the 1970s'. Planning the exhibition was a collaborative effort involving the gallery staff and the surviving folk who were part of the venture back in the 1970s. It has been a weird experience reconnecting with comrades from half a century ago, going back together in time to a different epoch when we genuinely believed that we were involved in a wider movement to create an alternative society. In part we felt we were contributing through the exemplary action of how the venture was organised as a collective, but we also saw ourselves as providing a printing and publishing service for local community groups and grassroot activists further afield.

We saw in the case of the 2021 Myanmar civil resistance against the military junta's seizure of power how, in the midst of the most intense confrontations and public protests, there were groups focused on providing medical services, monitoring human rights abuses, providing legal support, and sending reports to local, national and international media outlets. In some neighbourhoods local groups also organised themselves to provide needed community services such as garbage collection and transport facilities. We also saw, in the case of the protracted civil resistance movements in Europe that culminated in the 1989 collapse of the state socialist regimes, how the different parallel institutions established by dissidents – community centres, social clubs, production and distribution of samizdat literature – fulfilled an essential role, maintaining the communication channels and networks of trust that kept the dissident movements alive during the years of severe state repression.[7] Perhaps one of the most valued services provided by and for activists has been that of accompaniment: unarmed volunteers supporting the work of local

---

7   One of my friends, the British nonviolent activist Michael Randle, 'smuggled' a duplicating machine into Czechoslovakia in the early 1970s, to support the samizdat movement there. See Levy, 2021, p. 212.

human rights activists in conflict zones by their physical presence alongside them, intending thereby to open up the degree of space necessary for them to fulfil their chosen role.

10. Constructive action lacks leverage when push comes to shove

Whilst writing these concluding pages I began to feel I was trying to 'sell' constructive modes of action and resistance, trying to list all the 'positives' of this approach to making change happen. Now is the 'Ah but' time – and for me the most important 'ah but' is the fact that in most contexts constructive modes of nonviolent direct action on their own lack the 'umph' - the leverage power to bring about the collapse of authoritarian regimes. As we saw in the case of Kosovo, in and of themselves constructive modes of resistance lack the coercive power to impose the level of costs on the opposition necessary to force them to concede. Most modes of constructive resistance lack that degree of drama necessary to grab the attention of broad swathes of the public, including third-party publics and their political leaders, and convince them that 'something must be done'.

Going back to the Palestinians struggling to end the occupation, their constructive modes of resistance, however laudable in themselves, lack the degree of drama to arouse that sense of urgency necessary to grab the attention of significant third-parties (state and non-state) with the leverage power to impact on Israel's commitment to its colonial project. Sumud and other forms of quiet 'semi-resistance' have their significance as 'holding operations', keeping alive important facets of Palestinian culture, history and identity, but they are never going to bring about an end to the occupation.

Constructive modes of resistance are processes, not events. They lack the emotional punch of clashes between unarmed protesters and violent oppressors, images that can encapsulate and communicate a powerful morality tale of good versus evil. Such symbols can attract the attention of the global media and other significant agencies in a manner that the more mundane methods of constructive action cannot hope to attain. Furthermore, constructive modes of resistance are unlikely to sway opponents if we are to judge by the

Kosovan and Palestinian experiences. The social distance between the opposing sides is such as to render attempts at 'shame power' relatively ineffectual.

Perhaps part of the answer to this kind of dilemma can be found in Gandhi's approach. As noted in chapter three, when Gandhi initiated struggles against particular instances of injustice and oppression, he emphasised not merely the aim of overcoming evil, but also the importance of creating positive alternatives to the violent structures and practices that were being challenged. Hence, when he urged people to boycott British made cloth, he also encouraged them to produce their own clothing, hence the powerful symbolism of khadi. In confronting the British by refusing to pay the Salt Tax, he also emphasised the importance of people making and distributing their own salt. In these campaigns the constructive dimension was integrated into the protest itself, and added to its emotional impact and hence its power of leverage. A North European variant on this theme – my Scandinavian friend (and publisher and woodworker) Jørgen Johansen told me of an action when he and other activists attempted to block the entrance to a nuclear power-station with a windmill they had constructed.[8]

11. Constructive action and the temptations of 'internal exile'

In his account of his personal involvement in Israeli solidarity groups working alongside Palestinians to resist the worst abuses of the ongoing occupation, the writer and scholar David Shulman explained how, before he became active during the first Intifada, he became more and more appalled at the changes he was witnessing in Israeli society. He wrote:

> … for many years I, like many of my colleagues, went into a kind of internal exile, becoming more and more alienated from wider Israeli society. The rise of the Israeli right, from 1977 on, shocked me, infuriated me, and undermined my faith in the world I lived in. A raucous, viciously self-righteous tone came to dominate public life …. The results, in my view, were

---

8   Personal communication, 20 July 2021.

catastrophic; I watched in horror as Israel rapidly transformed itself into a paranoid, smug, and rather violent ghetto.[9]

These words struck a strong chord in me. Not only did they remind me of the friends I have made amongst Israeli peace activists as they have struggled with conflicting pressures – to stay and fight or go into exile, external or internal. It also brought back to me the numerous times I have joined local and national protests against British militaristic ventures in the Middle East and elsewhere, carrying a home-made placard proclaiming - 'Not in my name!' As I have grown older, and my levels of energy have declined, I confess that it becomes more difficult to resist the temptation to withdraw into internal exile. I try to fight the seductive appeal of the quietist response of disassociation from all the evil perpetrated by governments and agencies who claim to be acting on behalf of citizens like myself. Moreover, I can try to appease my sense of guilt by claiming that I continue to try and act as a caring and compassionate cosmopolitan citizen within the interstices of my everyday life. But, whilst I am sure that internal exile can be a wise response in certain circumstances and contexts, in liberal democracies such as the UK it is not enough. There is still the need for nonviolent protest and contestation, we still need to explore the means to create the friction necessary to prevent the smooth functioning of agencies driven by narrow, self-serving interests rather than concern for the well-being of humanity as a whole – alongside committed efforts to sow the seeds of a sustainable future.

---

9   D. Shulman, *Dark hope: Working for peace in Israel and Palestine*, Chicago: University of Chicago Press, 2007, p. 4.

Bibliography

Anderson S. & J. Larmore, eds., *Nonviolent struggle and social defence*, London: War Resisters International, 1991.

Avruch K. & R.S. Jose, 'Peace zones in the Philippines', in Hancock & Mitchell, eds., 2007, pp. 51-70.

Arunachalam K. & C. Sadler, *On the frontiers: Essays in honour of Rev. Dr R.R. Keithahn,* Madurai, TN: Koodal, 1977.

Arunachalam K. & K.M. Natarjan, eds., *Integrated rural development*, Madurai, TN: Koodal, 1977.

Armytage, W., *Heavens below: Utopian experiments in England 1560-1960,* London: Routledge & Kegan Paul, 1961.

Bamburg, J., 'Mondragon through a critical lens', *Fifty by fifty: Employee ownership news,* 3 October 2017.

Bartowski, M., ed., *Recovering nonviolent history: Civil resistance in liberation struggles*, Boulder, CO.: Lynne Rienner, 2013.

Bell, A., *Only for three months: the Basque children in exile,* Norwich: Mousehold Press, 2007.

Bhave, V., *Moved by love: The memoirs of Vinoba Bhave*, Wardha: Paramdam Prakachan, 1994.

Bickle R., 'An atmosphere of cooperation', *The Ecologist*, 22 March 2007.

Black, M., *A cause for our times: Oxfam the first 50 years*, Oxford: Oxford University Press, 1992.

Blumer, H., 'What is wrong with social theory?', *American Sociological Review*, v. 18, 1954, pp. 3-10.

Boserup, A. & A. Mack, *War without weapons*, London: Frances Pinter, 1974.

Brock P. & T. Socknat, eds., *Challenge to Mars: Essays on pacifism from 1918 to 1945*, Toronto: University of Toronto Press, 1999.

Brockway, F., *Inside the Left*, Leicester: Blackfriars Press, 1947.

Brown J. & A. Parel, eds., *The Cambridge companion to Gandhi*, Cambridge: Cambridge University Press, 2011.

Buber, M., *Paths in utopia,* London: Routledge & Kegan Paul, 1949.

Buchanan, T., *Britain and the Spanish Civil War*, Cambridge: Cambridge University Press, 1997.

Carter, A. 'People power and protest: The literature on civil resistance in historical context', in Roberts & Garton Ash, eds., 2009, pp. 25-42.

Carter, A., H. Clark & M. Randle, *A guide to civil resistance: A bibliography of people power and nonviolent protest*, London: Merlin Press, 2013.

Clark, H., 'The limits of prudence: Civil resistance in Kosovo, 1990-98', in Roberts & Garton Ash, 2009, pp. 277-294.

Ceadel, M., *Pacifism in Britain, 1914-1945: The defining of a faith*, Oxford: Clarendon Press, 1980.

Chabot S. & M. Sharifi, 'The violence of nonviolence: Problematizing nonviolent resistance in Iran and Egypt', *Societies without borders*, v.8, n. 2, 2013, pp. 205-232.

Chandra, B., *India's struggle for independence*, New Delhi: Penguin, 1989.

Chaudhuri, E. R., *Planning with the poor: The nonviolent experiment of Danilo Dolci in Sicily*, New Delhi: Gandhi Peace Foundation, 1998.

Chenoweth E. & M. J. Stephan, *Why civil resistance works: The strategic logic of nonviolent conflict*, NY: Columbia University Press, 2011.

Chester G. & A. Rigby, eds., *Articles of peace: Celebrating fifty years of Peace News*, Bridport: Prism Press, 1986.

Chomsky, N., *American power and the new mandarins*, New York: Pantheon Books, 1969.

Chomsky N. et al, *Climate crisis and the Global Green New Deal: The political economy of saving the planet*, London: Version, 2020.

Clark, H., *Civil resistance in Kosovo,* London: Pluto Press, 2000.

Clark, H., ed., *People power: Unarmed resistance and global solidarity,* London: Pluto, 2009.

Clark, H., 'The limits of prudence: Civil resistance in Kosovo, 1990-98', in *Civil resistance and power politics: The experience of non-violent action from Gandhi to the present*, edited by A. Roberts & T. Garton Ash, Oxford: Oxford University Press, 2009, pp. 277-294.

Clark, H., *Making nonviolent revolution*, London: Peace News, 2012.

Clark, S., *Echo in my soul*, New York: E. P. Dutton, 1962.

Coates, C., ed., *Utopia Britannica: British utopian experiments: 1325 to 1945*, London: Diggers & Dreamers, 2001.

Coleman, F., *The Marcel Network: How one French couple saved 527 children from the Holocaust*, Dulles, VA: Potomac Books, 2013.

Coluccello, R., *Challenging the Mafia mystique: Cosa Nostra from legitimisation to denunciation*, Basingstoke: Palgrave MacMillan, 2016.

Coppo, L., *The color of freedom*, Monroe, ME.: Common Courage Press, 2005.

Crosby, E., *A little taste of freedom: The Black freedom struggle in Clairborne County, Mississippi*, Chapel Hill: University of North Carolina Press, 2005.

Crouch, D. & C. Ward, *The allotment: Its landscape and culture*, Nottingham: Five Leaves, 1997.

Dalton, D., *Indian idea of freedom*, Gurgaon, Haryana: Academic Press, 1982.

Darley, G., *Villages of vision*, London: Paladin, 1978,

Darweish, M. & A. Rigby, *Popular protest in Palestine: The uncertain future of unarmed resistance*, London: Pluto Press, 2015.

Davidson, C., 'The Mondragon Cooperatives and 21st century socialism: A review of five books with radical critiques and new ideas', *Perspectives on global development and technology* , v.11, n.1, Jan. 2012, pp. 229-243.

Dean, B. & G. Scharnhorst. 'The Contemporary Reception of Walden', in *Studies in the American Renaissance*, 1990, pp. 293-328.

Dolci, D., *The outlaws of Partinico*, London: MacGibbon & Kee, 1960.

Dunseath, T., 'Teachers at war: Norwegian teachers during the German Occupation of Norway 1940-45', *History of Education*, v. 31, n. 4, 2002, pp. 371-383.

Duong, B., 'Despite a rocky start Cleveland model for worker coops stands test of time', *Shelterforce,* 9 March 2021.

Egan, D., 'Rethinking war of manoeuvre/ war of position: Gramsci and the military metaphor', *Critical Sociology*, v. 40, n. 4, 2014, pp. 521–538.

Elliott, A., 'Ella Baker: Free agent in the Civil Rights Movement', *Journal of Black Studies* , v. 26, n. 5, May 1996, pp. 593-603.

Fairbairn, B., *The meaning of Rochdale: The Rochdale Pioneers and the cooperative principles*, Saskatoon, CA: University of Saskatchewan, Centre for Study of Cooperatives, 1994.

Fukuyama, F.. 'The drive for dignity', *Foreign Policy*, 12 January 2012.

Galtung, J., *Non-violence and Israel/Palestine*, Honolulu: University of Hawaii, 1989.

Gandhi, M., *Constructive programme: Its meaning and place*, Ahmedabad: Navajivan Publishing, 1941.

Gandhi, M., *Hind swaraj or Indian home rule*, Ahmedabad: Navajivan Publishing, 1938.

Garnett, R. G., *Cooperation and the Owenite socialist communities in Britain, 1825–45,* Manchester: University of Manchester Press, 1972.

Gerth H. & C. Wright Mills, eds., *From Max Weber: Essays in sociology,* London: Routledge & Kegan Paul, 1967.

Grant, J., ed., *Black protest*, New York: Fawcett, 1968.

Grose, P., *A good place to hide: How one community saved thousands of lives from the Nazis*, London: Nicholas Brealey Publishing, 2014.

Gross, M., 'Jewish rescue in Holland and France during the Second World War: Moral Cognition and Collective Action', *Social Forces*, v. 73, n. 2, December 1994, pp. 463-496.

Guha, R., *An anthropologist among the Marxists*, Delhi: Permanent Black, 2001.

Gunnarson, C., 'Changing the game: Addiopizzo's mobilisation against racketeering in Palermo', *European Review of Organised Crime* v.1, n.1, 2014 , pp. 39-77.

Hancock, L. E. & C. Mitchell, eds., *Zones of peace*, Bloomfield, CT: Kumarian Press, 2007.

Hardiman, D., ed., *Nonviolence in modern Indian history*, Hyderabad: Orient Blackswan, 2017.

Hardy, D., *Alternative communities in nineteenth century England*, London: Longman, 1979.

Hardy, D., *Utopian England: Community experiments 1900-1945*, London: E & F.N. Spon, 2000.

Harrison, J.F.C., 'The Owenite socialist movement in Britain and the United States a comparative study', *Labor History*, v. 9, n. 3, pp. 323-337, July 2008.

Havel, V., *Living in truth*, London: Faber & Faber, 1990.

Hayes, D., *Challenge of conscience: The story of the conscientious objectors of 1939-45*, London: George Allen and Unwin, 1949.

Herzon, S. & A Hai, 'What do people mean when they say people-to-people?', *Palestine-Israel Journal*, v.12, n. 4, 2005.

Higgins, A.G., *A history of the Brotherhood Church*: Stapleton: Brotherhood Church, 1982

Hill, C., *The world turned upside down: Radical ideas during the English Revolution*, Harmondsworth: Penguin Books, 1975.

Hoe, S., *The man who gave his company away*, London: Heinemann, 1978.

Holman, M., 'The Purleigh Colony: Tolstoyan togetherness in the late 1890s', in M. Jones, ed., *New essays on Tolstoy*, Cambridge: Cambridge University Press, 1978, pp. 194–222.

Houck D. & D. Dixon, eds., *Women and the Civil Rights Movement, 1954–1965* , Jackson: University Press of Mississippi, 2009

Huxley, A., *Science, liberty and peace,* London: Chatto & Windus, 1947.

Isenberg, S., *A hero of our own: The story of Varian Fry*, Kindle, 2017.

Jamieson, A., *The anti-Mafia: Italy's fight against organized crime*, NY: St. Martin's Press, 2000.

Judah, T., *Kosovo: War and revenge*, New York: Yale University Press, 2000.

Kahn, K., 'Evergreen cooperatives adapt and grow', *Fifty by Fifty*, 31 March 2021

Kaplan, O., 'Protecting civilians in civil war: The institution of the ATCC in Colombia', *Journal of Peace Research,* v. 50, n. 3, 2013, pp. 351-367.

Kaplan, O., *Resisting war: How communities protect themselves,* Cambridge: Cambridge University Press, 2017.

Koestler, A., *The lotus and the robot,* London: Hutchinson, 1966.

Kostovicova, D., *Kosovo: The politics of identity and space,* Abingdon: Routledge, 2005.

Kumarappa, J. C., *The economy of permanence: A quest for a social order based on nonviolence,* Wardha: Maganvadi, 1948.

Legarreta, D., *The Guernica generation: Basque refugee children of the Spanish Civil War,* Reno, NV: University of Nevada Press, 1984.

Leval, G., *Collectives in the Spanish Revolution,* tr. Vernon Richards, London: Freedom Press, 1975.

Levy, C., ed., *Colin Ward: Life, times and thought,* London: Lawrence and Wishart, 2013.

Levy, M., *Ban the bomb! Michael Randle and direct action against nuclear war,* Stuttgart: Ibidem, 2021.

Lewis, N., *The honoured society: The Sicilian Mafia observed,* London: Eland, 2003.

Lindley, M., *J.C. Kumarappa: Mahatma Gandhi's economist,* Mumbai: Popular Prakashan, 2007.

Ling, P., 'Local leadership in the early Civil Rights Movement: The South Carolina Citizenship Education Program of the Highlander Folk School', *Journal of American Studies,* v. 29, n. 3, 1995, pp. 399-422.

London Committee of 100, *Beyond counting arses,* 1962.

Lupo, S., *History of the Mafia,* New York: Columbia University Press, 2011.

Mahoney L. & L. E. Eguren, *Unarmed bodyguards: International accompaniment for the protection of human rights,* West Hartford, Ct.: Kumarian Press, 1997.

Malcolm, N., *Kosovo: A short history,* London: MacMillan, 1998.

Mantena, K., 'Another realism: The politics of Gandhian nonviolence', *American Political Science Review*, v. 106, n. 2, May 2012, pp. 455-470.

Martin, B., 'Making accompaniment effective', in H. Clark, ed., 2009, pp. 93-97.

Martin, B., *Backfire manual: Tactics against injustice,* Sparsnas: Irene Publishing, 2012.

Mazgaonkar, A., 'India – macro-violence, micro-resistance: Development violence and unarmed grassroots resistance', in H. Clark, ed., 2009, pp. 76-85.

Maybin, E., *After the prawn rush: The human and environmental costs of commercial prawn farming,* London: Christian Aid, 1996.

Mogensen, M., 'The rescue of the Danish Jews', in M. B. Jensen and S. L. B. Jensen, eds., *Denmark and the Holocaust,* Copenhagen: Department for Holocaust and Genocide Studies, Institute for International Studies, 2003, pp. 33-61.

Moses R., 'The Algebra Project: Organising in the spirit of Ella', *Harvard Educational Review,* n. 59, Winter 1989, pp. 423-43.

Navarro, V., 'What about cooperatives as a solution? The case of Mondragon', *CounterPunch*, 30 April 2014.

Nepstad, S. E., *Nonviolent revolutions: Civil resistance n the late 20th century*, Oxford: Oxford University Press, 2011.

O'Connor R. & P. Kelly, *A study of industrial workers' cooperatives,* Dublin: Economic and Social Research Institute, 1980.

Ostergaard G. & M. Currell, *The gentle anarchists: A study of the leaders of the sarvodaya movement for non-violent revolution in India*, Oxford: Clarendon Press, 1971.

Ostergaard, G., *Nonviolent revolution in India,* New Delhi: Gandhi Peace Foundation, 1985.

Overy, B., *Gandhi as an organiser: How he shaped a nationwide rebellion: India 1915-1922,* Sparsnas, Sweden: Irene, 2019.

Paczkowski, E., 'The Marcora Law: An innovative way to promote entrepreneurship', *Medium*, 24 December 2020.

Paoli, L., *Mafia brotherhoods: Organized crime, Italian style*, Oxford: Oxford: Oxford University Press, 2003.

Payne, C., *I've got the light of freedom: The organizing tradition and the Mississippi Freedom struggle* , Berkeley: University of California Press, 2007.

Peck, J., *Freedom ride*, New York: Grove Press, 1962.

Pollin, D. & A. Guyot, *Thirty two acres of paradise: Varian Fry and Air-Bel, Marseille,* Kindle, 2015.

Rakopoulos, T., *From clans to co-ops: Confiscated Mafia land in Sicily*, New York: Berghahn, 2018.

Randle, M., *Civil resistance*, London: Fontana Press, 1994.

Reinders, R. C., 'Toynbee Hall and the American Settlement Movement', *Social Service Review*, v. 56, n. 1, March 1982, pp. 39-54.

Rigby, A., *Alternative realities: A study of communes and their members*, London: Routledge & Kegan Paul, 1974.

Rigby, A., 'Practical utopianism: a Gandhian approach to rural community development in India', *Community Development Journal*, v. 20, n. 1, 1985, pp. 2-7.

Rigby, A., 'Be practical, do the impossible: The politics of everyday living', in Chester & Rigby, eds., 1986, pp. 90-105.

Rigby, A., 'LAFTI—Making offers the landowners cannot refuse', *Community Development Journal,* v. 22, n. 4, 1987, pp. 310-321.

Rigby, A., *A life in peace: A biography of Wilfred Wellock*, Bridport: Prism Press, 1988.

Rigby, A., 'Pacifist communities in Britain in the Second World War', *Peace and Change*, v 15, no 2, April 1990, pp. 107-22.

Rigby, A., *Living the intifada,* London: Zed, 1991

Rigby, A., *The legacy of the past: The problem of collaborators and the Palestinian case*, East Jerusalem: PASSIA, 1997.

Rigby, A., 'Gram Swaraj versus globalisation: Popular resistance against the spread of prawn farms in India', *Peace and Change*, v. 22, n. 4, October 1997, pp. 381-413.

Rigby, A., 'The Peace Pledge Union: From peace to war, 1936-45', in Brock & Socknat, eds., 1999, pp. 169-185.

Rigby, A., *Palestinian resistance and nonviolence*, East Jerusalem: PASSIA, 2010.

Rigby, A., *The first Palestinian Intifada revisited*, Sparsnas, Sweden: Irene, 2015.

Rigby, A., 'The nonviolent activism of the radical Gandhian, Jagannathanji, 1912 -2013', in Hardiman, ed., 2017, pp. 179-206.

Rigby A. & M Sørensen, 'Frontstage and backstage emotion management in civil resistance', *Journal of Political Power*, v. 17, n. 2, June 2017, pp. 219-235.

Rijke A., & T. van Teeffelen, 'To exist is to resist: Sumud, heroism and the everyday', *Jerusalem Quarterly*, n. 59, 2014, pp. 86-99.

Rings, W., *Life with the enemy: Collaboration and resistance in Hitler's Europe 1939-1945*, NY: Doubleday, 1982.

Roberts, A., *Civilian resistance as a national defence: Nonviolent action against aggression*, Harmondsworth: Penguin, 1967.

Roberts A. & T. Garton Ash, *Civil resistance and power politics: The experience of non-violent action from Gandhi to the present*, Oxford: Oxford University Press, 2009.

Roy, S., *Failing peace: Gaza and the Palestinian-Israeli conflict*, London: Pluto Press , 2007.

Rowbotham, S., *Edward Carpenter: A life of liberty and love*, London: Verso, 2008.

Sammallahti L. & I. Doherty, 'Why has the number of worker co-ops increased 20-fold in the UK since 1970?', *Mutual Interest Media*, 31 March 2021.

Sampson, R., *The anarchist basis of pacifism*, London: Peace Pledge Union, 1970.

Schofield, S., *Oceans of work: Arms conversion revisited*, London: BASIC, 2007.

Shehadeh, R., *The third way: A journal of life in the West Bank*, London: Quartet Books, 1982.

Shehadeh, R., *Going home: A walk through fifty years of occupation*, London: Profile Books, 2019

Schock, K., *Unarmed insurrections: People power movements in nondemocracies,* Minneapolis: University of Minnesota Press, 2005.

Schock, K., *Civil resistance today,* Cambridge: Polity Press, 2015.

Schock, K., 'Gandhian struggles for land in India', in Hardiman, ed., 2017, pp. 207-229.

Schutz, A., *Collected papers I: The problem of social reality*, The Hague: Martinus Nijhoff, 1971.

Scott, J.C., *Domination and the arts of resistance: Hidden transcripts*, London: Yale University Press, 1992.

Semelin, J., *Unarmed against Hitler: Civilian resistance in Europe, 1939-1943*, London: Praeger, 1993.

Sharp, G., *Waging nonviolent struggle: 20th century practice and 21st century potential*, Boston: Porter Sargent, 2005.

Shaw, N., *Whiteway: A colony on the Cotswolds*, London: Daniels, 1935.

Shridharanai, K., *War without violence: A study of Gandhi's method and its accomplishments,* London: Victor Gollanz, 1939.

Shulman, D., *Dark hope: Working for peace in Israel and Palestine*, Chicago: University of Chicago Press, 2007.

Siedman, M., 'Work and revolution: Workers' control in Barcelona in the Spanish Civil War, 1936-38', *Journal of Contemporary History* , v.17, n.3, 1982, pp. 409-433.

Siedman, M., 'Agrarian Collectives during the Spanish Revolution and Civil War', *European History Quarterly*, v.30, n.2, 2000, pp. 209–235.

Smolar, A., 'Towards "self-limiting revolution": Poland, 1970-89' in Roberts & Garton Ash, eds., 2009, pp. 127-143.

Soliman, M., *Mobilisation and demobilisation of the Palestinian society towards popular resistance from 2004-2014*, Coventry University, unpublished Ph.D. thesis, 2019.

Spann, E., *Brotherly tomorrows: Movements for a cooperative society in America, 1820-1920,* New York: Columbia University Press, 1989.

Stubbings, L., ed., *Community in Britain*, West Byfleet: Community Service Committee, 1940.

Sørensen, M.J. & B. Martin, 'The dilemma action: Analysis of an activist technique', *Peace and Change*, v. 39, n. 1, January 2014, pp. 73-100.

Sørensen, M. J., 'Glorifications and simplifications in case studies of Danish WWII nonviolent resistance', *Journal of Resistance Studies*, v. 3, no 1, 2017, pp. 99-137.

Thomas, A., 'The rise of social cooperatives in Italy', *Voluntas: International journal of voluntary and non-profit organizations*, v.15, n. 3, September 2004, pp. 243-263.

Thompson, M., *A paper house: The ending of Yugoslavia*, London: Vintage. 1992.

Thoreau, H.D., 'Civil disobedience', in P. Mayer, ed., *The pacifist conscience*, Harmondsworth: Penguin, 1966, pp. 140-159.

Tjerandsen, C., *Education for citizenship: A Foundation's experience,* Santa Cruz, CA: Emil Schwartzhaupt Foundation, 1980.

Tolstoy, L., *The kingdom of God is within you*, New York: Cassell, 1894.

Vejvoda, I., 'Civil society versus Slobodan Milosevic: Serbia 1991-2000' in Roberts & Garton Ash, Oxford: 2009, pp. 295–316.

Vieta M. et al, *The Italian road to recuperating enterprises and the Legge Marcora framework*, Trento: European Research Institute on Cooperative and Social Enterprises, Research report n. 15/17, 2015.

Vinthagen, S., *A theory of nonviolent action: How civil resistance works*, London: Zed Press, 2015.

Wainwright, H., 'When the workers nearly took control: Five lessons from the Lucas Plan', *Open Democracy*, 29 November 2016.

Ward, C., *Anarchy in action*, London: Freedom Press, 1996.

Ward, C., *Cotters and squatters: Housing's hidden history*, Nottingham: Five Leaves, 2002.

Weber, M., 'Politics as a vocation', in Gerth & Wright Mills, eds.,1967, pp. 120-126.

Weber, T., *Gandhi's peace army: The Shanti Sena and unarmed peacekeeping*, Syracuse, NY: Syracuse University Press, 1996.

Widmer, K., 'The limits of pacifism', *Anarchy 52*, v. 5, n. 5, June 1965, pp. 161-66.

Yeo, S., 'A new life: The religion of socialism in Britain, 1883-1896', *History Workshop Journal*, n. 4, 1977, pp. 5-56.

Index

Abadi, Moussa, 130, 131
Aberdeen Peoples Press (APP), 81, 83, 209, 210, 212, 214, 225
Accompaniment, 124, 150, 151, 152, 153, 225
Acquiescence, 53, 180
Addiopizzo, 160, 17-72, 178-186, 188-89
Affinity group, 46
Agricultural colonies (Second World War), 38
Agriculture, 27, 56, 61, 76, 177
Alternative society, 21, 39, 40–41, 82–83, 227
Anarchism, i, 20, 33, 194
Anarchy, 16-17, 20-21
Anchor institutions, 206, 208
Anti-Mafia Commission, 169, 172, 186
Arizmendiarrieta, Jose Maria, 201, 203, 205
Ashram, 50-51, 55, 60, 75
ASSEFA (Association of Sarva Seva Farms), 63–64
Athletics front (Norway), 143

Baba Amte, 75, 220
Backfire, 2, 153
Backstage, 10, 12, 87
Bader, Ernest, 193, 216
Baker, Ella, 112–113, 118
Barrow Alternative Employment Committee, 211
Basic needs, 75, 124, 147, 176, 221
Basque refugees, 125, 126
BDS movement, 12
Benn, Anthony Wedgewood, 214
Bhoodan ((land gift), 56-59, 61, 63-65
Bickle, Richard, 218
Bihar, 65-66, 165
Birmingham, 9, 26, 111
Blood feud, 97
Bodhgaya Monastery, 66
Borsellino, Paulo, 172-174, 181, 183
Bradford, ii, 29, 45-46, 157, 201, 211, 213, 215
Brotherhood Church, 35, 37

Brown, Judith, 50
Buber, Martin, 8, 191-192
Burn-out 14, 87, 89

Cadbury, George, 9, 29
Campaign for Nuclear Disarmament (CND), 16
Carbon-footprint, 43, 206
Carpenter, Edward, 31-34
Ceadel, Martin, 215
Cetta, Anton, 97
Chandra, Bhipan, 14, 53-55, 69-71, 73, 222-223
Chavez, Cesar, 159, 170
Chhatra Yuva Sangharsh Vahini, 165
Church networks, 90, 93, 144, 146
Ciotti, Luigi, 174-175
Citizenship rights, 85, 111
Citizenship schools, 114, 116-118, 220
Civil disobedience, 3, 13, 47-48, 51-52, 54-55, 69, 77, 88, 222-223
Civil resistance, 2, 5, 8, 10,14, 16, 46-47, 51-52, 81-90, 92-103, 105-107, 110, 120, 139-140, 142, 209, 219, 221, 224-225
Civil rights movement (US), 111-115, 118-119, 219
Civil society, 9, 84, 90-91, 101, 105-106, 144, 146, 153, 175-176
Civil war, 22, 24, 125-126, 154, 156, 192-195, 197-198, 201
Clark, Howard, ii, 46, 75, 83-84, 95-97, 99-100, 124, 153
Clark, Septima, 112, 114-118
Cleveland, Ohio, 206-208
Climate crisis, 9, 43, 79, 212
CNT (Confederation National de Trabajo), 195
Coercion, 34, 65, 197, 199
Collective leadership, 113
Collectives, 193-195, 197-199, 212-213
Colombia, 154, 156
Coluccello, Salvatore, 167-168, 171
Communal living, 25, 34, 37
Communal unity, 50, 52

241

Communism, 25, 31, 56, 194
Communist Party of Spain (PCE), 194
Community leaders, 115, 117
Community mobilisation, 111, 220
Community organising, 55, 111-112, 118, 121, 219
Community Service Committee, 37
Complicity, 20, 170, 177, 181, 184
Concept (sensitising), 7
Confrontations, 2, 5, 16, 51, 70-71, 95, 100-102, 119, 122, 222-223, 227
Congress of Racial Equality (CORE), 119
Constructive action, i-iii, 1-3, 5-10, 12-14, 16-17, 21-22, 30, 48-49, 51, 73, 81, 83, 92, 109-110, 120-121, 123-125, 141, 153, 156, 178, 191, 193, 209, 219-227
Constructive resistance, 1, 5-7, 12, 14-15, 82, 84, 86-87, 89, 94, 96, 99, 110-111, 127-129, 131-132, 137, 142, 149, 159, 187, 221, 226
Constructive living, 4, 37, 124, 142-143
Constructive solidarity, 10, 11
Conversion, 32, 65, 99, 193, 211-212, 215
Cooperative Development Agency, 214
Cooperative movement, 29-30, 199
Cooperatives, 9, 24-30, 35, 38-40, 116, 165, 175-177, 183, 186, 189, 191-193, 197-209, 212-214, 216, 218
Counter-culture, 39-41
Courage 49, 90, 115, 121, 122, 132, 139, 146, 147, 206
Coventry, ii, 5-6, 225
Cranks/ eccentrics, 4, 41
Creative living, 37-38, 215
Credit union, 202
Culture (way of life), 87, 94, 108, 110, 112-113, 140-142, 149, 163, 175, 180, 182-185, 187, 207, 209, 221, 226
Czechoslovakia, 90-94, 125, 139, 221, 225

Dalla Chiesa, Carlo, 173
Danish Jews, 138-141
Darley, Gillian, 9, 27, 29
Darweish, Marwan, 13, 52, 107, 152

Davidson, Carl, 202
Democracies, constitutional, 2, 85, 228
Democratic League for Kosovo (LDK), 96-97
Denmark, 128, 137-141
Dictatorship (of ritual), 92
Diggers, 12, 22-24, 84
Dilemma action, 166
Direct action,
  Confrontational, 119
  Nonviolent, 1, 2, 5, 8, 45-46, 71, 159, 192
Discrimination, 110, 112
Dolci, Danilo, 159-172, 184-186, 220
Drama, 98, 110, 226
Dumpster diving, 7

Education, 30-31, 34, 59, 94-97, 102, 111-112, 114-119, 146-149, 163, 168, 173, 183, 186, 188, 220, 222
Ekta Parishad (Unity Forum), 77, 221
Emergency Rescue Committee, 128-129
Engels, Friedrich, 25
English Civil War, 22
Ethical consumption, 34, 182
Ethical tourism, 183, 188
Everard, William, 23
Evergreen Cooperatives, 206-208
Everyday life, ii, 10, 12, 19, 21, 32-33, 38, 40-41, 43, 47, 87, 109, 121, 141, 146, 157, 221, 224, 228
Everyday resistance, 11-12

Factory council, 195-196
Fagor, 203
Faith, 26, 37, 63, 128, 134, 136, 157, 215, 227
Falcone, Giovanni, 172-174 183
Federation, 202-204
Fisk, Robert, 123
Free schools, 40
Freedom riders, 119
Free-riders, 198
Friction, 2-4, 10, 12, 16, 86, 221, 228
Front-stage, 12, 16, 87
Fry, Varian, 129

Gandhi, M.K. ii, 13-14, 35, 45, 47-57, 60-62, 65, 69-73, 77-78, 84, 160, 163, 170, 216, 220, 222-223, 227
    Constructive programme, ii, 13-14, 48, 50, 52, 54-55, 60, 70, 75, 222-223
    Swaraj, 13, 48-50, 56, 61, 68-70, 73-74, 77
Gandhigram, 48, 61
Germany, 7, 25, 93, 125-126, 132, 136-138, 147-148
Goodman, Paul, 20
Goodway, David, 21
Gram sabha (village assembly), 58, 68
Gram swaraj, 61, 68-69, 73-74, 77
Gramdan (village gift), 56-59, 61-63, 65, 79
Gramsci, Antonio, 14, 53
Grassi, Libero, 180-183, 187
Green new deal, 212
Gunnarson, Carina, 180, 186-187

Hardy, Dennis, 378, 200
Havel, Vaclav, 91-93, 224
Hayes, Dennis, 38
Hebron, 151-152
Hezbollah, 106
Hidden transcripts, 11, 87
Highlander Folk School, 114-115
Hill, Christopher, 22-24
Horton, Miles, 115-116
Humanitarian constructive action, 124-125
Humanitarian constructive resistance, 128-129, 131-132, 137
Hypothesis, 86, 94, 11

Identity, 75, 87, 92-94, 99, 108-110, 120, 130, 134, 136, 142, 146, 149, 156-157, 221-222, 224, 226
Impastato, Giuseppe, 174, 181
Impunity, 172
Indira Gandhi, 65-67
Industrial Common Ownership Act (1976), 200
Industrial Common Ownership Movement (ICOM), 214
Innerdalen, 1
Intentional communities (communes), i, 9, 25, 21, 37, 40

Internal exile, 227, 228
International networks, 131, 135
Intifada, 99-102,104-107 110, 227
Israel, 6, 11, 14-15, 72, 95, 100-110, 121, 132, 151-153, 221, 226-228
Israeli settlements, 104, 106-107 ,152
    Israeli-produce, 111
    Occupation, 11, 13-15, 52, 95, 100-110, 152-153, 221, 226-227
    Separation barrier, 107

Jagannathanji, 48, 60, 74, 78, 223
Jai Jagat, 79
Jato River, 164
Jayaprakash Narayan (JP), 58, 64, 159, 165
Jenkins, Esau, 116
Jerusalem, 12, 15, 85, 100, 103-104, 107-108, 110
Johansen, Jørgen, ii, 1, 227

Kaplan, Oliver, 154-156
Keithahn, R.R., 60-63
Khadi, 50, 55, 227
Kilvenmani, 64
Kindertransport, 125, 127
King, Martin Luther, 111-112, 117, 170, 220
Kocherry, Thomas, 75
Kosovo, 84, 95-100, 226
Kosovo Liberation Army (UCK), 98
Krishnammal Jagannathan, 48-49, 60-69, 73-75, 78, 223
Kumarappa, J.C., 61-62

La Torre, Pio, 172-173, 176
LAFTI – Land for the Tillers Independence/Freedom, 67-68- 70-71, 73
Le Chambon, 123, 124, 125, 126, 127, 128, 132-137
Leadership, 47, 55, 69, 76, 95, 100, 110-113, 115, 117-118, 133, 148-149, 156, 166, 185
Leverage, 78, 87, 94, 105, 110, 151, 188, 226-227
Levison, Stanley, 112
Lewis, Norman, 161-162
Libera, 175-179- 185, 192
Libera Terra, 176-178, 192

Libero Futuro, 182
Lifestyle, 33, 43
Liverpool, 123, 127, 213
Living in the truth, 91-92, 110
Lucas Aerospace, 209-210
Mafia, 159-162, 164-186, 188
Malcolm, Noel, 96
Marcel Network, 129-132
Marcora Law, 208-209
Marshall, Peter, 23-24
Martin, Brian, ii, 2, 153, 166
Martyrdom, ii, 13
Marxists, 61, 191, 213
Merton, Thomas, 20
Michnik, Adam, 91-92
Milosevic, Slobodan, 91, 93, 95
Mobilisation, 15, 31, 54, 70, 74, 78,
    93-94, 97, 101, 106, 111, 145-146,
    174, 180, 186, 220-223
Mondragon, 193, 201-208, 217
Moses, Robert, 111-112
Mother Theresa Association, 96
Mudie, George, 200
Mussolini, Benito, 161
Mutual aid, 10, 39, 199, 201, 209
Myanmar, 87-90, 225

Narmada Bachao Andolan (NBA), 75
NATO, 95, 98, 100
Navarro, Vincent, 202-203
Neutrality, 137-138, 154-156
New Harmony, 26, 28
New Lanark, 26-27
Nieuwlande, 132-137
Nonviolence, 19, 34, 39, 45-47, 54,
    60-61, 63, 72, 78, 85, 97, 100, 136
Norwegian clergy, 144

Oslo Accords, 104
Ostergaard, Geoffrey, 48, 57-59, 54,
    58, 59, 63-65
Overy, Bob, ii, 45
Owen, Robert, 25-31, 199-200, 202
Owenism, 29, 31

Pacifism, i, 16-17, 19-20, 39, 45, 123,
    159, 215
Paktar, Medha, 76

Palermo, 160, 162, 164, 167, 169, 171-
    174, 178-180, 182-186, 188
Palestine, 13, 72, 100-101, 105, 107,
    109, 152
Palestine Liberation Organisation
    (PLO), 100
Palestinian Unarmed resistance, 13, 15,
    102-103, 106-107
Palestinian Authority (PA), 104, 106
Palestinian resistance, 13, 52, 85, 100-
    101
Parallel structure, 90, 93-94, 96-98,
    149, 225
Parks, Rosa, 111
Partinico, 164, 166-168, 185
Passivity, 97
Patriarchy, 41
Payne, Charles, 113-114, 117-120
Peace Brigades International (PBI),
    150-151
Peace News, ii, 4, 20, 37-39, 45, 83,
    159, 215
Peace Pledge Union (PPU), 19, 39, 126
Peace studies, ii, 45, 157, 201, 211,
    213, 215
Philippines, 153-154
Poland, 90, 93-94, 125, 138, 145, 147,
    149, 221
Political education, 111
Political factions, 100, 103
Political impotence, 110
Political mobilisation, 94, 221
Post, Johannes, 133, 135
Prague Spring (1968), 90
Prefigurative, 8, 11, 234
Production, 1, 9, 23, 30, 50, 56, 92,
    177, 191-193, 196, 199, 201, 203,
    208, 210-212, 215, 225
Prophetic witness, 38
Protest,
    Contentious, 2, 13-14, 16, 111
    Levels of participation, 13
    Nonviolent, ii, 1, 14, 84, 228

Quakers (Society of Friends), 9, 24-25,
    29, 31, 126-127, 216
Quisling, Vidkun, 144-145

Ramallah, 108
Randle, Michael, 44, 84, 93, 225, 230, 234
Rank, Carol, iii, 189
Regime pillars, 46, 89, 92
Regimes,
  Authoritarian, 3, 11, 16, 46-47, 85, 87, 89-90, 120, 219, 221, 226
  Occupation, 5, 85, 94-95, 99, 141, 143-145
  Repressive, 3, 16, 90, 120, 170
Repression, 11, 66, 86, 90, 92, 96, 100, 120-121, 149, 151, 221, 225
Resilience, 14, 93, 107, 109-110, 132, 187, 209, 218
Resistance,
  Defensive, 86, 102
  Offensive, 86, 89, 94, 101, 222
  Polemical, 85, 101
  Symbolic, 15, 85, 101
  Unarmed, 13, 15, 75, 96, 102-103, 106-107, 120, 124, 153, 157
  Everyday, 11-12
Reverse strike, 165-167, 184, 189
Revolution,
  Nonviolent, 56, 59, 83
Richmond, California, 205
Rigby, Andrew, 9, 13, 38-39, 42, 49, 52, 60, 63, 67-68, 85, 87, 99-100, 102-103, 107, 110, 152, 165, 215-217
Riina, Toto, 173
Rizzotto, Placido, 176
Robinson, Bernice, 116, 118
Rochdale, 30-31, 200
Rognoni-La Torre Law, 173
Rosenstock, Odette, 130-131
Rowbotham, Sheila, 31, 33-34
Rugova, Ibrahim, 96-98
Ruskin, John, 31
Rustin, Bayard, 11

Sabotage, 16, 138, 149, 165, 196
Safe spaces, 92, 111
Safe-havens, 13, 119, 127-128, 132, 155
Salt March (1930), 47, 51, 78
Saltaire, 29
Saltini, Zeno, 162

Sampson, Ronald, 19
Sanctions, 3, 6-7, 12, 86, 92, 98, 101, 120, 151, 221, 224
Sanctuary, 127, 131-132, 136, 140, 153-154
Sarva Seva Sang (Association for the Welfare of All), 56, 63
Satyagraha, 45, 47-49, 51-52, 55, 62-65, 68-71, 73, 75, 78-79, 223
Schofield, Steve, 211-212
Schutz, Alfred, 6
Scott Bader Commonwealth, 193, 216-217
Scott, James, 11, 87
Second World War, 37-38, 40, 85, 99, 123-124, 127, 132-133, 135, 137, 139, 141-143, 147, 150, 194
Self-reliance, 39, 49-50, 54, 59, 77
Semelin, Jacques, 124, 139-140, 142-146, 149, 157
Semi-resistance, 95, 98-99, 226
Serbia, 91, 93-96, 98-99, 221
Shakers, 25
Shame power, 99, 227
Sharp, Gene, 46, 85
Sheffield, 31-33
Shehadeh, Raja, 108-109
Shiva, Vandana, 72
Shopping,
  selective, 11-12
Shulman, David, 227-228
Sicilian Documentation Centre, 174
Sicily, 159-164, 166, 168-173, 176-180, 182-183, 187-189, 192
Slobodan Milosovic, 91, 94
Social enterprise, 175-177, 186
Socialists, 16, 25, 28, 31-34, 57, 65, 81, 135, 144-145, 176, 191, 194-195, 199-200, 215, 225
  utopian, 25, 31-32,
Solidarity, 10-12, 64, 75, 92, 97, 99, 101-102, 106, 124, 135, 146, 149-151, 153, 156-157, 167, 170-171, 183-184, 187, 196-198, 200, 203, 218, 227
Solidarnosc, 90, 93
Soliman, Mahmoud, 14-15
Sørensen, Majken, 87, 137, 166

Southern Christian Leadership Conference (SCLC), 112,114, 117-118
Spain, 125, 129, 192-194, 199, 201, 203-204, 206, 217
Spann, Edward, 25-26
Statist fallacy, 219
Student Nonviolent Coordinating Committee (SNCC), 113, 118-120
SUMA, 213
Sumud, 14-15, 107-110, 221, 226

Tamil Nadu, 48, 60-61, 63-64, 66-67, 69 72-73
Teachers, 55, 88, 96, 114, 116, 118, 133, 144-149
Thatcher, Margaret, 201
Third parties, 86, 103, 110, 125, 128, 226
Thompson, William, 200
Thoreau, Henry David, 3, 4
TNGSM (Tamil Nadu Gram Swaraj Movement), 69-72, 74
Tolstoy, Leo, 19-20, 34-35, 37
Torness Gathering, 13
Total revolution, 64, 66,165
Totalitarianism, 38
Trade unions, 128, 196, 204-204
Trappeto, 162, 164, 166-167
Trocmé, André & Magda, 133-134
Trust, 66, 70, 77, 94, 106, 116-117, 136, 188, 206, 216-217, 221-223, 225
Trusteeship, 216-217

UGT (Union General Trabajodores), 195
Underground, 31, 93-94, 135, 137, 147-149, 222
United Kingdom (UK), 2, 5-7, 16, 21, 30, 42-43, 93, 123, 126, 128, 163, 193, 199, 208, 210, 212-214, 217-218, 228
United Steel Workers (USW), 204-205
Utopian, 23-25, 31-32, 34, 40-41, 63, 73, 83, 191, 199, 209, 215

Vichy regime, 128-129, 132
Vietnam War, 40

Village council, 155, 197-198
Vinoba Bhave, 56-58, 60-63, 65, 67, 79, 159
Vinthagen, Stellan, 8, 11

Ward, Colin, 9-10, 20-21, 92
Weber, Max, 42, 65
Wellock. Wilfred, 38-39, 72, 215-216
West Bank, 14, 102, 104, 106, 108, 151
Whiteway, 35
Widmer, Kingsley, 16-17
Winstanley, Gerrard, 12, 22-24
Women,
  Migrant, 5-7
  Palestinian, 6, 101-102
Women in Black, 93
Women's liberation movement, 41
Workers cooperatives, 40, 193, 201, 213
Workers councils, 192
Wright, Cyril, 38, 39

Yeo, Stephen, 32
Youth Against Settlements (YAS), 152

Zones of peace, 124, 153

This is a unique book that explores a neglected aspect of many well-known movements in world history, drawing out examples of "constructive action" employed in very different struggles. Rigby draws both from a life-long experience with radical activism, and from social science, discussing how it might be helpful to view different types and tactics of movement activities as "constructive" or as "resistance," and sometimes as "constructive resistance." This is the perfect book for anyone interested in an overview of how constructive nonviolent direct action can be integrated into everyday life and thereby contribute to processes of change, even during wartime and against organized crime.

Stellan Vinthagen, Professor of Sociology, Director of Resistance Studies Initiative, University of Massachusetts, Amherst.

Learning about constructive action for social change, making the world better by joining with others to make it the way you'd like it to be, sounds like it could be boring. But with *Sowing seeds for the future* it is just the opposite: you learn by being taken on an engaging journey through fascinating campaigns, with Andrew as your personal guide.

Brian Martin Emeritus professor, University of Wollongong, Australia

Printed in the USA
CPSIA information can be obtained
at www.ICGtesting.com
LVHW020214271023
762320LV00009B/322

9 789188 061546